The
POO
BOMB

The
POO
BOMB

True Tales of Parental Terror

Jeff Vogel

**Andrews McMeel
Publishing**

Kansas City

To Mariann, who had to give birth to her.

No plan survives first contact with the enemy.

—Helmuth von Moltket

Contents

Prologue: Confessions of an Ambivalent Parent

This is a book of humor about babies.

Wait! Come back!

I'm not about to tell you any stories about this adorable thing my daughter said. Or about this cutesy, wootsy thing my little snugglymuffin did. Or how my baby brought me a level of bliss and enlightenment beyond your comprehension and that the parenting experience has been nothing but this big, juicy, one-year soul orgasm.

I can't stand that shit. I hope you can't either, because if it's parenting porn you're after, you got the wrong book.

This book contains everything funny that happened in our daughter Cordelia's first year of life. It is as honest, sharp, and cute-free as I can make it because, in my view, babies are slimy, irritable, black holes of need. And I mean that as literal truth. They're wailing little goblins, and only hormones, occasional cuteness, and felony statutes keep them from being anonymously left at a thrift store.

Raising an infant is paying your dues. It's what you endure until the kid is old enough to walk and talk and draw houses and thank you for its life. There are plenty of books out there that will pretend otherwise. This isn't one of them.

Beware, though. As I found out, taking this view is a great way to earn the disapproval of friends, family, and everyone else around you. Being someone who doesn't like babies around my family is like being an atheist around snake handlers. Any sort of honest accounting of the downside of having an infant in one's house was forbidden, upon threat of being thought unworthy to breed. If not outright dangerous.

But I stood by my guns. Before the baby arrived and the parenting experience ate my brain and turned me into this soft, dazed creature who could endlessly discuss feces color and say "Children are our future" without irony, I had to tell everyone my exact feelings on the subject. Lucky them. I believed (and still believe) that anyone who has the right to have a child also has the right to be unhappy about how much it is going to suck.

When Cordelia was born, my wife Mariann and I were supposed to obtain our joy from the intangible benefits of loving and caring for our child and from the pleasures of guiding a new, young life. This was as opposed to before, when we got joy by doing things we liked. We had to get our fun from the many minor thrills of being the sole support for a tiny, young person, as opposed to before, when we got our fun by doing things that were fun.

Facing that and the responsibility that came with it filled me with a complicated combination of emotions: Terror and fear. And horror. And terror. And that was well before I knew that the baby would repeatedly barf on me.

When I expressed these reservations to people who were already parents, especially older parents, I tended to get a shocked, offended look. They'd stare at me with that beaten-down, cultish, thousand-yard, glassy-eyed parent stare and express confusion that anyone would be unable to immediately see the joy that has been ground into their souls.

But, honestly, how could I feel any other way? First off, I was about to have to care for a ridiculously frail infant life. Read any baby book. Read the lists of warnings and missteps, any of which will treat your infant to a speedy, horrible death. You aren't supposed to let a small baby sleep with blankets on it, because they might

STRANGLE IT. Blankets! Strangle! Even if you haven't read any books, if the prospect of being a new parent looking after a helpless baby does not fill you with at least a moderate helping of worry, I'm sorry. There is something wrong with you.

And as for the part about parenthood being fulfilling, I suppose I believed it on a theoretical level, like I believe in other things I can't see, like black holes or elves. But the good things about being a parent are very theoretical and intangible, and the bad things are very real and imminent.

I had no idea what it would feel like to have my daughter look up at me and smile, or to hear her talk for the first time, or to see her graduate from college. On the other hand, I knew exactly what it's like to not get any sleep. And I'd had lavish experience with long periods of time without sex, so I wasn't too thrilled about that bit either.

When you weigh both sides of the equation, when the bad is so imminent and easily understood and the good is so intangible and distant, the question is not how one can be unhappy about having a child. The question is how anyone can bring him or herself to produce a sprog in the first place. Why are so many first-world countries having a hard time keeping their birthrate above the replacement rate? Because people aren't idiots!

I wanted to raise a little human. A real human, that could talk and play and be crushed by me at Nintendo. Unfortunately, to get there, I had to escort it through its gooey, fresh, prehuman, larval stage. I was willing to pay that price. But there was no way I would pretend it was a good deal.

It's not selfishness. Being ambivalent about having practically everything you value in your life, including such trifles as freedom and sleep, stripped away is not selfish. It's reasonable.

It's not uncaring. I would love my child. That's what makes it so terrifying. If I didn't know I'd care about my unborn daughter so much, I wouldn't have been so afraid.

I wasn't irrational. The risks are real. The costs are real. I'm not making any of this stuff up.

And I most definitely wasn't stupid. If I was going to go into this thing and give it my best, I was going to do it with eyes wide open. If I thought, based on the information I have, it would suck, that's how I felt. Why pretend otherwise?

Anyway, that was my attitude. I didn't pretend. I was the turd in the punchbowl. And believe me, it didn't make me any friends.

So, when you get stuck with a little squealer of your own, when you have a baby in a sling and your balls in a vise (or, if you are female, your metaphorical balls in a figurative vise), here is my advice to you.

Give in!

Don't say you won't become one of those parents whose minds are eaten by parenthood. Screw that. Be insufferable! Any of your friends who don't have children should hear ceaselessly how much more fulfilled their lives would be if they did and how meaningless their little problems and stresses are compared with the gut-churning nightmare that is having an infant child. Any of your friends who do have children should find you incapable of having conversations about anything but developmental milestones and feces. And have a baby shower. A *big* baby shower. Make your friends bring you lots of shit!

Your little angel is going to be such a ray of sunshine in your life. It will be beautiful. It will not die early. And you will be happy beyond your capability to withstand it.

As for me, I had a year with the baby. And my brain didn't turn off, though there were many times when I wished it would. Some of the stuff that happened was pretty funny. I'll tell you about it. And I promise, I won't get all cutesy on you.

If babies expect us to feed them and carry them around and teach them to talk and give them ponies and cars, it's only fair for us to get to sit around and make fun of them sometimes.

Some questions that may occur to you while reading this book.

Q: Is there one grand thesis that you want me to take away from this book?

A: There is no aspect of human life that cannot have all pleasure utterly stripped away by the presence of a small child.

Q: Don't you think that Cordelia is going to be upset that you wrote all this about her?

A: If she is, I will buy her a pony.

Q: Why did you use so many dirty words when writing this?

A: I do not feel that it is possible to write honestly about parenthood without using a lot of obscenities.

Q: I notice that you don't seem to regard your baby as intelligent and perceptive beyond what is humanly possible. Also, you don't feel that parenthood is a constant source of perfect joy and fulfillment. Doesn't that mean that you don't love your baby?

A: You're an idiot.

Dramatis Personae

This book is about one specific family and one specific baby. They are much like any other family, except of course for the baby being cuter, smarter, and just generally of higher quality than yours. No offense.

The characters in this tale are as follows:

Jeff—The Dad.

That's me.

About thirty-two years old. Six feet tall. Bespectacled, not thin, bearded, mediocre posture. Computer nerd.

I was an only child. My experience with babies, prior to having one, was basically nonexistent. Thus, the decision to become a parent was a very dramatic leap of faith. I would like to say I had a child because I wanted to make the world a better place, or because I thought it would cure cancer, or something. But I really did it because I had an entirely unsupported hunch that it would, in the very long run, lead me to a happier life. Plus, giving my parents a grandchild would get them to stop bugging me.

But no experience is no experience. Thus, my vocabulary for most of the first year was two words: "Ewww" and "Huh?" And my main activity during the first year was watching Cordelia for signs of human intelligence, so that I could communicate with her and thus blame her for what she was doing to me.

Mariann—The Mom.

My wife.

About twenty-eight years old. Five feet two. Hungarian immigrant. Background in electrical engineering. Computer nerd.

Mariann came from Hungary when she was six years old. That was early enough to make her indistinguishable from a normal person, but late enough to make her freaky in mysterious immigrant ways. She may seem sensible and reasonable for months at a time, but then you'll walk into the kitchen and find her busily rendering pork fat. Or plotting revenge against the Turks for some shit that happened eight centuries previous.

Mariann had a heavy hand in raising her brother, who was about nine years old when Cordelia was born. Thus, she went into this knowing what babies, toddlers, and children were like. That she had actual experience and was still willing to have babies was a source of great reassurance to me.

But then, I can't be sure. Maybe this is some weird Old Country thing where she has a subconscious desire to have as many babies as possible so she can send them off to fight the Russians.

Mariann and I work together. We run a small, cute software company. That isn't false modesty. It really is small and cute. We make and sell computer games over the Web. This means, among other things, that Cordelia will be able to use a Nintendo joystick before she can walk.

Cordelia—The Baby.

Human female baby. Born January 18, 2002. Pretty average height and weight. No physical abnormalities of any kind.

Like all babies, she came out of her mommy's tummy with an undeveloped brain. The axons in her brain lacked the fatty myelin coating they needed to function properly. Thus, she was forced to rely for survival on a series of reflexes. Sucking. Breathing. Screaming.

Therefore, for most of this book, its main character will be unable to move, think, or communicate in any meaningful way. Not promising.

Eventually, Cordelia gained the ability to think. And, in all that time, she was a very well-behaved, normal baby. No colic. No diseases. No abnormalities that I could use to write a heartrending Made for TV Movie. In general, nature gave us absolutely nothing to complain about.

And yet, complain I will.

George and Sharon Vogel—My Parents.

My parents. Good, decent people. Who wanted grandchildren. A lot. I soon realized that we had to be very careful talking to them. Actual conversation:

Me: Mom, we got great news.
Mom: Mariann is pregnant!
Me: Uhhh, no. We got a new bedroom set.

So, of course, I was obligated to give them a grandchild. I figured, hey, they put up with me and gave me food and put me through college. I'll be a mensch.

My parents are part of the small, freakish subset of American culture that lives in RVs. They don't actually have a house. They spend all their time driving from place to place, lurking in graveyards researching genealogy and visiting all of the most stunningly dull tourist attractions this country has to offer. They're the sort of good, regular, American folks that can drive past the wonders of New York City without the slightest regret because a stop might make them miss Scranton's Museum of Vaguely Historical Knick-Knacks. How they raised a diehard city boy like me, who believes a life without five Thai restaurants within short walking distance is not a life worth living, is a mystery.

Fortunately, with Cordelia, they get a new, malleable child. Thus, their RV spends much of the time sitting hugely in our driveway.

Ilona Krizsan—Mariann's Mom.

Mariann's mother is a short, energetic whirlwind of activity and opinions, who rapidly found rural Hungary to be small, smoky, and insufficient. Thus, when my wife was six, Ilona packed her up and fled Communism for the Land of the Free. They settled in New Jersey, which must have, at the time, seemed an improvement.

Ilona worked for some time in this country as a nanny. Thus, unlike other grandparents, who could only present us with unsupported opinions about the poor quality of our parenthood, Ilona was backed up with professional experience. But she baby-sat for us a lot, which made her invaluable. After a certain point, I would gladly play host to a pack of rampaging wolverines if they provided reliable baby-sitting.

The Teletubbies.

Cordelia's favorite television show, from the time she gained the capability to actually watch anything. The Teletubbies are four short, furry, babbling imbeciles, who are served by machines and constantly surrounded by magical whimsy.

While I loathe them, it is only through their assistance that Mariann and I ever managed to get ten minutes of uninterrupted conversation.

The Sperm.

Microscopic wriggly things. Short-lived and stupid. Based on the evidence, I know that I have produced at least one of them in my lifetime.

Only about two weeks elapsed between when Mariann and I decided to have a baby and when I actually knocked her up. Based on that, I have determined that I produce sperm of exceptional speed and stamina. Remarkable, persistent creatures. Be careful. One may be crawling up your leg right now.

The Egg.

A tiny, biological Death Star, ready to blow my old, complacent life into tiny bits.

Pregnant Women: How to Deal with the Danger

This chapter is aimed at the men reading this book. It seeks to explain pregnancy to them. I don't feel any need to explain pregnancy to women, as knocked-up women will have no choice but to comprehend what's happening to them, whether they like it or not. The baby is in there. And it's coming out. Good luck!

But men could use a few friendly warnings . . .

Introduction.

If you are like most men (and, unfortunately, you probably are), one of these days you will find yourself legally bound to a pregnant woman.

It is, of course, common knowledge that pregnant women are radiant, lovely creatures, beaming with a soft, pure, inner glow. They have entered a higher realm, beyond the comprehension of us worshipful, hairy creatures below them. They are the future of the species, goodness incarnate.

At least, that's what you're going to say if you know what's good for you.

To be a parent is to be shackled to a creature that you love and who drives you up the wall in equal portions. Being around a pregnant woman is excellent practice for this experience. Here is a brief, helpful guide to prepare you for those nine particularly long months.

Do not underestimate the dangers that a pregnant woman can pose to you. She may be big and puffy, but she can attack quickly and without warning.

I. She will probably be nuts.

Everyone has heard the funny jokes about pregnant women and their cravings. They will send you out late at night and make you get pickles and ice cream. Ha. Ha.

You should be so lucky.

If that was the main problem, you would be golden. You would come home with the pickles and ice cream, toss them into the bedroom so your wife can feed, go play XBox, and try to ignore the sinking feeling.

The truth is that pregnancy fills women with a devil's brew of nausea, terror, and baby hormones. Not to mention that a big, slimy creature is going to rip its way out of her vagina headfirst, screaming all the way. Don't think she isn't thinking about that every damn minute.

Nope. Forget dealing with this issue with a few late-night trips to the supermarket. She's gonna be a whirling dervish of crazy, and you're within arm's reach.

How will you deal with this? Well, I'm not going to tell you anything you couldn't have learned as easily by watching some fifties sitcoms. Smile. Nod a lot. *Lie.* Really, sometimes the corny old solutions are the right ones.

Also, when you're at the ultrasound, when you see that twitchy little creature on the black-and-white monitor, do not say, "Oh God! What is that? Hit it with a brick!" This won't help.

II. Sex becomes very complicated.

Since you are with a pregnant woman, I will assume that you are the one who knocked her up. If this isn't the case, your life is too complicated for this book to help you. Run!

If, on the other hand, you are the father, that means you have probably been having sex with her. Which means that you probably want to have sex with her again. This is where it gets tricky.

First, you have to get over the idea that, past all the fun body parts, there is a little, squishy person in there. This is unnerving, at best. Fortunately, if this really bothers you, a good two or three months without sex will make you a lot less squeamish. Three months of private, gloomy self-pleasure makes anything look hot.

Then there is the size issue. The mother's size. Now, I don't want to buy into our society's unrealistic, patriarchal, sizeist ideals of feminine beauty. But, at the same time, I must point out that sex with a pregnant woman is like making sweet, gentle love to a beanbag chair.

I dealt with this by closing my eyes and imagining I was having sex not with one very large woman but two very small women.

Finally, just so you know, very late in pregnancy, sex is one of the things that can induce labor. In fact, if the baby is late coming out, sex is sometimes recommended to encourage the process.

Please, please, please. Try to think about this as little as possible. Remembering what the sex you're having is about to do to your life will lead to some very bittersweet orgasms.

III. She will be sick as a dog.

Pregnancy is a highly unpleasant ailment, in which a seven-plus–pound parasite develops in the lady's tummy. This sickness has a variety of side effects, all of them unpleasant. If you are anything like me, you are now wondering, "This isn't going to inconvenience me, is it?"

The answer to that question, fortunately, is no. Her swollen ankles, nausea, back pain, and difficulty sleeping are not contagious. They are also low-level, constant, annoying problems, the sort that lend themselves to suffering in grim, stoic silence.

As long as you occasionally hold her hair back when she vomits and practice making a sort of sympathetic "Hmm" sound, you should be in the clear.

Oh, and you will be occasionally have the chance to go along with her to appointments with the lady-doctor. Go to all of these you can. This will, with a minimal time investment, earn you valuable "Good Daddy" points, which can be redeemed with a vengeance when things get really, really terrible a few months later.

IV. Farmer pants.

Finally, pregnancy tends to cause women to wear overalls, due to their roomy nature. This can be a problem because, of course, overalls should not ever be worn under any circumstances.

Unfortunately, this can't be helped, so you might as well make the most of it. If you have been nurturing any "Initiate Large, Virginal Farmgirl into the Mysteries of Womanhood" fantasies, your time is now.

In Conclusion.

Pregnancy is a time of trial and difficulty, and it won't be so hot for you either. Fortunately, with the correct attitude, the problems can be reduced to a small and manageable level (for you). This will help you clear your mind and focus on the main fact: Soon the baby will be born, and your life will be completely and totally over.

The First Three Months:
Baby Learns to Breathe

And So It Came to Pass.

On the evening of January 18, at around 8 P.M., my first child, Cordelia Krizsan Vogel, entered the world. She came out of Mariann, my wife. She got her mother's facial shape, her father's irritability, and her mother's genitalia. The event was the joyous conclusion to fifteen hours of labor. This is not as horrible as it sounds, because, as it turns out, epidurals RULE.

(For the uninitiated, when you get an epidural, what happens is that a nice person enters the room, sticks a needle into your spine, starts a steady flow of anesthetic into it, and leaves it there. For hours and hours. It is a good measure of how horrifying childbirth is that, when it is taking place, leaving needles in your spine sounds like a great option.)

Once the baby was out and cleaned off, it didn't do much. It just sort of sat there and twitched. That's what they do. For the first three months of life, a baby is much more similar to a potato than a human.

They can't move. They can't see correctly and, even if they could, their brains don't know now how to process the images their optic nerves are sending. Of course, the baby's brain can't actually think. Baby brains are not structurally developed during the first year. They have no long-term memory. All newborn behavior is reflex only, without consideration, without comprehension, without thought. They cannot love in any way we adults can comprehend.

Suck on that, new mom and dad.

Newborns are human in appearance only. The only things they can do are suck and squeal. And it's a funny thing. Now that I think about it, it's really hard to see why having a newborn was difficult. It was just a lump, wrapped in terry cloth.

And yet, it was difficult . . .

Week 1—Birth, and Other Really Gross Things

The fun stopped at 6 A.M. on January 18. I had only just gone to bed. (Nintendo is a harsh mistress.) Mariann roused me from a peaceful sleep to inform me that it was time to go to the hospital. After a spirited internal debate, I got out of bed and submitted to her will.

Deciding to be born just after I had gone to bed, thus depriving me of any rest at all, was one of the first merry little tricks Cordelia played on me. This is why I recommend that anyone about to have a child do nothing but sleep. Never, ever get out of bed. This guarantees that, when the quote-happy-event-unquote happens, you will be nice and rested.

Upon arriving at the hospital. Mariann was thoroughly questioned by a nurse. It was determined that my wife was not a crackhead. Then we were put in a nice room with a little bed and left to simmer. Time passed. The contractions got gradually more painful. I read the paper and wished I was asleep. Bagels were eaten.

Within an hour, the pain really started. Mariann, being a nice practical girl, immediately summoned an anesthesiologist to fire a bullet of blissful nothingness into her spine. Once she had lost all feeling from the waist down, we got calmed down and settled in. I know I'm repeating myself, but this is a key point. Epidurals RULE.

(Please do not pick a fight with me over the joys of natural childbirth. Unless, of course, you want me to explain at great length how I plan to have my wisdom teeth taken out without anesthesia, so that the intrusive evils of Western medicine don't get between me and the purity and joy of my dental care.)

On the bright side, once the drugs arrived, the labor was, while tiring, surprisingly pleasant. We compared notes on local restaurants with the nurses, hung out, and occasionally napped. Fifteen hours passed. There was a lot of grunting and pushing. Eventually, a baby plopped out.

On the upside, the baby was healthy. Two arms. Two legs. One head. On the downside, at the end of it, well . . . While the mother doesn't want me to go into too much detail, let's just say that her genitals looked like the first thirty minutes of *Saving Private Ryan*.

Meeting My Child

After Cordelia came out, I went over to where they were cleaning off the slime and moist unpleasantness so I could get a good look at her. The nurse said, "Say something to her." The first words she will ever hear from her father. The words that begin the journey, where I help her develop from a helpless primate into a productive member of society. But no pressure.

Being groggy and about eight seconds into my first experience with newborns, I said the first thing that came into my mind: "Hello, Cordelia. Welcome to the world. It's not going to get much better."

The nurses did not approve. I don't feel too bad about it though because
  i. I stand by my statement, and
  ii. As far as I know, my daughter does not yet speak English.

For Some, the Big Payoff Is Had

My parents, George and Sharon, were out of the room while all this was happening. I do not know exactly what they were doing during this time, but this is what I picture: I see them whirling madly around the waiting room, shrieking joyously, engaged in a savage, feral dance of triumph to celebrate the successful conclusion of years of nagging me to give them grandchildren.

Eventually, they came into the room. George took pictures. Sharon held the baby and glowed. Out of profound courtesy, they decided to wait a little longer before starting to hint about when they would get their second grandchild.

Amount of Time Elapsed Before I First Poked a Sleeping Baby to Make Sure She Was Still Alive

About six hours.

It Has Always Been This Night. It Will Always Be This Night.

The first night of Cordelia's life passed without incident. Occasionally, she would make this cute, whiny, little squeak, sort of a proto-cry, and one of us would pick her up, and she would quiet down immediately and look adorable. "Oh, this is easy, we can do this," we thought, being idiots.

The next night went something like this.

Midnight—2 A.M.: Baby screams whenever she is set down because she is hungry. Parents do not sleep.

2 A.M.—4 A.M.: Baby screams whenever she is set down because she really, really has to pee and has not figured out how to pee. She also screams whenever she is picked up. Parents do not sleep.

4 A.M.—6 A.M.: Baby, having been fed and having peed prodigiously, screams whenever she is set down or picked up because, in her tiny brain, all she can ever remember doing is screaming, and, to her, it is the perfectly reasonable and expected thing to do. Parents do not sleep.

6 A.M.: Parents give up this weird iron-man, "I WILL outlast the baby" thing they are doing and let nurses take baby away for a little while. Baby instantly stops screaming and goes to sleep like an angel. Father thinks baby is a little suck-up.

8 A.M.: Baby is returned to parents. Screaming instantly resumes.

Please understand that all of this is completely accurate and free of exaggeration. Daddy has a bad feeling about this situation.

The Unbearable Grossness of Being

I am cursed with the ability to be interested in just about anything. Plus, I'm a jerk. This is a bad combination, as any of my friends who have had the concept of meconium explained to them by me in sticky detail can testify.

(*meconium,* n. the first fecal excretion of a newborn child, composed chiefly of bile, mucus, and epithelial cells. —*Random House Webster's College Dictionary.* How cool is that?)

As a result, we have many sweet and charming childbirth photos:

- Baby's first time being held by mother.
- Baby's first scream.
- Baby's first flinch when startled by a camera flash.
- Baby's first angst.

I also have a number of other photos:

- Mother's first epidural.
- Mother's first epidural, better angle.
- Baby's first placenta.
- Baby's first meconium.
- Baby's head (which looks like it had just been squeezed out through a tube, because, you see, it had just been squeezed out through a tube).

We plan to have a lovely baby album, suitable for presentation to relatives, friends, and passersby. I also plan to have a second baby album, a secret, special baby album, henceforth known as Baby Album B. This will be a horror show, kept for my own private amusement, and only revealed as a surprise at a later date if Cordelia ever brings home a boyfriend I *really* hate.

A Word About Dealing with the Grossness

I was extremely worried about my ability to deal with, not to put too fine a point on this, shit. You know, feces. I thought it would completely gross me out.

Yet, much as a terrified young man oft becomes a bloodthirsty killer when faced with the immediate reality of battle, fatigue and necessity made the grossness absolutely no problem at all.

To clarify the point. When the baby was crying on its first night, the nurse and I placed it on the changing table to check if the diaper was dirty. Not wanting to deal with the bother of rediapering if I removed the diaper and it was clean, I jammed my finger inside and felt around without hesitation, not being sure what I would find.

While I will not go into further detail, rest assured that what I found was warm, moist, and sticky. It adhered to my skin, sinking in instantly, so that I might never feel clean again.

It was at this precise moment that my soul left my body.

And then I dealt with the situation as required.

I am no longer worried about grossness. Sure, the feces will become much more smelly and voluminous than they are now. I am *so* unconcerned.

To paraphrase the idealized movie version of General Patton, "Now, some of you are wondering whether or not you'll chicken out under fire. When you put your hand in a pile of goo that an hour before was your daughter's lunch, you'll know what to do."

Then We Went Home

After two nights, the hospital kicked us out.

Before we were allowed to leave, the nurses forced us to install Cordelia in the car seat in front of them, to make sure we could do it right. They were very surprised that we got it right the first time. It made me wonder what sort of troglodyte mouth-breathers were having children in the rooms around us.

We were very relieved to get home. Instead of failing to get sleep in the hospital, we could fail to get sleep in our own bed. It's much more comfortable that way.

Oh, and One Other Thing

Our daughter is named after King Lear's nice daughter.

She is *not* named after the character on *Buffy the Vampire Slayer*.

Week 2—Parenting Books Never Did Anyone a Damn Bit of Good

The first week passed. It all started to sink in. Parents of a newborn are like a buffalo that's been shot in the brain. It's dead. It's just too dumb to know it yet.

Mariann and I struggled to develop the basic parenting skills necessary to care for a completely helpless creature. We were armed only with determination, a checklist provided by the hospital, and my parents, who were staying with us. We frequently handed Cordelia to them like a ticking bomb, hid in the bedroom, and discussed which of us was more to blame for the mess we were in.

We also spent a lot of time with The Checklist. The hospital gave us this journal we were supposed to keep, meticulously recording Cordelia's body temperature and how much filth came out of her lower holes. This inspired me to start keeping a journal of how often I go to the bathroom and in what quantities. I think, in a year, it will make inspired reading.

We were also warned about all the bizarre health problems newborns can have. The skin flaking off her head. The smell of rotting flesh from her belly button. Her entire body being covered with fungus. The doctor warned us about all the concerns we might have and invited us to, if we got worried about something, piss off and not bother her.

Cordelia is developing quickly, as babies just out of the dark, wet place are supposed to. She is now the personification of infant charm and beauty. And her head doesn't have that lumpy, freakish pear shape anymore.

She also has skills. Today, at the doctor's office, to everyone's amazement, she rolled over on her own. Many babies can't do that until they're two months old. And, every night, she can stay awake from midnight until 8 A.M. I couldn't do that until college.

How Evolution Destroys My Life

Our child spends several hours in the middle of the night screaming. Every night. I do not say this because it is in any way exceptional. It isn't. I just mention it for purposes of background.

Now that I have a kid and talk to other parents about it, I find that everyone's kid does this. Why didn't anyone tell me? What was the big secret? And when I saw my friends' kids, why were they so quiet and adorable? And why is my kid only adorable when other people are around? They go, "Oh, what an adorable child," and it's hard not to say, "Want her? She's priced to move."

Why is that?

At first I thought it was because she's just a little suck-up. I suspected she would end up the sort of kid who reminds Teacher that she forgot to give homework.

Then I realized that it must be evolution. It makes sense. Babies being quiet when nonparents are around has two obvious selective advantages:

i. It makes people who haven't bred yet think that babies are actually (snicker) cute and (chuckle) nice, fooling them into breeding themselves. Thus the genome is spread. Suckers.

ii. In caveman days, when we were much less restrained than we are now, it was a good idea to be quiet around a stranger—if you were noisy and annoying, it made it that much more likely that that particular stranger would squish you with a rock. The squeaky wheel gets greased.

Books Never Did Anyone a Damn Bit of Good

It is a well-known fact that reading is never good for anything for anyone for any reason. It's true. It's been proven by science.

This is extra-true for books on parenting. We have to take care of this little alien beast, and the slightest misstep could result in disaster, articles about us in the tabloids, and jail. So we spend all our time reading books.

Right now, I can't give much advice to parents, but I can say this: Parenting books only exist to make you feel like shit.

Every parenting book is 20 percent actual true stuff based on science (e.g., change its diaper when it pisses itself, don't shake the baby, don't let it play with plastic bags) and 80 percent completely unsupported axe-grinding on the part of the author (e.g., don't feed your child meat, don't use a pacifier, don't bind feet).

Watch out for the author's own personal bitterness. In five hundred pages of book, something will always slip through:

"Infants can have a wide variety of hair color, and those colors may not stay constant through their childhood. Contrary to popular myth, hair color has no bearing on a child's personality, even if she has red hair like MY BITCH EX-WIFE."

My advice to you: Get several books. When you get confused, if all of the books tell you to do the same thing, believe it. If they tell you to do completely different things, someone (if not everyone) is talking out their ass. Do what you want.

On the other hand, if your personal cherished parenting ideas aren't covered in any of the books, you might want to rethink them. Seriously, no matter how crackbrained a theory is, someone's got a book on it out there. Every parenting aid short of enemas and voodoo (and probably those) is covered. If you have some bright, new idea but you can't find a book that says you're right, it's time for you to come back from Cloud Cuckoo Land before your kid has to make a run for it.

Who Gets My Things When I Die?

Before Cordelia was born, my wife and I wrote a will. This is an amusing activity, and is highly recommended for everyone.

When you write your will, you get to play the "Who gets your kid?" game. Here's how it works. The lawyer says, "Who gets your kid when you die?" and you think hard and come up with an answer. Then the lawyer asks, "Who gets your kid if they die?" And you answer. Then the lawyer asks, "Who gets your kid if *they* die?" And you repeat this process until there is nobody left you can even bear the thought of giving your child to and you have to spend ten minutes wincing and pondering how your child's life would be spent with your funny uncle who believes that all of the body's ailments can be cured with magnets.

Eventually, after fifteen minutes of the game, I asked, "Look. Can't I just say, if it gets to this point, that all of my child's possessions will be stripped away and she must roam the Earth, friendless and alone, righting wrongs and fighting injustice, like Caine in *Kung Fu*?"

It turns out, you can't put the words "righting wrongs and fighting injustice" in your will.

Also, while filling out the will, I got to have this conversation:

Me: "What is this space for?"
Lawyer: "You can specify what happens with your body after you die."
Me: "So I can choose 'Buried' or 'Cremated.'"
Lawyer: "Yes."
Me: "Can I choose 'Boiled'?"
Lawyer: "Yes. But only if, afterward, you are buried or cremated."

I realized that this is not technically correct. There are other options. I could be buried at sea. Or I could be sold to that artist who soaks cadavers in hot liquid plastic until they are preserved as a statue. A shiny, sexy statue. Either option would kick ass.

But I didn't push the issue. If I have learned anything from my short time in this world, it is this: Don't get on your lawyer's shit list.

A Philosophical Aside

When deciding whether to have children, I spent some time agonizing about whether I wanted to do so for a bad reason. Now, in the thick of the fight, I see the truth. There are no bad reasons to have children.

For there to be bad reasons to have children, there have to be good reasons to have children, and I can see clearly now that there are no good reasons to have children.

Actually, that's not quite right. I can think of a bad reason to have children. You shouldn't have a child in order to dry it out and sell it as an aphrodisiac for Asian businessmen.

Short of that, though, it doesn't matter much either way.

How My Child's Mind Is Developing

Being a new parent, I feel a great responsibility to delude myself into thinking that my two-week-old child is capable of actual thought.

Occasionally, she practices focusing her eyes, giving her a look that I can easily confuse with piercing intelligence. While struggling to control her facial muscles, she accidentally adopts expressions my mind interprets as smiles, or frowns, or looks of confusion. Sometimes I make faces and stick out my tongue at her, seeing if I can get her to imitate me, and, a short time later, she makes some random movement similar to what I did, making me think she is copying me.

Based on all of this, I can say that my child is possibly smart. Of course, based on such evidence, I could say exactly the same thing about a sufficiently active poodle.

A Brief, Tender Vignette

A friend asked me if I "love" my child. I answered that I don't know yet. I haven't had time to feel much of anything, "love" or not. When I get a chance to take a breath, I'll figure it out.

On the other hand, my daughter and I did have a moment the other night. It was late. She was in my lap, well into one of her all-night screaming and pinky-sucking sessions, when, just for a minute, she quieted down. She looked up. Her eyes focused on me. And her mouth twisted, for whatever reason, into a shape that looked a lot like a smile to her daddy.

I took her in my arms, lifted her, and held her close, overcome with a feeling of warmth, happiness, and optimism. At this point, my daughter spit a large globule of milk onto my chest, mixed with a good measure of mucus for texture.

Every time I have a moment that could be used as the punchline for a *Baby Blues* cartoon, a little bit of my soul shrivels up and dies.

But do I love her? Well, I don't have what my wife refers to as "foo foo" feelings. No warm fuzzies. But I strongly suspect, if necessary, I'd get hit by a car for her.

And if anyone wants to take her to Asia, powder her, and use her as rhino horn substitute, they'll have to pay me some *serious* folding money first.

Week 3—I'll Happily Lose the War If I Can Just Get One Victory

The second week of our daughter's life was a time of great learning and transition. For example, we learned that my parents were leaving. We then made the transition from borderline to psychotic.

In that time, my wife and I went from being tired and confused but loving guardians of a young life to The Worst Parents Ever.

So, Cordelia, my daughter, when you someday read this, bear in mind that your issues are not your fault. Mommy and Daddy permanently screwed you up.

We gave you a pacifier.

The Joy of Pacification

Here is a general rule of thumb about parenting books: Their main purpose is to make the experience as painful as possible. And unpleasant and inconvenient.

After we fed our daughter, she wanted to suck on things. Constantly. Her blanket. Her lower lip. She would latch onto the side of my hand while I was changing her. Experimentation revealed that she would attempt to gain sustenance from the back of a spoon or the tip of the TV remote. (I washed the end of the remote in soap and water first. I'm not a monster.) I tried to see if I could get her to suck on the wall, but the angle wasn't right.

And if I didn't give her something to suck on, she would scream. A lot. Given the chance, she would suck my wife's nipples until there was nothing left there but a bare patch, like a Barbie. And sure, that would be totally sexy. But then our next kid would have nothing to eat.

Despite all this, we didn't give her anything just to suck on. Well, occasionally I would put the tip of my little finger in her mouth for a minute, just to quiet her for a little. But the books said that giving the child things to suck on should be avoided, if at all possible, so I didn't.

Then we took her into the doctor's office for a checkup, and inside of five minutes of observation the nurse said, "Maybe you should get her a pacifier."

So we did. And we received, as a reward, twenty-four hours of joyous silence and peace. Then our daughter, using some bizarre, random thinking process in her tiny, empty brain, decided that she didn't like the pacifier anymore. Now she just sucks on the tip of my little finger. For hours.

But at least the screaming stopped.

Why Some People Who Work in Minimum Wage Jobs Should Probably Continue to Work in Minimum Wage Jobs

Me: "Where can I find a pacifier?"

(Pause.)

Target Employee: "For a baby?"

Maybe I'm the jerk. Maybe they do sell pacifiers for adults, and I just don't know about it. And, if this is the case, I want one NOW.

Suckin' That Sweet, Sweet Teat

So giving our child a pacifier (or my finger, nature's pacifier substitute) was only the first step in our becoming the Worst Parents Ever. Then our pediatrician, noting that my wife's breast milk supply was sufficient to keep our child healthy but not happy, suggested supplementing breast milk with the occasional bottle of formula.

Want to feel like a heartless jerk who would sell out your kid for an hour's free time and a handful of Skittles? Then crack a few parenting books and read what they have to say in their sections on formula. You'd think I was feeding my kid room temperature Mountain Dew with a pig urine chaser.

Sure, my wife could have decided to supplement her milk by going to a "lactation specialist," but she wanted to go with the formula. And I can't blame her. Because breast-feeding is a pain in the ass.

Oh, I know. Breast milk is nature's own baby food, and it helps the mother develop a special bond with the child, and blah blah blah. All I know is that my wife is looking forward to weaning the way I look forward to porn.

It's ironic. I've spent my whole life fantasizing about being married to someone who's been reduced to livestock, lying on the couch and getting milked eight hours a day, occasionally getting up to ease my tensions manually before returning to a prone position to have her nutrients drained again. Every guy dreams about this. Imagine my surprise to find that the reality is not quite as glorious as the fantasy.

Breast-feeding is a good thing. Good for the kid. Fine. But don't pretend it's necessarily this Glorious and Fulfilling La Leche League Mommy-Experience™. It's like when safe-sex educators start getting a little funny in the head and start insisting that condoms are not only necessary and safe (sure), but that they don't make sex less enjoyable. Look, idiot. Don't piss on our legs and tell us it's raining. We'll do the right thing, but don't browbeat us into thinking we have to like it.

Oh, and about that "special bond" breast-feeding helps you develop? Come on. If you clenched a spiral-cut ham to your chest for eight hours a day, you'd develop a "special bond" with it too.

A Helpful Quote, to Provide Background Information for the Upcoming Breast-feeding Rant

From *The Baby Book,* by William and Martha Sears, regarding babies who take a very long time breast-feeding: "If you have the time and baby has the desire, cherish every lingering meal, as breast-feeding is a phase of life with your baby that passes all too quickly."

Learn from my experience. Do not read this quote to an exhausted woman at the suckee end of a 3 A.M. marathon feeding session, unless you want her to do something to you with her free hand that you will neither "cherish" nor want to "linger" over.

And William and Martha Sears, I got somethin' you can cherish, right here.

What Baby Learned This Week

1. She learned that she can derive happiness by sucking her hand. She seems to try to maneuver her hand to her mouth. Because of her near total lack of motor control, this results in her either punching herself in the chin or poking herself in the eye. Sometimes, she accidentally flips Daddy off. I generally watch this process until the laughter makes me start to hyperventilate.
2. She learned to piss whenever we're changing her. As soon as the diaper's off, she cuts loose. Once, she did it four times in twenty-four hours.

This is inconvenient. But, since boys get the ability to pee standing up and she doesn't, I do not begrudge her these few precious months of urinary freedom.

Why I Got Rid of All of My Large Pots

Having a baby around makes it much harder to manage the voices in my head. I mean, before, they just told me to do horrible things to myself and my wife. But my wife knows Tae Kwon Do and could kick my ass, and I can't do anything painful to myself because I'm a big wuss. So that was all right.

But now I spend all of my time having internal conversations like:

Me: "Oh, Hell. Did I remember to put out the diapers so the service can pick them up?"
Inner voice: "Boil the baby."

Or,

Me: "Phew. She's finally asleep. I can get some work done."
Inner voice: "Boil the baby."

Or,

Me: "I'm hungry. I sure could use a ham sandwich."
Inner voice: "Boil the . . . wait. Did you say ham?"
Me: "Mmmmm. Sandwich."
Inner voice: "Mmmmm. Sandwich."
Me: "Better clean this plate."
Inner voice: "Put the baby in the dishwasher."

But the voice in my head didn't get its way. I wasn't able to fit the baby in the dishwasher rack.

Fortunately, my wife is understanding. She put Post-It notes on all of our large cooking vessels. Each says, in large, clear letters, "Don't boil the baby." It confused my parents when they came over. When they asked about it, I said, "What? Are you saying it's a good idea to boil the baby?" Then they changed the subject really quickly, so I think everything is going to work out okay.

The Law of Conservation of Personalities

Conservation of Personalities is my term for the way children tend to become the opposite of their parents. I tormented my huntin', fishin', fresh-meat-guttin' father with my bookworm, computer programming ways.

Now, as I am a professional computer game designer, my daughter will have access to all of the technological goodies, computer games, and fun books she could possibly absorb.

Thus, based on The Law of Conservation of Personalities, I believe that she will turn out to be an Amish Jock.

I'll Happily Lose the War If I Can Just Get One Victory

One bottle of formula a day didn't seem like much. But our house has a lot less screaming in it now. And my wife's nipples look a lot less like a prop in a David Cronenberg movie.

And Cordelia, if you're reading this and you turned out to be a twisted wreck with ruined health and an inability to love, I'm sure you can trace most of that back to days 8–14. Sorry.

Week 4—Don't Worry. Their Legs Always Fall Off. Nothing to Worry About.

We managed to complete a month of parenting. Only 215 more months until she turns eighteen and leaves home and *we win*.

We just had to survive a few days of parenting without a grandparent helping. For the first two weeks, my parents were around, doing a bit of low-impact nurturing before getting into their RV and driving to Mexico. Meanwhile, my mother-in-law Ilona lurked, like Gollum in *The Lord of the Rings,* waiting to pounce the moment my parents were gone.

Ilona is here to stay with us and help out. She walked into the house, summoned up all the authority gained from her years as a nanny and millennia worth of accumulated Eastern European ancestors, and blasted me out of the room with her disdain. She couldn't have done a better job with a laser beam. I disappeared, and she rescued Cordelia from our clutches.

So, most of this week, I hid. Occasionally, someone tells me how my daughter is doing.

And How Is the Little Angel Doing?

Cordelia is growing nicely, and she sleeps five to six uninterrupted hours every night. All to the good. On the other hand, looking into her eyes, I can't see any sign that she loves me. Or recognizes me. I just get this blank stare.

I'm a reasonable person. I'll give her one more month, and then she has to start loving me. Otherwise, I'm not sure this will work out.

I Sleep Much Better Now That the Baby Is Here

My wife and I have dramatically offset sleep schedules. She sleeps from 10 P.M.-ish to 7 A.M.-ish (sometimes getting up to be milked) and I sleep from 4 A.M.-ish to noon-ish. The baby sleeps during the short overlap.

It's eerie. I am sleeping better now than I did for months before the child arrived.

Of course, you may be one of those parents who has a kid that never sleeps at night, or never sleeps except in tiny patches. In this case, all I have to say is: HA HA HA! I am SUCH a better parent!

Since the first month ended with us being in good shape, I am now convinced that the rest of our child's infancy will go by completely easily and without incident. There will be no colic or other difficulties. It is impossible. I am not jinxing it. And I will not get any sort of ironic comeuppance.

A Thought About Checking Your Child in the Middle of the Night to Make Sure She Is Still Alive

When Cordelia was on the way, I asked my parents and uncles if they ever went into the bedroom and poked their kids to make sure they were still alive. They all said yes.

I know now that that answer was incomplete. When I am asked the same question, my answer is, "Yes, of course. But the first time you wake your child up from a sound sleep and she immediately starts screaming, you cut down on that shit REAL QUICK."

Now I'm down to only checking my little darling every half an hour. With a few years of work, I'm sure I can get it down to only checking her every thirty-one minutes. I'll probably keep this up until she's sixteen and it starts to totally creep her out.

Don't Worry. Their Legs Always Fall Off. Nothing to Worry About.

I am a science geek, so I prepared for being a parent like any good science geek would. I read books. I went to Web sites. You can't deal with an engineering problem without fully understanding the specifications and boundary conditions of the objects involved. You know. Mass. Coefficient of friction. Tensile strength. Flammability. That sort of thing.

Then I picked up a copy of the omnipresent best-seller *What to Expect the First Year*. I found out that pretty much every child's default state is "Broken." A few of the more memorable examples:

Chapter Four—Acne? Normal. "Explosive Bowel Movements"? Normal.

Chapter Five—Hernia? Nothing to worry about.

Chapter Thirteen—Child smashing his head against the walls of the crib? Perfectly reasonable. Even if knocks itself unconscious? Fine. Child occasionally holding his breath until he passes out? One in five kids do this.

Damn.

Kids are messed up. I kept expecting to turn the page and read

Child on Fire—
Occasionally, you will look in the crib and see that your baby is on fire. This happens to most children at one time or another and is perfectly normal. If the fire does not go out on its own within two or three hours, consider calling a doctor.

I expect to have this conversation on the phone with Cordelia's pediatrician:

"Hello, Doctor."

"Hello. What seems to be the problem?"

"Well, my daughter is . . . well . . ."

"Yes?"

"She is covered with ants."

"Oh? That's nothing to worry about. That happens to one in three children before age two."

"Really?"

"Oh, yes. The ant is the natural enemy of the baby."

"So I shouldn't worry about it?"

"Well, call me again if they're still there next week. Or if they start to lay eggs."

"Okay, thank you, Doctor."

Also, our daughter shits and pisses herself constantly. And she vomits a lot. It's really upsetting, especially since I heard somewhere that other babies do this, too. I'm almost starting to suspect that, if I left Cordelia completely alone, she wouldn't be able to function well at all.

Whoops. There Goes Another Rubber Tree Plant.

Sometimes, you have to escape. And sometimes, the law requires that you take what you're escaping from with you while you're escaping.

That's why Mariann and I took Cordelia out to lunch with us the other day. We're getting out of the house as much as we can while our daughter is, for all practical purposes, noisy luggage.

While we were eating, I noticed that a lone ant was in the carrier, climbing up the blanket toward our baby's face.

Now you sort of have to feel for this ant. I mean, here it was, walking on the best food source its colony could ever know. Soon, it would reach the face, get one taste of that sweet, sweet spit-up, and run back to the queen, and soon ants are everywhere. That is the sort of pluck and can-do spirit we're brought up to respect in this country.

That is why it really broke my heart to have to pick the creature up and flick it away. Granted, letting your baby get covered with ants is probably a perfectly reasonable thing to do from a Darwinian, red in tooth and claw, nature-centered perspective. Lord knows it's only fair.

But, as a father, I felt it was the sort of thing I should be doing. So there we are.

Baby's First Vocalization

Baby said her first recognizable, non-crylike sound the other day. It was "Goo."

That's right. She said quote-Goo-endquote. It's perfect. It's like if a dog said "Bark."

A New Skill

Cordelia is now the Spit-Up Princess. She is the real Vomit Comet.

I am amazed by the aplomb and dignity with which she can spit up milk. It's like nothing to her. She makes a little face, she squirts milk and digestive fluids on Daddy, and, in a moment, she's back to normal. When I vomit, it's this huge production with me bending over the bowl and gagging and brushing my teeth and everything. Cordelia, on the other hand, barfs with such practiced ease that it's as if she was born to do it. I think she's gifted.

Of course, maybe she's not just spitting up. Maybe she's three weeks old and already bulimic. I am a little worried about this, though if this is the case, it's not all bad. At least she knows how important it is to be pretty.

Daddy Quote of the Week

"She's putting on a lot of weight. She's starting to look less like a human and more like a baby."

Week 5—The Poo Bomb

And like that, all the grandparents were gone. They got their look-see, and they returned to peaceful, happy lives. Now it's just me, Mariann, and the baby. Everything that goes wrong from now on is our fault.

Now that Cordelia is over a month old, it has become that much easier to delude myself into thinking that she is showing signs of alertness and humanity. Sometimes she looks up and makes eye contact with me with such a piercing gaze that I can't help but believe that there are the beginnings of consciousness in there.

Then I watch her spend a furious minute trying to suck sustenance out of her upper lip, and I come to the cold realization that my daughter has spent the previous month growing from a seven-pound dope up to an eight-pound dope.

The Poo Bomb

One of the fascinating things about new parenthood is the way I had in my mind certain basic assumptions about how the process would work that were, in fact, to any actual parent, so totally and obviously wrong that there was no perceived need to point out that they were wrong. The wrong things I thought were seen as so obvious that nobody bothered to say otherwise.

For example, I recently rooted out one such assumption: that a diaper is capable of containing all the waste produced in any one "fecal occurrence."

Then, the other night I experienced an incident I have christened The Poo Bomb.

I watched TV, peacefully, with Cordelia lying on the couch next to me. She made some mildly fussy noises. I picked her up, took her into the nursery, and checked her diaper. I then found that she had shat out, conservatively, about 70 percent of her body weight. The waste product flowed around the diaper like the wind passes by a stick. I had to cross myself. It was majestic.

It was like, well, imagine an anaconda swallowing a warthog. But in reverse. And the warthog is made of poo.

I am almost positive that she can unhinge her hip bones.

I am starting to develop calm, firm parenting instincts. So it was obvious what I had to do next. I got the camera and took some pictures. Someday, Cordelia will bring home a boyfriend I don't like.

Then I cleaned up everything. And I mean everything. I probably had to clean stuff in YOUR house.

And the next morning, in direct violation of the Laws of Physics, she detonated another Poo Bomb. I swear to God she feels lighter.

Now She Can Fail!

Now that Cordelia is a month old, I can finally start measuring her up against development milestones.

I've been using the popular tome *What to Expect the First Year,* since it breaks down baby abilities into categories of decreasing likelihood (should be able to, may be able to, etc.). For example,

> "By the end of this month, your baby
>   . . . should be able to:
> • Breathe.
> • Scream.
>   . . . will probably be able to:
> • Stay awake from 10 P.M. to 10 A.M.
> • Urinate the moment its diaper comes off.
>   . . . may even be able to:
> • Be cute and adorable whenever nonparents are around.
> • Shit out 70 percent of its body weight in one go.
>   . . . may possibly be able to:
> • Repair an automotive transmission."

So now we can grade Cordelia. She is only a tiny sack of half-formed organs, and we can already evaluate her like a used car. And why shouldn't we? We're parents now, prisoners in our home. We don't have anything better to do. So we check the lists, making careful notes of the many things she might be able to do, but can't.

If our daughter is gifted, she is clearly not *that* gifted. I foresee 1,400 combined on the SAT, tops. She's a Yale child, at best. Clearly not Princeton material.

May Even Be Able to Train Mommy and Daddy

On the other hand, Cordelia did recently develop the ability to manipulate Mommy and Daddy. She can now cry to communicate nothing else than her desire for the parent holding her to get up off the nice comfortable couch, stop watching TV, and haul her around for a while.

I suppose I am proud of this.

Okay. If I Don't Hear a Clear Breath, I'm Only Going to Stand Here Ten More Minutes.

I am still obsessed over my daughter's ability to breathe. Which is, I suppose, reasonable. She still sleeps every night bracketed by those ridiculous foam "don't let the baby roll over" bars, and I still do breath checks every hour or so (but *very* quietly).

When looking after Cordelia, I'll always remember the little rhyme my grandmother taught me when I was little:

"If she's pink, stop and think.

If she's blue, nothing to do."

Hmm. Now that I think about it, I'm not sure that's right. Oh well. If something is wrong, I'm sure it'll come to me.

Yet Another Reason to Hate Parenting Books

Those who have read this far have probably picked up, at this point, my general lack of respect for parenting books. Well, maybe not lack of respect. I respect parenting books as much as I respect any class of medical text that freely interchanges science and guesswork.

My suspicions in this regard began while I was reading *The Birth Partner, Second Edition,* by Penny Simkin. The section on getting babies in the breech position to turn, in particular. The first technique described was the Breech Tilt position, in which the mother lies on a slanted board, with her ass above her head, in the hope that the child will turn around in the uterus. The section ended with this particularly choice quote:

"The position seems to encourage some babies to turn, but it may not work. Research studies have not found the breech tilt to be clearly more effective than doing nothing."

What?

WHAT!?!?!?

Okay. A baby is in a breech position. The mother is upset. She's frantic. She feels a desperate need to do something. In this case, people should be MORE careful about what they're saying, not LESS. And you CERTAINLY shouldn't just throw out random shit! I mean, why stop there? Why not say jumping jacks, wearing chains of daisies, and playing music down by the woman's vagina might get the baby to decide to turn around.

Oh. Wait. That last one was actually suggested. My personal hero, Penny Simkin, next recommends (I am not making this up) playing music at waist level in the hope of drawing the child's head down to hear better. If this doesn't work, she recommends having the father speak into the vagina like a microphone. This is so obviously ludicrous that she doesn't bother to mention the lack of scientific validity for this entertainment.

Actually, if playing music by mom's private parts can get the baby to turn its head down, we'd all better be careful that no music plays by the mother's head. Then the baby might turn itself breech to hear better! Oops!

If a mother manages to keep reading the book and gets past all the crap then, finally, Breech Version is described. In this procedure, the mother goes into an actual hospital, where actual doctors will attempt to physically turn the baby around in utero. This is painful, difficult, and has the minor, negligible advantage of actually working sometimes. Because it sometimes works and involves actual doctors, I'm frankly surprised it made it into the book.

(By the way, in all fairness to Penny Simkin, the dopey exercises are recommended in many, many other places, and most don't have the intellectual fortitude to mention there is no evidence they work. In fact, on lamaze.com, they even suggest specific sorts of music that seem to help the baby to turn. Bach and Vivaldi, in case you were curious. Also, *What to Expect When You're Expecting,* to its credit, simply says that there is no evidence that these exercises work, but they don't do harm either. Of course, the same thing can be said for just sitting and playing Nintendo.)

Don't get me wrong. I'm all in favor of empowering parents. I love the idea of getting the mother involved. This warm, fuzzy sentiment stops at exactly the point that giving emotionally strained parents random directions to keep them busy begins.

Week 6: Yet Another Way I Screwed Up My Kid

As of this writing, our darling daughter is forty-three days old. We have been parenting without a net for a bit over a week now. No grandparents. No baby-sitters. Just us and the baby. Cordelia's persistent survival is an unmistakable sign that things are sort of working out.

Mariann and I have come up with a number of nicknames for our daughter. The most commonly used are Miss Prissypants, Daddy's Little Fussbucket, and Poo Princess. We will develop more as time and circumstances allow.

Spending lots of time with Cordelia, however, is making me think about my responsibilities. After all, as I understand it, if I don't say exactly the right things to her at the right times, it will break her brain forever.

I'm Daddy. Say Daddy. Daaaaaaady. Daddy. Daddy. Daddydaddydaddy. Daddy, goddammit. Daddy. Daaaaady. Daddy.

Now that Cordelia is well into her second month and starting to edge into consciousness, the need to educate her is starting to weigh heavily on my brain. I've been talking to her constantly ever since she was squeezed out, but I've been talking like I do normally: Long, complex sentences with lots of obscenities. Since hardly anyone around me can understand what I'm saying, let alone a baby, I've begun to make an effort to talk in a more accessible way.

What this means in reality is that, when she looks at me, I say daddy a lot. Daddy. Daddy. Daaaaady. I'm trying to make this her first word. If she says "Daddy" before she says "Mommy," *I win.*

Mariann saw me doing this, so she took Cordelia and started saying "Daddy daddy daaady" too. Which is cheating! And I'm, like, "What sort of weird, crazyass, gender-bending, Greenwich Village shit is this?" So Mariann now says "Mommy" to Cordelia, unless I'm not around.

Sometimes, after I say "Daddy daddy daddy" a bunch of times, my daughter gets this irritated look on her face. I know it's just my imagination and that it's just a random twisting of her facial muscles, but I would swear that this look is meant to say, "Yes. You're Daddy. I get it. Retard."

Baby's First "Smile"

Speaking of random twisting of the facial muscles, Cordelia is smiling frequently now. There's no real rhyme or reason to it. She smiles when she sees Daddy. She smiles when she's about to poo. She smiles when she's about to start screaming.

I feel I should be doing something to communicate to her that she should smile when she is happy. So, whenever she smiles, I lurch forward, rub her belly, and say in a loud, happy voice, "Is that a smile? Is THAT a SMIIIIILE? You're such a good girl! A GOOOOOOD GIIIIIRRRRLLLLL!"

I strongly suspect that this scares the shit out of her. She smiles a lot less now. I think I am training her to never smile. I'm learning the error of my ways, though. The next time she smiles, I'm going to put her down and run out of the room.

A Few Brief Words on the Vagina

Now don't get me wrong. I have no problem with the vagina. I consider myself a big fan of the vagina. Sure, it's a temperamental and
overly complicated piece of machinery, but many has been the time
the vagina helped me happily while away the half hour between *Law
& Order* and *Letterman.*

However, to me, the vagina is like the work of Picasso. I can
admire and respect a Picasso and occasionally even highly enjoy a
Picasso, even while I don't claim to always understand Picasso. But
I don't think I want a Picasso on my wall. I don't want to live with
a Picasso.

And similarly, while I can admire and occasionally enjoy vaginas, I do not want to have to maintain one. I do not enjoy caring for
the machinery. And I am definitely not big on picking bits of feces
out of the vulva with a moist towelette.

(I know that these details are unpleasant. But the creation of
life is not for the squeamish.)

Which brings me to my daughter. If you read a lot of parenting
books and browse the sections on bathing, you will find frequent
references to vaginal mucous. Infant vaginas, like all vaginas, tend to
produce a reasonable amount of it. So what do you do with it?

One school of thought, popular in the more "modern" books, is
that this goo, like armpit hair, is a beautiful thing, and if nature put
it there it should be left alone. The other, less common, more old-
fashioned view, is *ewwww*! Clean that crap up! The decision of what
to do about this, as with practically every other parenting issue of any
import, is eventually dumped into the parent's lap.

The way I deal with it is by making sure to not be in the house
when my wife gives Cordelia a bath. My wife gets to make all the key
vagina decisions. Though I haven't seen it in a long time, I know my
wife has one, which makes her the resident expert.

In the meantime, I will care for my daughter's vagina in my
uncomfortable, don't-have-a-choice kind of way. I wipe it off when

she wets herself, while I'm humming songs, staring at the ceiling, trying to imagine what it's like in Spain, and engaging in other mental exercises to shrink my consciousness into a tiny, tiny thing.

And then, when she is grown up a bit more and can take care of the damn thing herself, I'm going to get so much therapy I'll make Woody Allen look like Ayn Rand.

A Brief Message to My Parents, Who I Know Will Read This:

I know you two fantasized for a long time about how great it would be to finally have a grandchild. And I am pretty positive that, in these fantasies, reading about your granddaughter's vaginal secretions played no part.

At this point, I must point out that you two raised *me*. Therefore, all this was written, in a very real, and, I suspect, legally binding, way, by you.

Yet Another Way I Screwed Up My Kid

Cordelia, if you are reading this, and you managed to get past the genitalia bits, you should probably know about another way I messed you up when you were little. I'll write it all down as soon as I'm through going upstairs, sneaking into your bedroom, and checking to make sure you're still alive. . . .

Okay. Back. You are still asleep. Thanks. Anyway. When you were just born, after you'd been out for a few hours, I ended up in the room alone with you. All the nurses were gone and your mom was in the bathroom dealing with her issues.

While I sat there holding you, I felt like singing to you. It was the first time you would ever hear music. And, being very tired, and not thinking, I started singing the song that was going through my head. It was "Forever in Blue Jeans."

That's right. The very first music you ever heard in this life, the song that was your introduction to that whole wonderful universe, was a Neil Diamond song.

I am so, so sorry.

By the time I finished the first chorus, I figured out what I was doing, and I sang the entirety of "Yellow Submarine." But I suspect that, by that time, it was too late.

I still sing to you, but I'm a lot more careful about the tunes I pick. I sing "Dust in the Wind" a lot. You seem to like that one.

College Fund

I've started doing research into college funds. This is so unredeemably complex and horrible that I can think of absolutely nothing funny to say about it.

My Current Fond Fantasy

I want to get a tape recorder and tape one of her loud, fussy screaming jags. Then I'll save the tape until she's fifteen. Then, late one night, I'll sneak into her room, play the tape at full volume, blast her ass out of bed, and scream, "How do *you* like it?"

I can't be the only person who has thought of doing this.

Thoughts from the Future

Occasionally, looking back at this journal, I am filled with awe at the depths of my own idiocy. Occasionally I will take the chance to point out moments of particular dumbousity.

For example, trying to teach a one-and-a-half-month-old child a word, any word, is a sign of poignant self-delusion. I could have spent that time in much more profitable activities. Such as, say, leaving her the hell alone.

But then again, she did say "Daddy" first.

Week 7: Dawn of the Neglectomatic

Cordelia creeps toward two months of accumulated life. Another month, another set of milestones. More weight to be borne by Daddy's delicate back. Larger deposits of feces. More sentience. Teeth.

Mariann and I have the routine pretty much down. I work a lot and watch the baby a few hours a day. She watches the baby a lot and works a few hours a day. It's halfway between a traditional setup and some sort of pure, utopian child-care situation where all the work is shared completely equally and the woman is a free, empowered spirit and the guy's balls shrivel up and fall off. Our system seems to be working for us, though, although the introduction of a baby-raising robot into the ecosystem would really take the rough edges off.

Looking ahead, my ten-year college reunion is coming up. Mariann has very kindly agreed to let me go, even though it frees me from parenting for a whole weekend and places me a thousand blissful miles from the baby to boot. Once there, I will get to brag that I have bred, thus lording my genetic, Darwinian superiority over the puny mortals!

The main problem we have with the baby, we have started to find, is all of the hours that need to be filled. Every night dumps several hours into our laps in which we have to stare at Cordelia and think, "What should we be doing? Are we doing enough? Is she bored? Should I be amusing her? How can I force her to love me?" We have been taking steps to fill these hours. While we do not have a baby-raising robot, we have found the next best thing . . .

Dawn of the Neglectomatic

We just got one of those electronic swing things. You know? Those things you put the baby in, and a little battery powered motor rocks it until it quiets down, simultaneously hypnotizing it into submission and churning the contents of its diapers into a frothing poo milkshake? Those things?

They're great. It feels like cheating.

Whenever our little fusspot is fed, burped, changed, and otherwise cared for in every way the law requires, if she's still fussing/whining/screaming/being heavy, we put her into the device one of our friends aptly named "The Neglectomatic." And it rocks her worries away.

I can actually watch the process on her face. Some little thing starts to bug her, and she carefully assembles the idea: "This annoys me. I should shout!" And then the rocking motion shakes the thought out of her head, like rolling a marble out of a hole in the bottom of a coffee can. And in the next minute, the process repeats itself.

Eventually, something bothers her for real, and the machinery is not enough to prevent her howls. Then Mariann or I take her out and see to her needs. Of course. But, as far as I'm concerned, if the problem isn't bad enough to keep Cordelia from enjoying the Neglectomatic, then Mommy and Daddy get to do their own thing for a while.

Now We Have to Buy a Goddamn Mobile

I can't escape my overachieving, idiot yuppie nature. You know how, if you put a dollar in the bank and let interest on it compound, eventually (in a thousand years or so) it will be a massive fortune? I can't help but feel that, if I do or say the right clever thing now, early in my daughter's life, it will compound and increase, like a snowball rolling downhill, into brilliance later on. Or, conversely, if I don't do enough during the precious moments of Cordelia's quiet alertness, instead of doing something I want to do (like sleep or play violent computer games), I will have, through my horrible inaction, cost my daughter a whole IQ point. Do this enough times, and she'll wind up a slack-jawed, burger-flipping, sorority-pledging, bottle-blonde troglodyte who can use the word "Booger" without irony. And then I will have to reabsorb her for her protein.

Nobody wants that.

So as it turns out, when Cordelia is lying in her crib staring up at the ceiling, I have to hang something above her that will stimulate her blank, gooey brainwad with its delightful shapes and colors. It's called a mobile. And I hate them.

If the selection at Target is any indication, mobiles cost about thirty bucks, are made of cheap plastic, play tinny versions of classical music, and look very colorful and interesting when looked at from the side (as opposed to from the bottom, the only angle the child will ever see it from). All of them conveyed one simple message to me, the consumer: "You are an idiot parent who will spend any amount on something for your baby, even if it's obviously stupid. *Give me your money!!!*"

But I'm not going to spend thirty bucks for three fuzzy pastel ducks hanging from strings, no matter how educational Target wants me to think it is. I'll sooner hang some power tools above her crib and hope they make her grow up to be a carpenter.

Since I left empty-handed, I am tempted to make my own mobile. The only problem here, besides my lack of artistic skill, time, and interest, is that a mobile has one other purpose. Based on what I read on the boxes, mobiles are also there so the child can hang itself when it unexpectedly learns to stand in its crib.

Damn it, if my darling Cordelia is going to hang herself on something, it's not going to be some shitty thing I threw together. No. My daughter deserves to meet a horrible and unexpected fate on the best educational device this world has to offer. And if that means dropping thirty bucks at Target, so be it.

Vogel's First Law for Dealing with Infants:

"It is impossible to underestimate the cognitive ability of a one-month-old."

I'm impatient. I am looking forward to the day when I can interact with my daughter as human. I sometimes like humans. Cordelia is not yet a human. She is ballast.

She hasn't even figured out that those pink things with all the little bits sticking out that occasionally cross her field of vision, what we grown-ups call "hands," are actually parts of her body, which she can control. If she even has a notion that she has an actual "body," a dubious prospect, considering her total inability to move it around.

And she doesn't realize that things she can no longer see still exist. Which means that, to her, Mommy and Daddy are just occasional phenomena, like the wind and the rain, which appear and disappear. She can recognize the appearance of the mommy-thing and the daddy-thing, and even greet that appearance with a display of what I think might possibly be happiness, but when the mommy-thing and the daddy-thing are out of sight, her blank little brain no longer recognizes that they exist.

If she even remembers them. The memory capability of the one-month-old is a very open question.

The practical upshot of all of this is that, when she's lying in her crib and I'm checking to make sure she's still alive, I have to make sure she doesn't see me. Because, if she does, her little goo brain seems to have this chain of barely coherent baby thoughts:

"Bzzzzzzzzz . . . ." (This is the sound of her empty brain, looking up at the blank ceiling, where the mommy-thing and the daddy-thing have neglectfully failed to put a mobile/strangulation device.)

"!!!!! Daddy-thing has appeared! It exists again!"

(I'm staring at her, looking for signs of breathing.)

"!!!!! Daddy-thing brings formula and carrying! Nutrients! Carrying!"

(Okay. Baby is not dead. I can go back to my movie now.)

"!!!!!!!!! Daddy-thing has disappeared! No more food! No more carrying! Forever!"

"Hey! Hey! Hey! Hey! Hey!"

In this case, "Hey!" is shouted aloud. It is the only word in Cordelia's vocabulary. However, her pronunciation skills are poor, so it sounds like "Waaahhhhh!!! Waaahhhhh!!!"

But I know that she means "Hey."

However, if I'm careful and keep her from seeing me, I don't exist, so she won't know to require anything of me. And then I get to watch a two-hour movie in less than six hours.

One More Thing About My Daughter's Crying

When she gets *really* upset, her cry sounds just like a dolphin who's been possessed by Satan.

The Recipe for Sleep. And Sweet Neglect.

My daughter reliably sleeps five to six uninterrupted hours a night, every night. It's fabulous. Part of the reason, of course, is that we are lucky. But part of it is because of me, and my recipe of strategic neglect.

Don't get me wrong. I have not adopted the borderline sadistic "Let her lie in bed and cry until she passes out" theory of parenting. I'm not a jerk. Yet.

Instead, I put Cordelia to bed using a complicated series of steps designed to strip away her ability to stay awake. Of course, since the system works well for me, it must be doing her incredible and irreversible harm. Here is how I achieve an infant take-down and the ways the literature tells me I am breaking her brain:

Step 1—Get Mommy to go to bed at 9:30 P.M.
Reason—Mommy will just interfere.
Harm to baby—Considerable. Mommy's absence lets Daddy take charge, which is just a bad idea.
Step 2—As soon as baby gets hungry (usually around 10:30), pack her full of formula until she couldn't possibly hold any more. When picking her up, I should hear a gentle sloshing sound. She should be as full as a pimple. When she cries from then on, feed her a little more formula.
Reason—Then it'll take hours before hunger wakes her up again.
Harm to baby—Mind-blowing. First, mother's milk is the baby's perfect food. I know this because it says it on the side of the bottle I'm using to feed her the formula.
Second, I am teaching Cordelia not only to always eat as much as she possible can, but that she should deal with being upset

by eating more. Eventually, she's going to end up as huge as any two people at a science fiction convention.

Step 3—Around 11:30 P.M., put the baby into a disposable diaper.

Reason—Keeps irritating and wakefulness-causing urine far from baby's delicate genitals.

Harm to baby—For once, none. The harm will come to future generations who have to clean up the landfills. Screw them. Let the cockroaches that evolve after all humans are gone deal with the diapers. I have my own problems.

Step 4—Put a pacifier in her mouth.

Reason—Even when packed full of formula (soy product and corn syrup solids . . . ewww), my daughter will squeal if she doesn't have anything to suck on. And she can't suck on her hands, because she doesn't realize she has them, and she can't suck on my little finger, because it will be busy being attached to me.

Harm to baby—Considerable. Using pacifiers as substitutes for affection will cause Cordelia vague and undefined but devastating harm. Mussolini used a pacifier.

Step 5—At midnight, swaddle her (i.e., wrap her tightly in blankets, so the cute, spasmodic arm motions she makes when she sleeps don't wake her up or, worse, knock the pacifier out of her mouth) and lie her down in her crib. Turn out lights.

Reason—So she can go to sleep.

Harm to baby—Likely death. According to *Complete Baby and Child Care* by Dr. Miriam Stoppard, the crib's mattress is supposed to have holes in it so that, if the baby rolls over, she doesn't suffocate. Sure, this is bizarre bordering on idiotic. But it's in a book, so it must be correct.

Step 6—Should the baby cry, put the pacifier back into her mouth. (The pacifier falling out is the number one reason Cordelia ever cries.) If she cries again, pick her up until she stops. Then put her back down and put the pacifier back into her mouth.

I don't know what to do if Step 6 doesn't work out, because it's never happened. She may want to get up, but the massive amounts of soy in her stomach weigh her down.

Harm to baby—Since I never actually let her be upset for more than a few moments, I don't think there is immediate psychological harm. However, I am slowly programming her to believe that anyone who comforts her will only do so for a few minutes. This will probably result in her having a lot of disappointing affairs with married men.

And that's all it takes to get a baby to sleep. Equal amounts preparation, optimism, and disinterest. All I ask you to remember is two things:

i. It will not work for you,
   and,
ii. Any night now, it will not work for me either.

When that happens, I'll see you in Hell.

Week 8—I'll Dress Her in Chain Mail, As Long As It's Free

It's taking extra time to write this week. I'm having to type everything while holding Cordelia in my lap. I'm writing one-handed. You would think my fourteen years on the Internet would have made me better at typing one-handed. I think I've been going to the wrong Web sites.

I'm writing this with one hand because the other is holding Cordelia upright. If I let her lie on her back, she will instantly start screaming. When I try to make amends by lifting her up again, she will cry a few more seconds to fully make her point. Then she will punish me with a withering infant look of irritation and disappointment.

I think this says something bad about me as a person, but I am far more pleased when she communicates irritation than happiness.

The smiles I'm supposed to be so impressed by might just be the result of gas. But those frowns are real. They're 100 percent pure, undiluted, "Hey, don't try to put one over on me, OLD MAN." It melts my heart.

What Makes My Daughter Happy

Sometimes, I want my child to be quiet and alert and happy and looking in my eyes with this sort of beautiful, sacred parent-child communication like in *Bambi*. At this stage of life, my overachieving yuppie spirit is not satisfied merely with having my daughter get to the end of the day without turning blue. I think I should be interacting with her. Or educating her. Or, at the very least, getting a reminder of what her face looks like when it's not asleep or screaming.

Sometimes, I can commune with her mushy little brain by planting my face the book-recommended eight to ten inches from hers and making barnyard noises. Mooing, barking, etc. This quiets her down and is usually good for a smile, but then I start to worry that she will learn to talk this way. She'll start to communicate exclusively in clucks and grunts. And then she'll flee the company of regular humans, with their strange, frightening language of sentences and vowels. And the next thing you know, she's living in a shack in the woods, spending her life naked and covered with squirrels, and it's MY FAULT.

Fortunately, this doesn't need to happen. If I want to spend time with a happy baby, I don't need to moo. There is a time when she is always quiet, alert, happy, and ready with a smile, never fail. And that is when she is not wearing pants.

In the time between when I've changed her diaper and put on her clothes, she is invariably happy. Blissed out. She kicks her legs up and airs out her parts, and she couldn't be more pleased. I had no idea how freeing and joyous it could be to free oneself from the cruel shackles of pants.

And yet, when I got jealous and tried it myself, it didn't work. I used the bathroom, rubbed myself down thoroughly with moist towelettes, took off my pants, hopped onto the bed, and kicked my legs in the air. It really made me feel cool and free (and quite fresh, thank you for asking), but not happy.

I wondered what it would take for me to attain Cordelia's pantsless ecstasy. I had Mariann come in and rub my belly. No help. I had her moo at me. While this intrigued me in a way neither of us are comfortable with, no extra happiness. My legs hurt. My back hurt. While my kid can hold that position forever, I had to lower my legs. And, eventually, I put on pants.

Yes, the joy of no pants, like my youthful innocence and enjoyment of Hostess cupcakes, is gone forever. But at least I can teach my daughter and help her experience the thrill of utter pantslessness. Before it's too late. It's the Circle of Life.

An Unnecessary and Brief Comment on the Subject of Vomit

My daughter, like all infants, spits up a lot. "Spit-up" is the cute euphemism we parents use for "barf" or "vomit" in an attempt to retain our sanity.

Until recently, her milky spit-up has smelled, well, like milk. A little musty, but not so bad.

Recently, however, her spit-up started to smell like what it is. Vomit. This was a strictly unnecessary stripping away of one of the cherished illusions that has been helping me get from one end of the day to the other.

The last thing in the world I needed was for parenthood to become more gross.

Yes. I Know Your Child Shits. And I Don't Want to Hear About It.

I was about to fill this space with a story about my child pooing in an interesting way. You will be pleased to know that I thought better of it.

It is only natural, I suppose. If you share your home with a creature that is completely uninhibited about when and where it excretes waste and has the ability to do so with astonishing force and range, you will get stories. *Everyone* with children has these stories. So why, God, why do we tell them?

These stories are corrosive to the soul, for the teller, the listener, and the subject. My parents have two of them about me. In one, I stood in the back of a pickup truck and peed on passing traffic. In the other, I peed on one of my grandparents' paintings. (In my defense, it's not exactly the greatest painting in the world.) Each of the dozens of times I have heard these stories, it has taken a week off my life.

Therefore, I now make a promise to you, the reader. No more stories about filth expulsion. Even really good ones, like the one I was going to write, which included the word "lampshade."

Of course, I reserve the right to break this promise, but only if something really, *really* good happens. But she'll have to piss on the Pope.

I'll Dress Her in Chain Mail, As Long As It's Free.

Mariann's timing in getting pregnant was excellent. When Cordelia was born, we knew four couples who had recently had their final child, and two more who just had a kid and were determined not to have another any time soon.

As a result, we were showered with tons of free shit. Parents, freshly freed from the burden of caring for infants, looked around and went "Aaah! What is all this crap doing in my house! If I ever see another sippy-cup, I will ram it through my head!" So they gave it all to us. Multiple copies of the same book. Spare bathtubs. His and hers strollers. And clothes. Tons and tons of clothes.

It seems like, every day, Cordelia is wearing an outfit I've never seen before. Jumpers with French writing on the chest. Masculine blue velour one-pieces. Ludicrous dresses edged in lace (which we put on her as a punishment). The fashion show never ends.

It turns out, I'll dress my kid in anything as long as it's free. A tinfoil pantsuit. Baby seal fur. The skin of a different, larger baby. No matter. An exhausted friend gives it to us in a paper bag, and it goes into the queue.

And, when something gets outgrown, it goes into a different bag. We already have two huge bags of obsolete spare garments. I'll tell you one thing. Our next friend who gets knocked up wins the lottery.

I Wuv My Widdle Hippie Girl

We got clothes at the baby shower too. A hippie couple we know made Cordelia a lovely pair of tie-dyed undergarments. It was an admittedly noble effort to turn our fresh new daughter into some sort of scumass, vegan, Nader voter.

My wife and I soon observed that whenever we put her into her tie-dyed outfit, she would, without fail, immediately urinate on it.

She is her father's daughter.

I Wuv My Daddy Tagboard Face

We bought a mobile to hang above her crib. It's some asinine educational thing. It's a set of four-inch-diameter cardboard circles with geometrical designs and crude, black-and-white human faces on them. I was surprised and displeased to find that Cordelia is actually fascinated by it. I didn't go through all the trouble of having my wife give birth to have a daughter who can be entertained by staring at circles.

It gets worse. Within hours of the mobile's installation, I looked into the crib and saw Cordelia staring at the cardboard face. She had this smiling, blissed-out look on her face. I recognized the expression instantly. It's the way she looks when she sees me!

Nothing strips a fresh parent of delusions regarding the depth of the emotional attachment of his child faster than seeing her give total adoration and allegiance to a cardboard disk.

But I knew how to handle the situation. The next time Cordelia was crying, I was, like, all "Oh? Something wrong? Need to be fed? Changed? Well why don't you have the *cardboard disk* do it, huh? What's the matter? The *cardboard disk* not there for you? Huh? Bet you don't feel so smart now! You backed the wrong horse, kid! The *cardboard disk* has got nothin' on me! Nothin'!"

> ## Thoughts from the Future
>
> Note, once again, my futile attempts to communicate with a two-month-old. It is very hard to come to terms with the fact that there are some humans you just can't talk to. They can't understand. There is no point. In general, you should talk to a two-month-old like you would to the average Rush Limbaugh fan.
>
> Oh, and when a couple we knew had a daughter, we dumped three huge plastic bins of secondhand baby clothes in their living room as soon as possible. It's their problem now.

Then my wife Mariann came in. Surprisingly, she was entirely unsympathetic to my viewpoint and took Cordelia off to deal with whatever she was whining about. It's easy for her to be that way. She doesn't realize how fickle and disloyal our child is. And I plan to make this extremely clear, just as soon as Mariann is speaking with me again.

Week 9—Now Baby Must Be Stuck with Needles

Spring is beginning to blossom, pollen is thick in the air, and the bright stillness of the morning is broken by the happy chirps of Cordelia.

Now over two months old and well over ten pounds, she has attained a major milestone in the eyes of her daddy. She has reached the size of a small but usable turkey. While I do not intend to stuff and roast her, I do take some satisfaction in getting her to the point where she would be useful for that purpose.

The First Doctor's Appointment

Her increasing age also led us (well, led her mom, as Daddy was asleep) to take Cordelia for her two-month doctor's appointment.

It was an informative trip. First, Daddy learned that his back pain wasn't in his head. His delightful little girl had ballooned to ten pounds and ten ounces of vertebrae-compressing baby. This is a gain of well over an ounce a day. A simple process of extrapolation reveals that, on her sixteenth birthday, she will be almost four hundred pounds, and we can get rich selling her to the circus.

Second, some tube in her right eye is all gummed up. This means her tears can't drain out. Instead, they stay in her eye, getting it permanently gross and crusty. Compared to the normal disgusting things that a baby exposes you to (up to and including spraying feces across the room and onto the lampshade), this is mild and almost endearing. We are assured that this will clear up on its own, unless it doesn't.

Finally, the big news. Our baby seems to have a heart murmur. According to the parenting books and Web sites Mommy and Daddy have been frantically scouring, this is a terrifying-sounding condition that many babies seem to have, though it can just be the way the heart sounds and not really anything, or if it is anything, it'll most likely clear up on its own, or . . .

Well, what the books say is "Don't worry." Great. What "heart murmur" means is that babies fall into two groups: babies who seem to have a heart murmur and are just fine, and babies who seem to have a heart murmur and will meet a horrible fate. Which a worried, irrational parent will invariably read as, "Tough break. Might as well conceive another one now." Why not let the other shoe drop and have the pediatrician run into the room shouting "Hello, your baby is going to die, die, DIE!!!"

The books say that the reason doctors freak parents out about this diagnosis, even if it is almost undoubtedly nothing, is that they want to make a note of it so they can look at it later. Sure. As if later they were going to just forget to check the heart. Look, if it's not worth doing anything about it until a certain point, couldn't you just freak me out about it AT THAT POINT?

Because now I have to tell my parents that their grandchild has a heart murmur, and they're going to freak out, and then I'll tell them it's nothing, and they won't believe me, and I won't believe me, and then everyone is running around in circles screaming except the baby. As if I didn't have enough reasons to pack a bag, head south, smuggle heroin in my rectum, and never be seen again.

On the bright side, we were told that Cordelia was, apart from the bad stuff, basically healthy and perfect. Though she was about to become drastically less healthy and perfect. Because they were about to impale her with needles.

Now Baby Must Be Stuck with Needles

The nurses at the doctor's office had it *together,* man. Cordelia needed to get four shots. Four! So two nurses came in and gave the shots in two pairs of two, one on each thigh, at the same time. The engineer in my soul applauds such efficiency. I also applaud my daughter, for learning how loud she can scream. I love my little bull-horn girl.

We did decide to vaccinate our child. For some people, this decision is controversial. A Web search for "vaccines" will bring up a host of Web sites, some of them even proofread, which explain why this is a bad idea. Some of them give sensible alternatives, like (ahem) homeopathy.

It is my firm belief that there is no belief so asinine, no course of action so bizarre, that it cannot have a half dozen Web sites strongly devoted to its practice. If these people ever learned to check their spelling, we might be in real trouble.

Antivaccination people are spooky. I'm not saying that vaccines should be mandatory, but everyone who doesn't have their infants take advantage of the miracles of modern medicine should be required to either provide a solid health reason why the vaccine will be harmful ("The last one made her burst into flames") or write a five-hundred-word essay entitled "Why Polio Isn't So Bad."

(Don't laugh. I had no trouble finding such essays online. At thinktwice.com, for example. Turns out, according to them, polio is not much to worry about. Phew! Thinktwice.com is also willing to

sell you selections from this fine collection of books on holistic medicine, so I can't recommend it highly enough, in a sixteenth-century
kind of way.)

The Joyous Blossoming of Pre-Colic

We are getting close to the age when colic can happen. Or, as I usually call it, "The 'C' Word," for fear that speaking that cursed word
aloud will summon it. Every night, I watch carefully for periods of
long, irrational screaming, afraid that I, too, have been touched by
the colic fairy and all happiness will be stripped off me like blubber
off a whale.

And Cordelia does not disappoint. When the evening comes,
she frequently treats me to long, uninterrupted periods of
screeeeeaming. Up to an hour. I do not call this colic. That would
be like stubbing my toe and shouting, "Ahh! I severed my foot!"

But I know enough to be afraid. I watch carefully, waiting for
signs or screaming jags that last over an hour. And if the squealing
does start to last that long I will . . . will . . . well, I won't do anything, actually. But I will complain a lot more.

Fortunately, I am prepared for the worst. I am able to simultaneously hold Cordelia, make comforting noises, and surf the Web.
If she's going to be screaming anyway, I might as well have some
fun.

Now It Can Be Told. The Advantages of Parenthood.

I didn't have one major, overarching reason for wanting a child. I
had a lot of little tiny reasons.

For example, I wanted to free my parents from the horrible, soul-
grinding future they made abundantly clear a life without grandchildren offered them. I figured, "Hey. Be a mensch. They put me
through college. It's the least I can do."

But I think the main reason, or at least, the slightly more important reason, is that I never, ever, ever wanted to have this conversation again:

Me: "What do you want to do tonight?"

Mariann: "I dunno. What do you want to do?"

Me: "I dunno."

There is nothing like having a baby to temporarily dispel all angst from your life. Now we have this conversation instead:

Me: "What do you want to do tonight?"

Wife: "Keep the baby from turning blue."

Me: "Great! Let's do it!"

My Baby Can DO Something!

My baby has just achieved a huge milestone, apart from her new, previously mentioned roastability.

She has figured out that she has a "hand." She can now amuse herself for up to an hour at a time by lifting her right hand to her mouth, sucking on it for a little bit, forgetting that that was what she put her hand there for, letting it fall out of her mouth, and then repeating the process. Throw in the occasional, accidental, self-inflicted punch in the nose, and it's surprisingly entertaining to watch.

This is a big thing for me because it's the first time I can see her actually *do* something. She wants something, she controls her body, and she makes it happen. Actually, activity is a huge relief after two months of basically taking care of a big, gooey, pink larva.

The mobile still hypnotizes her to a degree that I find, frankly, disturbing. Last night, she spent a half hour staring up at the mobile while sucking on her hands. Tonight, an hour. Between the mobile and her hand, she can achieve total relaxation. For me to be that relaxed, you'd have to put a bullet in my head.

It's the baby girl equivalent of me spending a peaceful afternoon sitting on the couch watching TV and scratching my balls. There is nothing more beautiful than seeing my daughter take after her daddy.

"Honey, This Is Britney Spears. Daddy Thinks She Is Sexy."

I also set up a little stereo in her nursery. I played a CD of Classical Music for Babies. She listed to it intently for a while. I found myself

Thoughts from the Future

Don't worry. The heart murmur turned out to be exactly nothing. This isn't going to turn into one of those baby books where I suddenly wave around an alcoholic relative or a dead child to teach you valuable lessons about how you should value life and make every moment count or whatever. Believe me, I am the last person you should take life guidance from.

Nothing poignant happens in this book. Though I do drop the kid on her head in a few months.

struck with a sudden, irresistible desire to beat her up and take her lunch money.

So I put in some Led Zeppelin. Some people claim that classical music helps baby brains develop better. This may be true (though I doubt it). But they don't say anything about what I should do to teach the babies *how to ROCK*.

Week 10—Baby's Life Among the Geeks

Cordelia is sailing smoothly through her third month of life. Her screaming jags gave me and Mariann strong motivation to develop new ways to distract, pacify, or psychologically anesthetize her. Be it a mobile, a CD of baby music, or Daddy's "special" formula mixture (lime juice, triple sec, tequila, shaken, salt on the nipple, and some vitamins for good health), she is turning into as quiet and well-behaved a little drool-girl as anyone could ever want.

She has made no advancements in the last week. Despite our encouragement and unnervingly constant observation, she is as dopey and glassy-eyed as ever.

Well, actually, there is something. Today, she used her razor-sharp baby nails to give her face both the deepest and the longest self-inflicted scratches ever. I think this means she is improving her strength and motor skills.

Bear with me. I'm grasping at straws here, people.

Baby's Life Among the Geeks

This weekend, we took our daughter on our first family trip. We went to stay in a hotel by the airport and attend a science fiction convention.

Our daughter comes from a strong nerd background, and she will be raised in an extremely nerd-heavy environment. Her nursery also serves as the storeroom for all my old Dungeons and Dragons books. Bearing this in mind, we figured, "Hey, why fight it?" We might as well immerse her in geekdom from day one, and see what happens. If worst comes to worst, we can sell her to the circus.

It is a difficult thing, exposing one so delicate and blank-brained to the sort of wanksticks who know how to speak Klingon, have memorized the *Rocky Horror Picture Show,* and think Doctor Who is good. But, then again, these are my people. And exposing Cordelia to them is my sacred responsibility.

As I understand it, my job as a parent is to completely program my child. Every belief, every preference, every behavior, good or bad, will be what my wife and I decide. If we deem that she will vote Republican, like clams, and hate jazz, she will do so. Those are just examples, of course. I can't stand kids and their crazy jazz music.

Therefore, the geek immersion. If we don't do this now, there is a chance that Cordelia will one day be capable of cheering for her high-school football team without irony. And we can't have that.

Mariann and I are *gods,* and Cordelia is the *clay* we mold, working her in our own image. So we took her to a hotel to spend a weekend around people wearing latex extensions on their foreheads.

Believe me, it made sense at the time.

So anyway. What we found out is that taking a two-and-a-half-month-old to a hotel for the weekend is aggravating. But so is having a two-and-a-half-month-old anywhere else. So no loss. And having a baby around lots of people is a great self-esteem builder. Strangers poke at your child and smile at you. If you ever feel down, just sling your sprog around a crowd, and at least someone will be impressed by it.

It is amazing something so cute and interesting could emerge from my sperm. And to think I spent all those years wasting it.

Why I Am the Worst Parent Ever

While I was pushing Cordelia in a stroller down one of the hallways of the convention, I walked past a young, attractive woman wearing an unusually skimpy costume. I was so distracted by her ass that I pushed the stroller into a pole.

Not, on reflection, my proudest moment.

Dopey, Dopey Baby

Spending lots of time in the presence of people who are neither me nor my offspring, however, makes it very clear how different my somewhat unsentimental view of parenting is from everyone else's. This becomes most clear when, in the presence of others, I refer to little Cordelia as "Dopey."

To their credit, they immediately jump to my daughter's defense, since she is far too blank-minded and oblivious to do it herself. They ask, horrified, how any parent could refer to his own little child as "dopey."

My response is simple. She *is* dopey. DOPEY DOPEY DOPEY. Have you ever looked in the eyes of a two-month-old? Taken a good, long look? There's nothin' there! Ever wonder what was going on in those tiny infant brains of theirs? Well, here's what it sounds like: "Bzzzzzzzzzzzzzz."

And I have to describe her as dopey, because it helps me come to terms with the fact that she might always be that way. Maybe I'm overly pessimistic, but how can I be absolutely sure that she's ever going to get any smarter? Concluding that my child's brain will develop just because every other kid's does strikes me as excessively naive and optimistic.

How do I know I won't still have to carry her around in a sling when she's in kindergarten? Can I be sure I won't have to drive at top speed to her seventh-grade class because the pacifier fell out of her mouth. Jesus, what if she takes up track and field in high school? I'll have to learn how to pole vault, just to haul her lumpy form over that damn bar. I don't want to be changing the diapers of a thirty-year-old! That's when she's supposed to be changing my diapers!

No. I'm going to face up to it now. She's a dopey, dopey little girl. And you can argue the point with me all you want. She won't mind. She'll be sitting there, happy and content, in a rapidly expanding pool of her own waste.

A Brief Discussion of the Five-Second Rule in the Context of Parenting

Of the many ways in which science has made it easier for us to live productive lives, I think the most significant is the Five-Second Rule.

For the unfamiliar, the Five-Second Rule states that, when food is dropped on the floor, if it is picked up and brushed off within five seconds, it is still wholesome and edible. Past that, it is considered "dirty" and must be discarded/given to the dog. I am sure that this rule was created and verified by Science, no doubt tested by hordes of bespectacled biosnackgineers, with clipboards and ear hair.

The Five-Second Rule is important because of Cordelia's dependence on her pacifier (known to science as a "Binky"), combined with her ability to occasionally spit it a long distance. Whenever she lands it on the floor, I swoop down as swiftly as I can, scoop it up, wipe off the bits of grit that have adhered to her saliva, triumphantly shout "Five-Second Rule!" and jam it back into her mouth.

But this makes me wonder. How are the five seconds counted? Suppose the Binky lands on the floor once for one second, is replaced, is spit out, and then lands again for two seconds. Do the seconds add up? When it's spit out again, do I have a fresh five seconds to grab it, or do I have only two seconds? Does her sucking restore the lost "floor time" slowly, or is it all regained the moment I put the Binky in her mouth?

Good questions, all, and ones that can only satisfactorily be answered by appealing to that sweet, fierce bitch-goddess which is Science. Infuriatingly, none of the parenting books I have consulted say thing one about the Five-Second Rule. I demand that this situation be rectified. I require rigid, laboratory-tested bounds for my laziness and apathy.

"Well, Why Don't You Just Wash Off the Pacifier Before Putting It Back into Her Mouth? Huh?"

Because then I would be spending ten hours a day washing off the goddamn pacifier. Also, germs build character.

Plus, I'm burned out on the whole sanitation thing. Before a nurse suggested we get a pacifier, Cordelia sucked on my little finger. I was washing my hands so often that I was getting big, flaky sores. It got so bad even obsessive compulsives were coming up to me on the street and saying, "Dude, you need to RELAX!"

Forcing Music Appreciation

There are lots of places to get advice on how to make your child appreciate music. There are music CDs you can buy to get your infant to develop a love of Mozart, or Bach, or some other crusty dead guy.

For example, at the baby shower, we were given a CD of classical music for babies. That is, it is perfectly good classical music, played in a way an adult imagines a tiny baby might enjoy. That is, short snippets of the greatest hits played on someone's Casio keyboard. It annoys Daddy, so baby loves it.

And yet, what I want to know is not how to create interest in my child, but how to prevent it. I am, frankly, indifferent about how Cordelia feels about Mozart. However, I am willing to exert considerable effort to keep her from ever liking jazz.

For that matter, I would gladly burn all potential for love of music out of her tiny brain before I'd let her spend several years tormenting me with that boy band shit. I know that this is years off, but I still dread it.

There must be a way to prevent this. Maybe, from the age of six, I'll play the Backstreet Boys constantly. I will dance to them, in my shambling, white guy manner. I will call them "phat" and "da bomb." A display like that should result in her treating boy bands like radioactive waste.

And, at the same time, she can't ever see me listen to music I like, or she'll hate it. For the next eighteen years, I can only listen to the Beatles and Led Zeppelin in the tiny crawlspace under the stairs, and I'll refer to Lennon in her presence as a "dirty longhair."

With hard work and patience, I'm sure I can give my little girl the freedom to choose to like what I do.

A Compromise on the Music Issue

In sixteen years, as now, I am sure that many pop stars loved by the young will be of the "Underage, sexually teasing jailbait girls" variety. Like Britney Spears. Jewel. Hanson. And so on.

There is room for compromise here. My daughter can plaster posters of her favorite stars all over the house as long as they are . . . well . . . how to put this delicately? Easy on the eyes.

All we have to do is work together, and I'm sure can all get our own little something out of the deal.

Week 11: "Look, Honey! Her Fontanel Is Throbbing."

Cordelia has entered a growth spurt. This means that, instead of sleeping six hours at night before needing more food, she sleeps five. You might not think such a small difference would make a big change in the tranquility of our household. You would be incorrect.

I work until late at night. Thus, for most of the night, Mariann can sleep while I take care of baby issues. When the baby wakes and wails, I change diapers, provide comfort, simulate affection, and so on. But when Cordelia wakes up because she's hungry, I have to walk into the bedroom, disturb my wife's peaceful slumber, and say, "Come on. Haul them boobs out. Need 'em."

Okay. I don't actually say that. But Cordelia's screaming conveys the message very well. This makes Mariann unhappy, so I am unhappy. Or, at least, made to be unhappy.

This is a real step down from the old days before Cordelia was born. Back then, I never had to wake Mariann up to get access to her breasts. Except for really special occasions.

So less sleep, all around. You might be saying, "Oh, so what! You think you have problems? My baby only sleeps one hour a night! And she never stops screaming! And she has a gun!!!" Well, I'm not saying my problems are worse than yours. What I am saying, though, from sort of a cosmic standpoint, is that it is better for you to suffer greatly than for me to be slightly inconvenienced. Just so you know.

Conversations with the Baby

Our baby is starting to enter the babble stage. She can spend long periods of time trying to get her mouth to make vowel sounds.

I can sympathize with her difficulties. Despite years of trying, I can not roll my R's. Mariann's family is Hungarian and, when they find that I can't roll R's, they look at me like I'm r-r-r-r-r-retarded. But I just can't do it. And for Cordelia, every single sound she'll need to make will be like me rolling my R's. Her mouth will need to be trained to make every single sound. Every way to pronounce every letter is a new challenge, which will take days of practice. So I'm helping.

When she is feeling talkative, I converse with her by repeating every sound she makes back to her. I delude myself into thinking it really encourages her . . . we can go on like this for an hour at a time.

"Ooo."

"Oooo."

"Oooo. Ohh."

"Oooooo. Ohh."

(I think, "God, I feel like a jerk.")

"Aaaaahhhoi!"

"Aaaahhhoooii!"

"Aaahh."

"Aaaahhh."

(I think, "But I suppose, if I didn't want to spend all my time looking like a complete idiot, I wouldn't have had a kid.")

"Uhh. Ooooh. Aoooah. Oi."

"Oooh. Aooooahh. Oi."

"Oi. Oi."

"Oi. Oi."

("Oi? What is she? A British soccer hooligan?")

Then, eventually, I get bored. So I spend time trying to teach her actual words.

"Uhhhh. Ohh."

"Defenestrate."

"Ooo. Goo."

"Colonoscopy."

"Oooo. Oi."

"Mellifluous."

"Uhhhh."

"Uh . . . Honey? Did I do 'colonoscopy' yet?"

"Yes."

"Okay, thanks."

"Uhhh. Aaaaoi."

"Colonoscopy."

"Gooo. Ooo."

"Androgynous."

Then, eventually, Cordelia just stares at me like I'm a jerk.

The process is interesting. If there was anything I was looking forward to about parenting, apart from being released from the pressure of having to perform sexually on a regular basis, it was seeing a squealing, blood-smeared little wad of pale flesh develop into a full human being. To see her learn to talk is to see her accept one half of her heritage as a full, empowered member of our species. As soon as her hands have developed enough to hold and aim a gun, she will be complete.

Secrets of the Baby Mutterer

One of the parenting books easily found in any bookstore is *Secrets of the Baby Whisperer*. Despite the sick-making, gut-churning title, it does not actually try to convince overeager parents that they can communicate with their children. Although it does divide babies into different "personalities." It turns out, there are options besides "bitchy."

This does, however, give me an idea for my own book. I'll call it *Secrets of the Baby Mutterer: Decoding Your Baby's Utterances So That You Can Understand It Perfectly and Realize How Smart the Little Sprog Is*. It will be full of shit I just made up, which will put it on the intellectual level of most parenting books.

A sample of translations:

"Waaaahhhh! Waaaahhhh!"—"Hey! Hey!"

"Gooo. Gah."—"I am noncommittal."

"Ehhhh. Ehhhhhh. Eh."—"I am having trouble breathing. Please totally righteously freak out now."

"Ahhh. Ah. Ahhhhh."—"I have absolutely no moral sense. If I was bigger and stronger, I would have no qualms about cracking your skull open to see if there's candy inside."

"Oi. Oi."—"I want to be a British soccer hooligan."

Hell Is Other Parents

When I found out that my wife was going to be bearing my child, I made to myself one silent, sacred resolution. I was not going to let parenthood eat my brain. I was not going to turn into one of *those* parents.

There is a certain sort of person who is invariably turned by parenthood into this sort of gaseous kvetch who responds to news of any difficulty, no matter how big or small, with a litany of woe from their parenting life. You will know who I am talking about, if you have ever had one of these conversations:

> Me: "My job is driving me nuts. I'm having real trouble working on this project."
>
> Them: "You should try having a baby. Then you'll know what trouble is!"
>
> Me: "Man, I'm tired. The baby was up all night."
>
> Them: "You think you have it bad now? Wait until she's had colic for two months."
>
> Me: "I just found out. The tumor in my stomach is malignant."
>
> Them: "Just wait until you've raised a teenager. Then you'll know what worrying is!"
>
> Me: "Help me. Oh God, please. I'm having a heart attack."
>
> Them: "Like that's a problem. Just wait until you've . . . Hey. Are you okay?"

I want to deal with this problem like I want to deal with any problem: with horrible, horrible violence. But they are parents, so small people depend on them for support and sustenance, so, in some tiny, moral way, destroying them would be wrong.

But one day, their children will have left home. They will be free. And if some senior citizens ever bitch to me about how tough parenting is, I'll boil them.

What My Baby Has Learned. What She Hasn't.

What she has learned: When she jams her entire fist into her mouth, it gives her pleasure.

What she has not learned: Trying to jam both fists into her mouth at the same time? Not so good.

Imperforate Anus!

I was browsing through *Complete Baby and Child Care,* by Dr. Miriam Stoppard, reading about the different, horrible afflictions Cordelia did not get. Every time I read about something awful we missed, I got a little thrill of relief. ("No Pyloric Stenosis! Phew!")

It was then that I learned about "Imperforate Anus." I am not kidding. What this means is that the baby is born, basically, with no asshole. This is kind of bad. If nothing is done, eventually, these babies *explode.*

Okay, that last sentence wasn't true. Unfortunately.

The only reason I mention this is because now, if you are anything like me, and I see no reason why you aren't, you will be unable to go through any conversation for the next several days without finding a way to work in the phrase "imperforate anus."

I've also started saying that my baby was born with "perforate anus." That sounds pretty good, too.

"Look, Honey! Her Fontanel Is Throbbing."

The fontanels are, of course, the soft spots in the baby's head where the skull hasn't closed yet. I am assured that they are sealed off with a strong membrane, which prevent idle poking from damaging the baby's sweet little brain. Bear in mind, it is still a bad idea to bonk the baby's head against things.

What they don't tell you, however, is that sometimes, for reasons known only to God and hydraulic science, the soft spot pulses. You can watch as it throbs vigorously up and down, making it look like the kid's brain is trying to tunnel its way out.

I have a strong stomach. I watched the birth. I watched Mariann's torn bits get sewn up. I prodded and poked the placenta. But when I saw Cordelia's brain throbbing, I was, like, "What sort of messed up horror movie shit is this?" It completely freaked me out.

When I expressed these feelings to my loving support network of friends and family they assured me that, yes, these feelings make me a total pussy. Turns out it's just another normal, expected, stupid baby thing. But I'm sorry. Diapers are one thing. But watching Cordelia's brain *pulse* is just icky.

It Has to Be Said

It's painfully banal, but it still deserves to be noted. I finally had my moment of Nightmare Parent Satori the other night.

That's where you're floating along, workin' it, gettin' it done, spongin' up the poo, getting from one end of the day to the other, and you stop, stunned, and say:

"HOLY SHIT! I'm a PARENT. Who let THAT happen?"

The second moment of Parent Satori will come in a few years when I open my mouth and my dad's voice comes out. I can wait.

Having my eyes opened too far sprains my head.

Week 12—It's the Casual Sadism That Makes Life Worthwhile

My darling little spud is rapidly approaching the end of her third month of life. As she is carried, inert and drooling, into her fifth trimester, I watch eagerly for signs of mental growth.

This week, I have not been disappointed. She has, for example, decided that she enjoys sucking on her hand and, at times, she even prefers it to the pacifier. My little darling still lacks the muscle control to reliably get her hand to her mouth though, so, while she lies in her crib, she can spent up to fifteen minutes at a time smacking herself in the face. Smack. Smack. Smack.

I'll be sitting in the next room, watching TV, and I'll hear it. Smack. Smack. Smack. Smack. Smack.

Eventually, she gets tired of practicing hand usage and starts to cry. I'll put the pacifier back in her mouth. She'll suck contentedly for a minute. Then she'll start smacking her face again.

Babies are funny.

I Am Her God

Recently, while I was doing computer stuff, little Cordelia developed a completely new variety of fussing. I would hold her in my lap or on my shoulder, as usual, and she would piss and moan and bitch. But then I would move her so she could look directly at my face. She would calm down, and a smile appeared that even I would call "adorable." Then I'd shift her to a position easier on my poor arms, where she couldn't see my face, and she would fuss. Then I'd let her see my face, and she would be ecstatic.

There are times in my life when I suspect that being almost completely cynical and pessimistic has its drawbacks. This was one of them. I know that this experience was supposed to completely melt me and warm me full of happy, gooey parent feeling. And I suppose it did, a little.

But I mainly thought two things. First, that I am completely unworthy of anyone else being so totally reliant on me for support and happiness. Because, as much as my baby wanted nothing more than to stare in awe at my glorious visage, all I wanted to do was answer my e-mail.

The second thing I thought was, "Yeah. Like this is going to last."

Well, I might as well get used to it. I'll manage. I'm already held up as an object of worship by my wife, friends, coworkers, and family. One more person who thinks I'm a Golden God won't make any difference.

"Honey, We Need Something to Moisten the Baby."

Mariann recently observed that our little girl's facial skin was dry. It was starting to flake a little. It turns out that flaking easily, while a good sign in cooked fish, is bad in the context of babies. I completely didn't notice this. I assume, had Cordelia been left solely in my care, she would have eventually wound up a small pile of bits of dried skin.

My wife went out, bought a humidifier, and installed it in her room. As advertised, it is now much more humid in there, which lends a pleasing softness to the shit smell. I'm sort of pissed about it, though. I had always assumed we were going to bake the baby. Now that she's being steamed, I need to completely rework the recipe.

Quiet Alert Is Neither Quiet Nor Alert. Discuss.

Background for the nonparents. Babies, simple, dopey creatures that they are, have only a few modes. We adults are complicated machines, with a wide variety of settings (sleeping, exercising, watching porn, pretending not to see homeless people, etc.). Babies on the other hand, spend the vast majority of their time either i) sleeping, ii) eating, or iii) bitching. Behaviorally, they're a lot like sheep, but without the keen, piercing intelligence. Or the ability to move.

But, for a short time every day, they are in what is charmingly and flatteringly called "quiet alert" mode. This is when they take in information about the world about them and try to figure out this whole "life" thing. And, if you're the parent, you better be on the goddamn ball and have some flash cards handy during this tiny window of alert time, or your baby will always be stupid. Which sucks because, if you're like me, you're counting on that bit of quiet time to finally get the dishwasher unloaded.

But anyway. It's called "quiet alert," which is not a very good term. First, it's not quiet. My baby makes a complicated, unbroken series of grunts, hisses, and whines, which I defy even a grandparent to find cute. She sounds like she's snuffling for truffles.

Second, and more importantly, I really don't think "alert" is the right mode. I think "alert" implies that she is really taking in, processing, and evaluating information about the world. When I look at her eyes, though, she sure doesn't look alert, not in any way I understand it. The world comes up to her eyes, pours through, and then gets lost in the hamster maze that is her undeveloped brain.

I picture her thinking process, at these times, to be a lot like one of those machines they use to pick lottery numbers. You know, with all the Ping-Pong balls with numbers on them, bouncing around randomly in that clear, plastic box? Except that there are a lot fewer balls and, instead of numbers, they all have "Waaah" written on them. That's what Cordelia's brain is like. She looks around and sees things, and a bunch of balls bounce around in the box for a minute, and then the winning number pops out: "Waaah. Waaah. Waaah. Waaah. Waaah. Waaah."

So I suppose we can call it "quiet alert," but I have a different idea. I say we call it "lucid dopeyness." It's not as good from a marketing perspective, but at least we aren't kidding ourselves.

A Mother's Words in Defense of Her Baby

When I express my opinions regarding Cordelia's "dopeyness," Mariann admirably leaps to her defense. She doesn't think that Cordelia is dopey and, in a very, very small way, she is right. Sometimes Cordelia gets a look so sharp, so attentive, that I can almost convince myself that there really are gears turning in that tiny head.

But I'm defensive of my girl, too! Just in a different way. I don't expect her to be anything but dopey. She's only three months old! Her brain has not yet fully developed in any way you care to name. But she is healthy, and she is growing fast, and she is cute beyond any reasonable human capacity for cuteness. And I think that is more than enough.

I don't need to convince myself she is smart. She has the whole rest of her life for that. To be blunt, I am made ecstatic by every day she gets through without turning blue.

It's the Casual Sadism That Makes Life Worthwhile

Cordelia frequently spits her pacifier onto the floor. As I am a firm believer in the Five-Second Rule (if it's on the floor for less than five seconds, it's not dirty), I don't have a problem with it. I pick it up, wipe off the ants, and pop it back in her mouth.

This disgusts Mariann extensively. However, her back isn't holding up under repeated trips to the floor for the pacifier any better than mine is. So she went to the store and got this thing to hold it onto Cordelia's clothes. It's a thin strap with a plastic clip on one end and a Velcro loop to hold the pacifier on the other. The clip attaches to her clothes. Now, if baby spits out the pacifier, it just dangles there in easy reach.

I love this handy invention, but for the wrong reason. I found that I can dangle the pacifier on a string just above the baby's mouth, so its tip brushes against her lips. When I do this, she'll snap at it, like a guppy. She'll get a little of it in her mouth, and I'll pull it back, and she gets this great expression on her face. It's so funny. It's like dangling a string in front of a kitten, except the kitten is paralyzed.

I want to pretend I engage in this casual sadism for instructive purposes, to teach her that, if she used her hands, she could just reach up and grab the damn pacifier. But the truth is, I'm just being a bully. I'd like to put some hip, funny, funky spin on it, but all I can do is promise to try to be a better person in some distant, vaguely defined future in which I'm getting sleep.

The Old Bait and Switch

When we embarked on the adventure of parenthood, we were promised the baby smell. The baby's head was supposed to smell good. It would relax us. It would be like that new car smell, or that new wife smell. It would be a minor aesthetic pleasure that would carry us through the dark times. And her head did smell good. For a while.

But time takes away the new car smell, and the new baby smell is the same way. Now, instead of smelling like freshness and hope tinted with talcum powder, our daughter's head smells like the beach at low tide.

To be fair, if I barfed on myself a dozen times a day, I'd get kind of funky too. But I still think nature pulled a bait and switch on us.

Smack. Smack. Smack. Smack. Smack.

Final developmental alert. She's about to gain the ability to hold objects. I tried pressing a rattle against her fingertips. She got a really good, firm grip!

Then she smacked herself in the face with it.

Is three months too early to get a baby therapy?

Week 13—Drool Is Like Diamonds

Cordelia just ticked over into her fourth month of life. It has been a full season, and she is still alive and functioning. And, as we look back on our accomplishments, Mariann and I can think of only one thing: *The grandparents can come here and give us a break any day now!*

Looking ahead, Cordelia is about to gain the ability to roll over. This means that, any night now, she will roll onto her stomach and suffocate.

Sure, this seems counterintuitive, considering the countless humans who have survived to adulthood before her. And yet, if this isn't a problem, why does Babies 'R' Us sell little padded devices designed to keep the baby from rolling over? And if this isn't a problem, why was I idiot enough to buy one?

Hand Sucking, a Progress Report

It is a simple mathematical fact of life that if something is good, twice as much of it is twice as good. Or so it would appear to the baby. And yet Cordelia has not yet learned that, while putting one fist into her mouth is satisfying, trying to jam both fists into her mouth at the same time is much less satisfying. It's far more amusing for Daddy though.

She's also working on proper management of her fingers. She happily sucks on her middle and index fingers. Then she jams them down her throat. The resultant gagging prevents the relaxation she was sucking on her fingers to obtain. Though, once again, providing amusement for Daddy.

Finally, Cordelia does not understand that physical objects have a reality independent from her, with certain invariable qualities. For example, they can't be in more than one place at once. Thus, if she lets her hand fall out of her mouth, it will no longer be in her mouth, no matter how angry she gets that it isn't there. Giving her laughing father angry looks will not remedy this situation.

When Cordelia realizes that I'm laughing at her and I am forced to stop, my job as a parent will become ten times harder.

Aural Violation

One of the biggest problems with becoming a parent is the way it exposes you to shitty things. Shitty food. (Lunchables.) Shitty books. (Teletubby books.) Shitty movies. (*Spy Kids*. Disney straight-to-video cartoons.) And shitty music. Oh God, the music.

With movies, there are good options I can present to her. I love cartoons as much as any developmentally retarded geek boy. Bugs Bunny. *My Neighbor Totoro*.

With books, there are good options. I get a big kick out of Harry Potter, and similarly overrated works of fiction. And I don't care how old you are. If you don't like Shel Silverstein, there's something wrong with you.

We can get her to eat good food. All we have to do is keep bad food from her. Then she'll have no choice. She has to eat eventually.

But the music. Oh God, the music. The vast bulk of children's music is synthed-up Deedle Doodle Deedle crap. Listening to it is like having spiders crawl into my ears.

Which brings me to a "gift" I just got from two of my "friends." It's a cassette tape called *Wee Sing Silly Songs*. It has forty-seven songs, accompanied with lyrics and sheet music. Because, if you are like me, and I'm sure you are, there's no better way to spend one's free time than to commandeer a piano and bang off a few spirited rounds of "Little Bunny Foo Foo."

(An aside. One of the best ways to inflict malicious mischief on friends in the guise of kindness is to give their kids music.)

But back to *Wee Sing Silly Songs*. Here are a few highlights from the *forty-seven* songs on this tape:

"Boom, Boom, Ain't It Great to Be Crazy?"—A charming serenade to the delights of mental illness.

"Hinky Dinky 'Double D' Farm"—Interesting coincidence. I have a video tape called *Double D Farm* in a shoebox under my bed.

"John Brown's Baby"—Apparently, before he seized Harper's Ferry, killed those people, and was hung by the neck until dead, John Brown had a kid who did the most adorable shit you ever heard of.

"Once an Austrian Went Yodeling"—There is no possible way that a song with this name could be good.

Also, half the songs or so are about some guy named Jesus, and how darn terrific he was. Screw that.

Facing Baby Eye to Eye

I love picking up baby and holding her facing me, eye to eye, so she can look at me with awe and adoration. Why else have a baby? What other point do they have?

But now, when I do this, she looks everywhere but at me. She looks left. Then right. Then left. Then right. And so on, turning her eyes past me without even a moment's notice. There are better balms for one's self-esteem than the experience of being blown off by one's own baby. It's like my Senior Prom all over again.

Belly Practice, Until the Screaming Starts

Since I don't want Cordelia to get a case of the SIDS, she sleeps on her back. That's what the books say, and we'd bathe our baby in soup if the books said that'd keep SIDS away.

Since Cordelia spends all her time on her back, our pediatrician advised us to occasionally put her on her stomach, so her belly muscles get exercise. Cordelia hates being on her stomach. Therefore, I have to transform myself into that most loathsome of all creatures, a gym teacher.

And she hates it more and more as time goes on. When I plop her down on her belly, she lifts her head, and points it face down toward the blanket, lets it drop, and then she can't breathe, so she lifts her head, points it face down, and drops it again. Splat. Splat. Splat. This process repeats until she really totally massively freaks out.

Repetitive, self-defeating behavior is rapidly becoming a theme in this journal.

I hate doing this to her. Who knows how this ordeal, repeated during her formative years, will warp her? Maybe she'll develop a total terror of being flipped onto her stomach. I developed that fear in my teenage years. But enough about summer camp.

A Question That I'm Sure Has Occurred to You, Too.

How old does she have to be before her hand muscle control is good enough to flip someone the bird?

That would be *so cute*!

Drool Is Like Diamonds

No matter how hard you fight to prevent it, being a parent reprograms your brain. This is clearest in the area of drool.

I always thought that baby drool was, like, *so* gross. Seeing a little baby with a long, sticky rainbow dangling from its slack, puffy mouth was enough to make me want to give myself a vasectomy with a ballpoint pen, right then and there.

But now I have a little girl, and it's all different. I see her jam her two chubby little fingers into her mouth, yank them out, and smear the saliva all over her lips and chin, and, to me, the viscous moisture looks just like a chain of little diamonds.

I envy her. It is a great ability. I wish more than anything I could drool on command. It would be a great trick. For example, you ever been cornered by a dull person at a party? A real wanker, who wants nothing more than to pinion you and spend hours describing his tormented childhood and the anguish of his bisexuality issues? Sure you have. And if you, like me, are cursed with a tiny trace of politeness, you've lingered there, boxed in, wasting time that could be spent harvesting the shrimp platter?

Well, at these times, I wish I could drool. I would gaze at the bore attentively and with apparent interest while, slowly, a trickle of drool runs down my chin and starts to soak into my collar. And then, as my shirt gets heavier and heavier with spit, my eyes lose their focus, and I slump against the wall. It would be the coolest trick.

And yet, I cannot drool. Believe me, I've tried. I just can't get it to work. It's the largest failure in my life, apart from all the others.

Yes, it would be great to be a baby again. She drools when I talk to her, just the way I dream it. If it wasn't for that whole unpleasant "Unable to walk, use hands, or talk" thing, it'd be a sweet life.

Thoughts from the Future

Cordelia never got SIDS.

She also eventually learned to walk, crawl, run, and jump. She somehow did this even though I stopped tormenting her by putting her on her stomach. Will these miracles never cease?

Intermission—Dealing with the Childfree

I would like to take a few pages to speak to those reading this who don't have children. All two of you.

Since this is a book of baby humor, it is unlikely that many non-parents (henceforth referred to as "childfree") will read these pages. The childfree tend to rightly regard baby humor as cutesy pats on the head for parents whose souls have been crushed. And rightly so. And yet, for the brave two of you reading this, I have to press on, for some things have to be said.

Some of us humans, due to misguided optimism or exceptionally cunning sperm, ended up raising offspring. Despite this, we still like to spend some time around the childfree, as you provide a pleasant reminder of what life was like when we were happy. Also, you aren't parents. Jesus, parents are annoying. All "Blah blah blah. Baby baby baby." Who needs to hear that?

And we're useful to you, too. If you want to have kids, we reassure you that it is possible. Our continued presence lets you know that raising a sprog won't actually kill you. And, if you don't want kids, we will provide limitless evidence to support your choice.

But if your tribe and ours are going to continue to interact, there are a few modest things I would like to request:

I. Don't invite us to a deathtrap.

True story. A friend of ours invited me, my wife, and our toddler to a party at his apartment. He is a juggler. On the coffee table in the room we were all to spend our time, we found an axe. An actual axe.

We don't expect you to fully baby-safe your apartment. You don't have to put gates on the stairs or plastic plugs in the sockets. The lack of these things will make us miserable, but such is our lot in life. We're always miserable.

But please. Show us some mercy. No axes on the tables, no knives on the floor, minimal open flames. Shards of glass kept to a minimum. Keep your porcupine in the garage and your scorpions in their cute little scorpion houses.

And if you insist on keeping lots of pretty, valuable, delicate things at knee height, don't invite me to your stupid house. I'll watch my baby. I won't duct tape her to the goddamn wall.

II. We don't give a shit if you have kids or not.

Some parents really, really like being parents, and they want to make sure you know what joy you are missing. Other parents really, really hate having kids, and they want others to join them in their misery. Both sorts of parents will try and convince you to breed. Yeah, I know. It's annoying as hell.

But, to be honest, we don't really give a shit whether you have kids or not. We may idly bug you about it sometimes, but we really don't care. The fewer kids you have, the more land will be left for mine.

III. We are miserable shut-ins.

When dealing with parents of very young children, treat them like you might treat an invalid. Current movies, concerts, restaurants, vacations, these are topics of conversation we will not be able to fully engage in. We have not seen the latest cool movie, the one with that hot new actress we haven't heard of. We probably aren't up on current events. We may not even have been out of the house. That glowing yellow ball in the sky, it may be terrifying to us.

Instead, discuss TV shows. Movies out on DVD. Local fast-food chains. The weather. This is our world now.

It is all right to help us catch up with what is going on in the world, within reason. Feel free to say something like, "Hey, there's a new movie out called *The Matrix*. You ought to get it when it's on DVD. Oh, and the president lost his leg in a thresher accident." This helps us keep up with our culture as it moves on without us.

IV. Don't take any crap from us.

You are our friends. We are counting on you to help us keep parenthood from eating our brains. Sometimes, tough love is in order.

Should we ever talk about the baby for more than five minutes, show you more than three photographs, or show you videos of the baby for any amount of time at all, feel free to reprimand us. I recommend a single, sharp slap, on the fleshy part of the cheek.

Nothing damaging. You aren't trying to dislocate the jaw. Just a quick shock to the system, as if to say, "Yeah. We know. Baby. Great. Shut the hell up."

V. Militant childfree people are assholes. Don't be an asshole.

For some couples, being childfree is enough. Minimal responsibilities. Two incomes. Freedom. Long vacations. Doesn't look like a lot of downside there.

But for a small minority, this isn't enough. To the militantly childfree, the mere act of procreating is offensive. Tax breaks and other governmental support for parents seems unjust, children are repellent, and cutting any slack to parents is something that must not be done.

(For various flavors of this point of view, from sort of sensible to outright crazy, do a Google search for "childfree.")

Just so you know, we people who are, at considerable expense and difficulty, raising kids are doing you a favor. You see, someday you will be old. You'll be creaky and wrinkly and dusty, and your joints will hurt. You will probably want, at some point, to take it easy.

To do so, you will need to eat food grown by young people. You will be kept safe by a military and a police force composed of young people. If your house catches fire, the flames will be put out by young people. The clothes you wear will have been made by young people, the water and electricity systems will be maintained by young people, and, God forbid, your ass may be wiped by young people. And if being supported by young people is offensive to you, you can drive on roads maintained by young people to a Walmart, where a young cashier will happily sell you a suicide machine.

Parents are doing nonparents an enormous favor. We earn our tax breaks. And, if this makes you upset, you might more profitably spend that angry energy blowing me.

VI. Your opinion is not important to me.

In a remote, ignored corner of my mind, there is a small, dusty box. This box is for parenting advice from nonparents. When you tell me something about raising children, it goes into that box and is never inspected again.

To the childfree, all parents look cruel, feebleminded, or both. I know how much better than me you think you would do. You would never let the kid watch TV. You would never do that thing I do where I rub my temples with my fingers and succumb to total despair. You would never pray for death's sweet release. And your child would be smart and clean and cheery and could bench-press three hundred.

But don't share with me your hot tips for parenting perfection. While I may nod in seeming agreement, I will be laughing at you on the inside. And then your comment will go into that little box.

You want to improve me? Do it by example. Have your perfect child. Blind me with the joyous radiance of your godlike offspring. And, until you've actually been a better parent, all I really need from you is human contact.

And pizza. Please. Bring pizza.

The Second Season: It Still Can't Move

Ah, the second three months. They are, barring colic or some other nightmare, the good months. Sure, you won't realize that they were the good months until long after they were over. But they were all right.

After three months, the surprise is gone. You know how to do what you need to do. The routine is down. The kid's natural inclination to sleep more during the night and less during the day has kicked in.

And yet, the baby is still inert. It's still an immobile processing machine, absorbing food at one end and excreting it (in processed form) at the other. You can haul the child around in a basket, and it will be incapable of freeing itself.

Sure, you'll be checking it in the middle of the night to make sure it didn't just decide to stop breathing. But this vague, existential fear is nothing compared to the very real, practical fear you'll be having when the kid is running in circles atop your kitchen table.

Also, it doesn't know how to take its diaper off yet. Know how good you have it.

In these months, healthy, reasonably directed babies will learn to do the following things:

   i. Flop over. A form of movement that is charming because it's so easy for parents to prevent it.

  ii. Learn to see. The baby will start to tease meaning out of the riot of colors and movements its eyes are pouring into its brain. And yes, if before now you thought that the baby was looking at you and thinking, "That is my mommy, and I love her," you were on crack.

 iii. Eat solid food. Though not consensually.

No dramatic changes, and nothing that enables the baby to harm you or your stuff. Enjoy this. It ends soon.

Week 14—My Daughter, the Evil Temptress

I wished, and I received. I am going to get a chance to reacquaint myself with this woman who I, at some point, married. And, just as importantly, I'll get a chance to temporarily unacquaint myself with the baby that has been the dopey focus of our lives for the previous months.

My parents have come to visit.

It's been a relaxing week here at parenting central. The care of my three-month-old daughter Cordelia has gone smoothly and easily. At least, that's my best guess about how it has been, as I have been absent for much of it.

I am very relaxed now, having partaken of these things the local savages call "restaurants" and "movies." These childfree ones are a strange people, with many delightful practices. And I will take my fill before I must return to my indoor pee-mopping lifestyle.

Handing Off to the Grandparents

This weekend, I was lucky to receive that one special blessing, that true and glorious treat that all parents of young sprogs lust after. My parents came to stay with us for a few days. It gives me a chance to make a transition. For a few days, instead of being a bad parent, I can be a bad son.

The moment my parents come through the door, looking for their adorable little grandchild, I dump Cordelia in their outstretched hands. Then, in the best Wile E. Coyote fashion, I run through the front door, leaving only a puff of smoke and a me-shaped hole behind.

Hopefully, my wife follows after me.

For the first eighteen years of my life, my parents were authority figures who I used to get what I wanted. Then, after I left home, they became distant, friendly presences, available for happy holidays and subtle interrogation regarding the availability of grandchildren. But now that I am a parent, too, my parents have finally adopted the true role nature reserved for them: authority figures who I use to get what I want.

And what I want is what any parent wants: three spare hours for dinner, a movie, a little bit of convo with the spousal unit. Please.

Oh, the conversations my wife, Mariann, and I have been having.

"And you are?"

"Jeff. And you?"

"Mariann."

"Oh, yes. The one with the breasts. How's that working out for you?"

"They are sore and useful. And how's your penis doing?"

"It hasn't caused anyone great suffering. Recently."

I am a terrible son. My parents arrive, and I can't get out of the house soon enough. Last weekend, I went to two plays and went out for two meals. I came home for a bit and my parents asked me how I was, and I told them quickly while casting about with my eyes for an escape route. It's exactly like my adolescence, except that then I didn't leave them to clean up baby shit while I was gone. Of course, I might be forgetting about something.

But then again, they get something out of the deal too. A chance to rent a baby for the evening. A generally adorable and sweet (if dopey) girl, who doesn't scream too much and who has not yet had her personality warped by her parents. It makes me feel good to give

Mom and Dad what they want so much. Then they won't make me pay them back for college.

Everyone Is Circling the Wagons

On the other hand, having Cordelia's grandparents around leaves me outnumbered three to one on the whole dopeyness issue. Wow. Write something on the Internet referring to your three-month-old baby as "dopey" and everyone acts as if I'd been carrying her around on the streets at 2 A.M., trying to trade her for a bus ticket and a used bong.

Well. I have a Webster's dictionary on my desk. Let's see what it says "dopey" means. Hmm. "Sluggish or befuddled, as from the use of narcotics or alcohol."

Well Hell, she must be sluggish. She hasn't moved around since we got her home. And if any word can be used to describe a three-month-old baby, it's befuddled. When she knows that I still exist even when she can't see me, and when she doesn't completely freak out whenever I blow lightly on her face, I'll deem her a little less fuddled.

But I give up. I'm outnumbered. Fine. She's not dopey. When she looks at things, it is with a clear, piercing analytical intelligence that understands what she is seeing. And when she punches herself in the face trying to get her finger in her mouth, it's because she is rationally investigating her pain tolerance. And she could repair an automotive transmission, if only she knew that the tools aren't food.

No, sir. Dopey she is not. Now, if you'll excuse me, she just shat herself, and I need to let her kick her ankles around in the feces while I try to get the diaper off.

Dawn of the Parent Nightmare

There are several nightmares that people share. Being in public without pants. Being chased and unable to run. A final exam you haven't studied for. Actors are afflicted by dreams where they are onstage and don't know their lines.

I just had the Parent's Nightmare. It was like this.

First, I learned that Mariann had been killed with saws while protesting the clear-cutting of some forest. (Which is already really weird, since that is very unlike my wife. My wife is the sort of person who doesn't like veal because it's not cruel ENOUGH.) Then I was at a barbecue with my family. Cordelia was feeling cold so, to keep her warm, I put her in the barbecue on low heat and put the lid on. Then I forgot about her. Eventually, I ran to the grill, lifted the lid, and saw what had happened. And I woke with a start, and that was pretty much it for sleep for that night.

Certain cultures believe that dreams are mystical journeys, and we take them so that spirits can teach us valuable lessons. If this is the case, one of my spirits wants me to know that I shouldn't put the baby in the barbecue.

Thanks, but I already kind of had a grip on that part.

An Experiment in Putting to Bed, and the Horrible Results

This is how I have been putting Cordelia to bed. First, I cram her full of food. Once she makes a sloshy noise when I shake her, I swaddle her really tightly. Once she looks like a sad little mummy, I put the pacifier in her mouth. Once she is being made artificially happy by a chunk of rubber, I set her down and turn off the lights. Presto. Sleeping baby.

But I started to think that this specific series of steps might not be necessary. I thought, since she can suck on her hands, she might not need the pacifier, and since she's three months old, she might not need the swaddling. So I tried putting her to bed without either.

Inside of five minutes, she was crying. She was trying to suck on her fingers, but her fingers were missing her mouth and poking her in the eye. So I put the pacifier in her mouth. Then she decided that she also wanted to be sucking on her hand. So she swung her hand up and knocked the pacifier out of her mouth. Then she poked herself in the eye again. So I swaddled her and replaced the pacifier. Mouth plugged and motionless, she slept.

And don't get me wrong. I have no problem with my child poking herself in the eye. It teaches her a valuable lesson: Don't do that. But she's not so bright. The last person she saw was me, and then someone was hitting her in the face. She might blame me for that! And then the baby punching incidents come up in hypnosis therapy, and off I go to Bad Daddy Jail.

So we're back to the mummy-plugged-with-rubber sleep technique. I bring all this up because I want people to know one thing. When I call Cordelia "dopey," it is not entirely an arbitrary judgment, free from all evaluation of actual evidence.

My Daughter, the Evil Temptress

I am pretty sure that this part is mainly a reflection of my parental bias. But I think that my baby is uncommonly cute. She is definitely not one of those ugly babies. She has all the right parts, in the proper proportions, and an occasional alert gaze that creates the impression that she doesn't spent most of her waking time inconveniencing Mommy and Daddy.

What's more, some social self-preservation gene in her little DNA makes her be exceptionally cute among strangers. The effect of this on people fills me with malicious glee. When I show Cordelia off, you can actually hear the womens' ovaries start to quiver, open, and expel eggs with little popping noises. The effect on guys is startlingly similar. After some guy took a long, loving look at our sprogling in a restaurant, I actually heard his girlfriend mutter to him, "Don't get too excited. You won't get one for a while."

When strangers ogled our child, it was tempting, at first, to go, "No! Run! It's a bait and switch! She's tempting you! Get away before it's too late!"

But now I just smile happily and say, "She's an angel." Let them learn on their own. Shared suffering is the best suffering.

Week 15—Three Days of Undaddy

It has been an eventful week in Cordelia's life. A week of exploration, learning, and growth. Or so I was told. Because I wasn't around.

It's been a good couple weeks for me. My parents left, casting long, mournful looks at their granddaughter and weeping bitter tears. And then I got on a plane.

For most of the week, I was Undaddy, a blissfully absent being, spending several days a thousand or so miles away at my college reunion. I am writing what I can of my baby's growth, doing my best to relay what I was told. I may make a few mistakes, but so what. A loss of information and truth is a small price to pay for nine hours of uninterrupted sleep in a hotel bed.

I take great personal risk writing this report as my wife, who stayed at home with the baby and her mother, got no such respite. But I must tell the truth, even though it puts me in line for a jealousy-driven ass-kickin'.

Three Days of Undaddy

Being a parent changes your whole perception of things. Parenthood lets you see the world in a whole new way, through the eyes of not having your child around.

It was a great delight to savor this strange world of baby not being around, in which people went to "restaurants," and "slept in," and spent lots of time not "freaking out." And being at a college reunion under these circumstances was perfect, because having successfully bred gave me all the key "not a loser" points without the indignity of being seen jamming my finger in Cordelia's diaper, pulling it out, and sniffing it to see if she needs changing.

Such things do not lead to the envy that is the eternally desired prize at any college reunion.

Having a baby is ultimate proof of non-loserhood. It means that you are a mature being, who has taken on great hardship and sacrifices to achieve the one true goal of passing on the genes to the next generation. Plus, it shows that I was actually able to get a woman to let my sperm enter her body and take root. It says to all nearby, "Remember what a dork I was in college? No more! Sperm! Egg! Genes passed to next generation! Me win!" This alone makes up for a lot of dirty diapers.

And then, after displaying my manliness in a peacock feather display of baby photographs, I went out for dinner. At restaurants, they have people who walk around and give you bread and refill your glass of water when you need it. It totally rules.

My Undaddy Badge of Pride

However, I have some pride. Reunions and similar events are an opportunity for the parental state to slip in and eat your brain, turning you into one of those goo goo parent zombies. If you have the proper, righteous amount of fear of this happening, do what I did:

i. Limit yourself to three photographs. Only. You can display them in five seconds, bang, bang, bang, and it's over with and you can talk like a human being again. I have three pictures that I showed. One of them was of Cordelia lying on a broiling pan, smiling obliviously, surrounded by bunches of fresh herbs. Best baby picture, ever.

ii. Limit talking about the baby to once per hour. Come on. You can do it. If you want to impress people, nothing will wow them more than that. And your childfree friends will be beside themselves with gratitude.

Talk about movies. You won't be able to mention anything not out on video, since your recreation options are now limited to anything with a pause button. (Though don't mention how much porn you're watching. Nobody needs porn like fathers of small children. That's what we should get on Father's Day, not shitty ties.)

Talk about politics. You may not know anything specific, but the Jews and the Arabs are always beating the shit out of each other, so talk about that. And talk about how sweet the good old days are. If your friends are in any way reasonable, they won't begrudge you a little nostalgia about the days before the fontanel cleared the birth canal and it all went horribly, horribly wrong.

A Sad Admission, and an Uncharacteristic Moment of Sincerity

Time until I missed my little girl—about 48 hours.

Ambush on Return

My absence was not difficult for Mariann. Her mother Ilona came to visit. Ilona is a former nanny. Thus, not only was Mariann not obliged to do much childcare, but she counted herself lucky to even catch a glimpse of Cordelia.

Ilona was still there when I returned. One glance made it clear what her opinion of my abandonment of my family was. So I hid in the bedroom and fantasized about restaurants. Sexy, sexy restaurants.

The First Goocramming Session

My wife Mariann has begun trying to feed Cordelia solid food. Admittedly, this is a bit on the early side. However, Mariann is very eager. You know that warm motherly glow women get when they breastfeed? Mariann gets the opposite of that. Mariann wants to wean so badly that La Leche League members have been trying to break in and hammer a stake through her heart.

So, for the first feeding attempt, we got some Earth's Best brand organic "First Apples" applesauce. They proudly proclaim on the tiny label, something like fifty times, that they use no genetically modified ingredients of any kind. Like I care. Give it five years and Cordelia will be screaming and running into walls until Mommy and I give her Twinkies. Even if genetically engineered apples made a difference, they wouldn't make a difference.

Also, the label smugly states that the applesauce inside is vegan. What a relief. We didn't buy any of that baby applesauce that had big chunks of ham in it. I bet the bulk of the baby food that my mom got me was vegan. But that was a simpler, happier time, when bragging that your food was vegan would get you pistol-whipped by a Teamster.

Anyway, after all that prelude, the final result was predictable. My wife spooned some applesauce into Cordelia's mouth. Cordelia responded by using her reflexive spitting capabilities, thoughtfully provided by nature for just such situations.

Poor Mommy. More breastfeeding for her.

But that's not the most noteworthy thing about Earth's Best brand baby food.

Vegans Are Up to No Damn Good

Earth's Best brand sells all sorts of baby crap. Rice cereal. Smashed fruit. And so on. And, on all of their labels, they have paintings of little babies, one year old or so, wearing cloth diapers (of course cloth, without plastic covers), working in a garden. Some of them are picking. Some are weeding. One has a shovel, twice as large as he is. The babies are all depicted as very happy. (Terrifying examples can be seen on their products page at earthsbest.com.)

But I know better.

To quote the back of their "Whole Grain Rice Cereal" box, "We fortify our cereals with iron because it is so crucial to early physical and neurological development." Yeah, sure! So you can put the kids to work in the fields that much *earlier,* you sanctimonious, child labor using *bastards*!

The front of the box says it all. Those blank-eyed kids, picking weeds without gloves, manhandling enormous shovels around with delicate baby fingers. Wearing cloth diapers without covers, so the urine and watery baby feces can leak out in little rivulets, drying and caking up as the noontime sun blasts their exposed baby flesh!

Yeah, I feed my little girl formula sometimes. But at least I don't put babies to work in the fields like vegetarians do. I had no idea that making baby food was such a sick, dirty business.

Week 16—The Amazing Rotatable Baby

And then the grandparents were gone. Mariann and I were left to several more months of actual parenting. I always feel very inadequate after the grandparents go. They are so much better at interacting with Cordelia than I am. They have experience. They know all the games, and they are tireless. When I feel the need to play with her, it's all I can manage to croak out a little song, poke her in a friendly manner with my forefinger, and collapse exhausted.

But this time, it's going to be different. I'm going to take charge of the situation. I'm going to stand tall, get out there, and do some *parenting*, by God!

Since Cordelia Krizsan Vogel is approaching the end of her fourth month in her position as First Child in her family, I called her into the head office for a bit of a discussion.

I informed her that, while we appreciated her contributions to the family unit so far, we were disappointed by her lack of progress. We don't have many positions in the Vogel/Krizsan family unit, you see, and while the options granted are very generous (including a lump sum of cash to be paid in full after the demise of both parental units), the expectations are high. I let Cordelia know that, if improvement was not forthcoming, we would have to let her go.

Parenting is great. I don't know why I didn't try it sooner. Our little girl bucked up, stiffed her little spine, and charted a firm course of improvement . . .

Mobility

There is nothing more terrifying than mobility. To relocate one's body is one of the first two signs of development, of humanity, of becoming an active and independent creature (more on the second sign later). The sort of active and independent creature that can destroy all of my valued worldly possessions.

Cordelia can roll over now. From her stomach, she can flop over onto her back. This is the first link in a long chain of destruction.

The physics of her movement is interesting. You see, Cordelia, like all small babies, has three body parts:

i. Her Gut Sac. The overlarge, lumpy torso that contains all life-support elements.

ii. Her Big Block Head. Hard, heavy, and with a hole in it. The hole serves as a conduit for nutritive fluid, carrying it from the outside world into the Gut Sac. When the hole is not filled, it makes shrill noises that alert us of its need for filling. Despite the considerable aptitude new parents have for self-delusion, the block head has no other purpose early on. Supposedly, there is some sort of cognitive activity taking place inside. Don't kid yourself.

iii. Her Dangly Bits. There are four of these. Eventually, they become arms and legs and are actually used for things. For now, they are only pleasant aesthetic accessories for the Gut Sac.

With such an odd and awkward set of parts, it's amazing that she can do anything but scream and excrete. But she figured it out. When she's on her stomach, she uses her flimsy little arms to hoist her block head into the air. Once her head mass is at a height, she flops it over to the side. With the help of a little twist of her Gut Sac, the weight of her head carries her right over and onto her back.

I want to move around by flinging my head places and letting it drag my body behind. That would be cool.

She still can't flop from on back to on stomach, though. I think the reason for this is lack of motivation. As science seems to currently think, if she sleeps on her stomach, she's much more likely to get the SIDS. Thus, when she flips onto her back, she is simply trying to say, "Daddy, I like to breathe!"

So she can move. We have to babyproof the house. Crap.

You Now Have One Item in Your Inventory.

But what key bit of human heritage she has claimed this week? Now, she can grab objects. She can see objects, reach for them (very slowly and carefully), and grasp them in her little hands. She is now only tiny steps from being able to wield a fork and jam it into a power outlet to dig for candy.

Once she has an object, she always does the same thing: jam it into her mouth. This is totally stereotypical baby behavior, and I love it. It's like living with a tiny Homer Simpson.

Now that she can move and take, all she has to learn to do is talk and she will have fully earned her social security number. She'll be an actual human, and we can no longer put her in a cardboard box, set her in front of the supermarket, and give her away like a puppy. ("We'd really like her to end up on a farm.")

I Like Babies. So Sue Me.

If I had a dime for every person in my age group who said he or she didn't like babies, I'd have a dollar. I used to agree with them, but then I spent huge amounts of time around an actual baby.

Babies are like stinky French cheese. They are an acquired taste. At first, you see the drool and hear the squealing and (if unlucky) smell the stink. You are repelled by the vacant expression and total self-interest. If you didn't know that it's a human, the rational reaction to encountering a squealy, drooly baby would be to hit it with a rock.

But babies have a certain charm that long-term exposure makes extremely clear. They have a combination of limitless, ambitious energy and doughheaded guilelessness that is nothing but charming.

They're not really people. But they want to be. My daughter can only really do one thing: grab things. And she only knows how to do one thing with items she collects: jam them into her mouth. That's all she can do, goddammit, so that's what she's going to do. She's going to jam every possible object into her mouth, and she's not going to stop until she can do something else.

In sum, babies have the same, adorable, limitless enthusiasm for exploring the world as puppies. And everyone loves puppies! But while puppies grow up to be big, dumb, slobbering dogs, babies grow up to be people. So babies are better.

The Thing I Usually Like to Say to People Who Talk About How Selfish and Obnoxious Babies Are:

"Well, if you were a mute quadriplegic, lying alone in your own waste, and really hungry and thirsty, you'd start screaming too."

Baby Feeding Status Report

Every once in a while, we jam fruit goo in the baby's mouth. She spits it out, while making adorable little hurt expressions.

Nothing makes me happier than being able to bother and annoy my daughter in the guise of being a caring, considerate parent.

The Amazing Rotatable Baby

Cordelia really likes to be picked up and slung around. I put my hands firmly around her ribcage, under her arms, hoist her up, and bounce her around. She loves it. I lift her up and balance her on my head, making her a "Baby Hat." It means that she now has an actual skill: being a hat. Mommy wants Cordelia to vomit down my back when I do this. This has not yet happened, disappointing Mommy.

Cordelia is also the amazing rotatable baby. I can lift her straight up and rotate her horizontal, ninety degrees right, then ninety degrees left, spinning her back and forth. She loves this. Or, at least, she smiles when I do this. But it could be a rictus of fear. Who can tell? I'm not going to second-guess smiles. I have enough to worry about.

Some of my idiot friends asked why I was rotating my child. I think that is obvious. You need to rotate your baby occasionally so that she wears evenly.

If you don't rotate your baby, you can have a blowout. And heck, if a baby blows out when you're going at a good speed, you could lose the entire family.

Cordelia's Current Status in the Family

The family unit set out a challenge for Cordelia this week, and I have to admit she met it. It's not like she went out and generated more sales or anything, but she did do the extra learning and development we required to keep from having to give her away at the supermarket.

But if our family has any slogan, it's "What have you done for me lately?" We expect development to continue. I'm sure you will find me perfectly reasonable when I say this: Complacency in our three-month-olds will NOT be tolerated.

Oh. And Why Things Are About to Suck

She has started teething.

Week 17—"Hey, Little Girl! This Is What Mild Discomfort Feels Like!"

So what is that word for when everything is going great, and everyone is calm and happy and complacent, and suddenly, almost overnight, everything goes straight to hell and you have no idea what is going on with anything anymore? What's that word again?

Oh yeah. "Teething."

There is a pleasing symmetry. Our darling little girl Cordelia is now four months old. And she is growing four tiny teeth. And she sleeps four hours a night. And her daddy is about to put her in the closet for four weeks.

Thoughts from the Future

Wearing my daughter like a hat was one of the most enduring games I played with her. I picked her up and placed her, belly down, on my head, supporting most of her weight with my hands. She loved it. Everyone around was horrified. It was great.

Then she became a toddler. Her legs grew strong. The baby hat game stopped about the point I realized that it was going to cost me a minimum of three teeth to continue.

On the other hand, you can keep rotating your child indefinitely.

"Hey, Little Girl! This Is What Mild Discomfort Feels Like!"

For the unaware, teething is the process by which the baby's first teeth (twenty in all) burrow through the gum into glorious life. This process causes a constant, low level of discomfort.

When grownups feel a constant low level of discomfort, we bitch a little, pop some ibuprofen, and get on with our lives. Babies, on the other hand, are not used to pain and not known, in general, for bearing up under adversity with dignity and stoic determination. Also, their clumsy, chubby little fingers can't get an ibuprofen bottle open. (Stupid babyproofing!) So they get through the ordeal with massive crying and complaining. Generally when they should be sleeping.

One thing the little ones do to ease the discomfort is to grab something (a plastic ring, ice cubes wrapped in a washcloth, a human nipple) and chew the shit out of it. Sadly, Cordelia is teething early, so her hands aren't capable of holding the chew toys in her mouth. Tee hee! Another of Nature's little jokes!

In olden days, frazzled parents would rub brandy or other strong liquor on a teething baby's gums to ease the discomfort. We modern adults are too delicate for such strong measures. My wife and I have been splitting the difference and liberally applying this treatment to each other.

Now I ask you. And, when I say "you," I mean a specific "you" who has some knowledge of biology. Is there any species who gives birth to offspring as hapless and useless as humans? Consider baby alligators. They are born with teeth. Little, cute, sharp ones. And they certainly don't spend weeks being reduced to reptilian basket cases learning to use those teeth. No, they come out of the egg loaded for bear, ready to rend a teething ring into tiny, yellow plastic bits, each with one of Snoopy's severed limbs printed on it.

"Oh, That Jeff. He Just Doesn't Like Babies."

Now I'm in for more shit from my relatives for describing babies as "hapless" and "useless." Well they don't move, they can't bear getting teeth, and sometimes they just stop breathing for no good reason. I love my little girl. She is adorable beyond words. But if I didn't watch her every minute, she'd be eaten by mice.

Loadin' Her Up with the Drugz

Fortunately, modern science has not left us high and dry regarding the whole teething situation. Being truly the parents of the path of least resistance, we dealt with this problem by going out and getting drugs.

We are the worst parents in the world. There is no problem so piddling that we can't find some way to weasel our way out of it, doing incalculable harm to our daughter in the progress. Pacifiers. Formula. Disposable diapers. Epidurals.

And now drugs. We just suck.

Even for one as jaded and apathetic as myself, the process of putting baby to bed has become rather disturbing. First, I load her full of food and swaddle her as usual. And then I get the baby Tylenol and give her a good stiff shot. And then she gets sleep, and I get guilt.

The idea of medicating my daughter to make her quiet and pliable, even with something as innocent as Baby Tylenol, is really depressing to me. I mean, why stop there? Why not get little baby doses of Ritalin? It won't get rid of the gum pain, but it'll drain the strength to object out of her. Heck, I could give her Valium, but Mommy and I are already taking it all.

But, on the other hand, what right do I have to *not* drug her? I drug myself as a matter of routine. If I was having trouble sleeping because I was in pain and someone refused me the medication that would provide a restful slumber, I would give that person a righteous ass-kicking. Or, at least, I'd do as much ass-kicking as my pudgy, nerdly form is capable of. Which, sadly, isn't much.

I suspect I'm overthinking this process. She's in pain. I make the pain go away. I'd just feel a lot better if, at some point, I'd deal with a problem by not taking the easy way out.

I think I'll buy her a pony.

Chompity Chomp Chomp

Although the whining and bitching isn't so cute, Cordelia does have one adorable habit. When one of my fingers gets close to her face, she lurches out and chomps on it. Then she gnaws on it with her cute, pink little gums. She's my widdle baby velociraptor.

Of course, it's great for me. My wife plays the same game, but with her nipples instead of her finger, and she has informed me that this habit is the opposite of cute.

An Admittedly Excessive Response to Three Out of Four People We Have Told That Our Daughter's Name Is Cordelia:

No. We have not yet thought of a nickname for her. Not Delia, or Dee, or Cor, or Lia. Her name is "Cordelia." Just "Cordelia." It is not Welsh or Sanskrit. It is not in some weird African language with pops and hissing noises. It is only four lousy syllables long. Is that so hard to say? What are we? Goddamn chimpanzees?

Oh! She's Gagging! It's soooo cuuuute!!!!!

According to *What to Expect the First Year,* some babies learn to cough a lot early in life. They make their parents think they are choking to death, in order to trick attention out of them.

This is why I love babies, for all their dopeyness. They do have a certain cunning ingenuity. They have very little to work with, but they leverage it as best they can.

Cordelia does this. She scrunches up her face, and then she sticks her little tongue way out and rounds her mouth into a little O, and she makes this cute "Keh! Keh!" noise. I know I'm being scammed, but I still pick her up. It beats screaming.

Other Milestones

The other night, I wiped the very, very first booger off of her nose. I should have saved it in the photo album, but we horrify our relatives with the pictures in there as it is.

Now My Corpse Is Really Worth Something

Finally, my life insurance has happened. My death is now worth two hundred and fifty thousand dollars to my loved ones. The agent patiently explained, also, that such a piddly amount would be seen by my survivors as proof that I didn't love them very much. And people think insurance salesmen aren't sweethearts!

So if you are reading this and you are one of my descendants and you think I didn't care about you because of the unsatisfactory monetary windfall my corpse resulted in, I have a message for you from beyond the grave: Bite me.

I had a small brain tumor removed when I was nineteen. Since then, I have had no problems in this area. No symptoms, or handicaps, or other growths. Yet, despite the thirteen years between that event and now, it was difficult finding someone who would give me any life insurance policy, let alone one that wasn't insanely expensive.

There is nothing that gives you an unnerving awareness of the temporary status of your mortality like a life insurance salesman getting nervous around you.

Week 18—Our Baby Could Kick Your Baby's Ass

Teeth should grow faster.

Now that Cordelia is well into her fourth month, I can fully see the reason to become a parent. If I hadn't gotten a kid, the last four months would just have flown by, click, click, click, click, without my even noticing them. Having a child, however, slows life down. It makes you reeeeeally notice that time is passing.

There are two sorts of time: nonparent time, and ass-wiping time. Guess which one goes slower.

Four months down. Two hundred and twelve more, and we can send her to college.

More Checking. More Impaling with Needles.

Mariann took Cordelia to a doctor. It turns out that she is pretty much exactly at the fiftieth percentile for everything. Weight. Height.

Decibels of screaming when suddenly and unexpectedly stuck with needles. However, she is exceptionally strong. If a parent holds her hands for balance, she can completely support her weight on her legs. This is our one show-off-the-baby trick. It's not very interesting, but it's not like you can teach a four-month-old how to juggle.

During our previous doctor's appointment, we learned that Cordelia had a heart murmur. Research indicated that it would almost undoubtedly disappear. This time the doctor found that, sure enough, it has disappeared. The mission of completely freaking out Mom and Dad unnecessarily was a success!

Actually, the doctor was disappointed to find that, this time, there was nothing she could use to send us into a downward spiral of terror and anxiety. So she simply closed the appointment by saying "And remember. One day, your baby will be dead." Pretty lame, but it was the best she could do given what she had to work with.

The Powerful Force of Parental Delusion

In a previous installment of this journal, I wrote that Cordelia's brain was developing. I gave as evidence that she was capable of seeing an object, reaching for it, and grabbing it. I am now, sadly, forced to retract all of this. Especially the brain developing part.

You see, our little girl likes to clasp both hands together and then jam them into her mouth. When I handed her a "thing," I was always positioning it where her hands always grab anyway. When I hold an object two inches higher than that, she reaches out, grabs thin air, and looks surprised. Then she gives a little mental shrug and shoves, like, twelve fingers into her mouth.

Repeated trials had the same result. She can't grab for things yet. This is so embarrassing.

I mean, I was trying so hard to be a teeny bit rational about gauging her development. She is a baby. Her brain is still a blank thing, and I thought I could be at least a little impartial and honest about judging when it started to become less unfull. I wanted to love her for her cheery blankness, instead of superimposing my own delusions onto her basically honest and straightforward behavior.

But it won't happen again. The next time I claim some development on her part, I'll have video documentation. Or maybe I'll just never believe she can do anything. She'll say, "Daddy! I love you! And I just made a robot." And I'll be all like, "Oh, look honey! Our little girl is making sounds. How cute!"

Responsible Opposing Viewpoints Are Present

My wife, on the other hand, gave up early. She woke me up today, plopped down Cordelia, and said, "Look! She can sit up sometimes!"

I watched the process with great interest.

(Wife carefully balances baby upright.) "Watch this." (Lets go. Baby instantly falls over. Thud.) "Okay, I'll try again." (Picks up baby. Carefully balances her again. Lets go. This time, baby stays upright for about three seconds before gravity claims her.) "See? She sat up!" (Thud.)

My response was: "Yeah. And sometimes, when I ask her what one plus one is, she grunts twice." I then learned that this is not the sort of thing you should say if you prize domestic tranquility.

Our Baby Could Kick Your Baby's Ass

Having a baby of my own makes me pay a lot more attention to the offspring of others. I'm always peeking into other parents' strollers and Baby Bjorns. And I can now say this with some confidence and authority: our baby is *so* much more attractive than the competition.

Oh, I know what you're thinking. I'm just a biased parent. I can't be trusted to judge. But believe me, if there was some scientific scale for baby attractiveness, our child would be near the top of the scale. She has bright eyes, smiles a lot, and has the proper proportions. She's not an obese little sack of butter, but she's adorably well rounded and just a teeny bit chubby. She's not like those twiggy lumps of gristle and bones other parents are trying to pass off as cute.

Face it. She's darling. Science doesn't lie.

And I don't say this to brag, and I'm not trying to establish the higher genetic grade of my sperm. I'm just concerned on the behalf of the other babies. I mean, I'm sure you've seen those, well, my wife and I call them Bug Babies. The tiny little scrawny things with huge eyes and haunted looks, the babies you want to grab and force-feed cream? Sometimes I see a baby and I just know that the mother's breasts are producing exactly 95 percent of the milk the kid should be getting, and she's trying to make up for the other 5 percent with pure force of will.

Sure, we supplement Mommy's milk with formula. We're sell-outs. We suck. But hey, I have never looked at Cordelia and shouted, "Shit! Honey, get this kid some ham, quick!"

Actually, I saw one baby, about a month old, that seemed to have gone through the Bug Baby stage and come out on the far side. It was pretty scrawny, but that's reasonable for one that young. But it also had this sad look and these enormous, terrifying bags under its eyes.

I swear, it was the eye bags that did it. It looked like it'd just come home from fourteen hours at the ad agency. It looked like it knew the family budget was tight, and layoffs were imminent, and there was an all-hands meeting scheduled for next week, and you know what that means. You can always tell when you're looking at a baby who thinks it could get pink-slipped at any moment.

"So What You're Saying Is That You Think Your Kid Is Cuter Than Mine?"

Not necessarily. Only nine times out of ten.

"Well, Screw You."

Hey. Science doesn't lie.

Yeah. It's a Baby. A Picture Is Five Bucks. Move Along.

It has been frequently observed that babies are chick magnets. When you're a guy, nothing beats a baby for getting unavailable ladies to come up and chat with you. Of course, I get nothing but grand-mothers and burly construction workers, but still. It's always nice to get attention.

One of the advantages of having an exceptionally attractive baby is the way we constantly get self-esteem reinforcement from total strangers. We counted a full dozen compliments during our last trip to the Farmer's Market. I'd try to bottle my baby's cuteness and sell it, but I don't know how to boil her down.

Sometimes, though, the attention is creepy. Like yesterday, I was walking her around in her stroller, and this guy, about forty, was completely smitten by her. He wasn't homeless or drunk or anything. Thin, moustache, tall, looked like he had a job as a carpenter or something else that involves actual work. Sensible, salt of the earth type. But the moment he saw the baby, it ate his brain. She was the most, most fanfrickintastic thing he had ever seen.

And then, after cooing over her for a minute, completely ecstatic, he turns to me, gives my hand a *very* firm shake, and says, I swear to God, "Marvelous." Then he went on his way. I think he wanted to compliment me on the quality of my seed, but his Spider Senses were detecting another baby just around the corner that was about to escape. And nothing is better than looking at a baby.

How does this happen? I like babies. They're cute, to an extent. But I can't imagine totally freaking out over them. So I've decided to go into a new line of work. Baby petting zoos. You pay five bucks, and you get to spend an hour in the presence of a dozen highly attractive, carefully selected babies. You can pet them, poke at them, change their diapers, whatever. Pay five extra bucks and we drag a toddler out of the back room to call you "Daddy."

It's brilliant. Easiest million bucks ever made. Venture capital is welcomed.

Week 19—When You Don't Play Computer Games, It Makes the Baby Jesus Cry

As I help raise Cordelia, I sometimes think wistfully back to the time when she wasn't awful.

Once, she was a quiet, happy, burbling baby, who loved life and stuffed animals and the five to seven uninterrupted hours of sleep she got every night. Then her cute, sharp little teeth started to push their way out through her gums and she turned into a pill. No, not just a pill. A fierce, primal little pill, like a fussy little dinosaur. A pillosaurus.

Now when she sleeps two uninterrupted hours, I do a little happy dance. I've said it once, I've said it a thousand times. If someone would have told me that having a baby is occasionally inconvenient, I'd never have had one.

Of course, when Cordelia is angry and pained, Mariann and I have our weapon: Baby Tylenol. Or, as I now call it, Vitamin T.

When You Don't Play Computer Games, It Makes the Baby Jesus Cry

Actually, I don't get it the worst. My wife does. I stay up the first half of the night, when the baby sleeps sort of okay. She handles the second half of the night, when the baby fights with every bit of strength in her floppy body the cruel clutches of Sleep, that evil, life-stealing Bitch-Goddess.

So, to make my wife less of a zombie, I started to stay up later, so that she could get more sleep. (Working at home has its points.) And the way I stay up later is to play computer games. And, at this point, I should point out that I am a lifelong computer game addict. So this development, while good for my wife, is very, very, very bad for me.

The worst thing that could possibly happen to me is to have staying up all night playing computer games become the kind, virtuous thing to do. This is like letting a jazz player live in a house made of heroin. It's as if someone had told me when I was a teenager that, every time I jerked off, it saved the life of a puppy.

Before, when I looked up from a play session to see the sun rising, I knew I was a big loser. Now, when this happens, I know that I am a Nice Man.

And I get my reward later, when my properly rested wife is feeling real friendly. If you know what I mean.

Another Good Reason to Keep Writing This Journal:

Someday, Cordelia will ask me "Was I a good baby?" If I were most parents, I'd have to give her a pained smile and say "Oh, of course you were. You were an angel."

But now, instead, I can consult the documentation and say "Well, generally. But there was a bad spot in week five and another in week thirty-seven. And from weeks sixteen to eighteen inclusive, you were a little pillosaurus. Shame on you. Now go to bed."

Intentionally Starving My Child for My Wife's Benefit

When Cordelia gets difficult, I tend to treat her like I would a malfunctioning computer program. I troubleshoot her, experimenting with different patterns of feeding her, giving her painkillers, walking her around, poking her with a chopstick, and other remedies, trying to find the right combination of stimuli that will turn her into a Good Baby. Or, at least, not a little shrieking wolverine.

For example, when I go to bed and leave the baby in my peacefully sleeping wife's care, I want her to be as content as possible. The longer Cordelia sleeps, the longer until she wakes up my wife, and the more friendly my wife is the next day, and the less I suffer. So I want to leave behind a pretty darn content baby.

That generally means that I need to pack the baby with as much food as possible before I go to bed. And that means I need to time her so that she is hungry when I go to bed, but not so hungry that she freaks out and screams and wakes my wife. So the hours before I go to bed are spent in a complicated dance of reassurance and neglect, feeding her just enough to sustain her, but not enough to satisfy her.

So, basically, I am underfeeding her to make my wife happy. I'm not sure how I bent my brain until it got to this point, but our baby is still a pudgy little lump of butter on the bone, so I'm not actually putting anyone in any danger.

Most nights, this system works pretty well. Or, at least, better than when I don't do it. Treating her like a complicated little computer program does tend to leave out a lot of what you humans call "love."

However, I intend to learn how to express warmth and empathy very soon. I think there's a chapter on it in one of my parenting books.

Temper and Self-Control

During a teething-related fit of pique, I handed Cordelia a rattle to soothe her. She looked at me and flung it away. I love it when she reacts to things the way a reasonable human would. If I was mad and sitting in pee and you handed a rattle to me to make it better, I'd be pretty pissed, too.

Of course, the main reason I was handing her the rattle was that I was totally trying to blow her off. All of our parenting books say at what month she can eat and crawl and walk, but none of them say when the baby can figure out that you're blowing it off. I think this is important information to have.

On the other hand, Cordelia hasn't learned that, when you flail your arms and legs around at random, they hit hard things. This makes you sad. But once Cordelia gets enough visits from the Pain Fairy, things will come together there, too.

Sometimes You Just Wanna Pick on 'Em.

Since Cordelia has been somewhat frustrating on occasion, I have been looking for ways to pick on her in a way that makes it seem like I am being a loving, careful parent.

For example, I try to feed her rice cereal. It's a good thing to feed her, and she hates it. She makes really cute frowny faces and spits and hisses and gets annoyed. This is currently my and Mariann's number one source of entertainment.

Also, parenting books say that we should be introducing her senses to new, interesting sensations. So sometimes I get my fingers wet and flick water onto her face. This really alarms her, but in a loving, educational way.

I asked Mariann if it was okay to do this. She said that she does it too sometimes. So now I know that it's all right.

Some Parents Talk About Getting a Layette

I'm not sure what a layette is, but here's my guess: It's a quick lay you try to squeeze in while the baby is sleeping.

Everything Is All New and Shiny

If there's anything that makes me think things are developing in my baby's brain thing, it's the focused way she looks around. It seems like she's really trying to take in what things look like. It makes sense. When I see something new and interesting, I'll stare at and really intensely admire it. Like a rhino, or a lovely sunset over the ocean, or an aerobics class.

But for Cordelia, everything around her is new and interesting, so she stares at it in the same way. A chair, or her stroller, or big, hairy Daddy walking around the house with no shirt. It's all as glorious as a sunset.

Now I can keep her from crying for large periods of time simply by pointing her in different directions. This changing view of mundane objects can keep her happily occupied for minutes at a time. Then her gums start hurting again, and it's off for the drugs.

Week 20—Reverse Colic

Babies are creatures of wild mood swings.

One week, she is a sleepless, finger-gnawing little terror. The next, she is a little angel. Not the sort of bullshit angel with wings and a harp you see on Hallmark cards, but the sort of angel that lets Mommy and Daddy get a good night's sleep and doesn't vomit on them all the time.

Last week, terror. This week, angel. Every week is a new spin on the Wheel of Parenting.

Reverse Colic

Cordelia now suffers from reverse colic. This is a condition where, in mid-evening, the baby is extremely happy and playful for no apparent reason. Side effects of this rare and temporary condition are improved parental interest and an increase in poking by delighted strangers.

Yes, she's one happy baby. Happy to be tickled. Happy to see Mommy and Daddy. Happy to be worn as a hat. And when nighttime rolls around, she's happy to go right to sleep. Sometimes, she even achieves this state without healthy shots of Baby Tylenol.

I think this signifies the end of teething. Or, at least, this round of teething. Her little pearly whites are almost in. But, as usual, I can't relax. Being as I am the father of Speedy Choo Choo Mood Swing Girl, all I can do is grimly record these events as a reference point to read back on nostalgically when she won't stop screaming. Like tomorrow. Or when she's thirteen.

My father, since I was wee, always thought that I was too "pessimistic." I don't like that term. I prefer "realist." Or, "burnt out, hollow shell of a human being." But these few days, I'm getting lots of sleep, and you can't feel bad about that.

Grabbing for Real

In a previous entry, I retracted my statement that Cordelia can grab for things. Now I retract the retraction. She definitely grabs things now. And not just double handfuls of Daddy's chest hair.

When she's in her crib, she can see something out of her reach and contort, twist, and arch her whole little body to grab it. Once snared, she will, in a sea anemone–like motion, pull it back and insert it in her mouth, for information processing and nutrient absorption. Books call this "mouthing." I call it "the systematic sliming of every object in the house."

Already, Cordelia is learning one of the most valuable lessons of life: you work hard in order to obtain things. The only good reason to exert yourself is to expand your collection of stuff.

Along these lines, I eventually intend to reward her with cash payments for good grades. Some frown on this procedure, saying it teaches children that the only reason to work hard is for comfort and financial gain, and that hard work for its own reward is for losers. Interestingly, this is exactly the lesson I want to teach her.

Decorations Are Very Important for the Development of Young Minds

An explanation is in order. My parents were in the meat business for a very long time. During that time, they obtained a number of interesting objects. Then they moved into their RV, and some of those objects were handed over to me and my wife for safekeeping.

So if you are ever in our house and enter the nursery and note that there are three large, steel meat hooks hanging in the closet next to the baby clothes, please be assured that there is nothing sinister going on.

Nothing You Can't Do on eBay

EBay is a marvelous Web site. You can buy and sell just about anything there. Pez dispensers. Pornographic Atari cartridges. A house. (Actually, I didn't make up any of that. They made pornographic Atari cartridges. How could you not want to bring a child into a world filled with such ingeniousness?)

But eBay is very strict about certain things you cannot sell there. You can't sell alcohol. You can't sell plants and seeds, or fireworks, or guns, or human organs. Porn is fine, of course, especially in Atari format. And surprisingly, you can buy and sell bits of baby.

Oh sure, it says you can't do this on their rules page. And most people believe this PR. But if you want to trade baby bits, you just have to look in the right place. First, click on Collectibles. Then Non-paper. Then Baby. And there you are.

For example, a Ziploc bag of freshly shaved baby hair goes for about twenty bucks. I thought this was weird at first, until I found out that it is used to make the highest quality baby wigs. I don't know why you want to go onto eBay to buy a baby wig. But I imagine I'd want to get one after I shaved my baby's head.

You can also get sealed jars of baby drool, for teething babies who ran out of their own. I ordered two.

Fresh baby teeth are sold in lots of twenty, for youngsters of an entrepreneurial bent blessed with a generous Tooth Fairy and parents who can't count.

So, if you need a few extra bucks and were saving your kid's drool anyway, keep this in mind. I think I saw some good deals there. But try to keep it hush-hush. We all got a good thing going here. I'm not sure why some Haitian dude is paying top dollar for my daughter's nail clippings, but I'm cool with it as long as the checks clear.

Rock-a-Bye Baby

A quick aside. Recent experience (and many a late evening a capella rendition) has made me realize what a wickedly funny song "Rock-a-Bye Baby" is. Especially the "bough breaks" bit.

If anything better expresses a parent's combination of love and loathing for a baby that refuses to sleep, I don't know about it.

A Way Being a Parent Reprograms Your Brain

Before, when a newborn baby was shown on a movie or TV show, I'd go, "Oooh! How cute!" and not give it another thought.

Now, though, experience has made me observe two peculiar things about filmed births. First, the baby always comes out impossibly clean. Second, it comes out impossibly huge. Now, instead of "How cute!," I'm more likely to say something like "Oooh! How cu . . . wait a second! It's a six-month-old! She gave birth to a six-month-old! Oh my God! She had it in her until the start of the sixth trimester! Look how big its head is! How did that thing fit out of her? It must have gutted her like a trout!!!!"

My nonparent friends love it when I talk like this. They could not possibly appreciate it more.

Week 21—Her Brain Outweighs Her Body

New milestone. It has now been five months since my daughter Cordelia came out of my wife and into our hearts. She's come a long

Thoughts from the Future

You still cannot sell your baby's body parts on eBay.

way since her first fragile moments. She's made a lot of advances. For example, she doesn't have an umbilical cord attached to her anymore. And she now has belly cellulite.

As time goes on, she is more and more able to focus on tasks with an intensity of purpose that scares me. She's starting to show will and intent. She's starting to become, to make up a word, persony.

It scares the shit out of me. She's starting to look at me. I mean, really *look* at *me*.

I remind Mariann about all these monthly birthdays. Mariann couldn't care less. But it makes me feel involved, so I keep at it.

Pain Disagreements

Teething has resumed. It occurs to me that if it weren't for the miracle of teeth, parenting might be almost kind of predictable. But instead, at the dawn of each new day, you never know how screamy it's going to be.

Every day, her little canines move a subatomic distance closer to the surface. At this rate, I estimate that her baby teeth will all be out about three months after her adult ones. I'd try to pinch the sluggish little bastards and drag them out, but that seems like cheating.

Cordelia seems very resigned to her teething situation. She's sort of at peace with it. Sometimes, based on extra irritability and unusually persistent inability to nap, I suspect that her teeth hurt. But I can't be sure. They only hurt enough to cause a massive screaming jag occasionally. I'm positive that she's hurting sometimes, but she's learned to, on odd days, be a little stoic about it. Except for the long periods of naplessness, so far so good.

When I give her Baby Tylenol, naplessness and fussiness end quickly (and she gets these adorable looks of disgust when her mouth is filled with the sweet, sticky red goo). But this is where I and my wife part ways. My wife is loath to pack a little baby with drugs, any drugs, unless there is strong and convincing evidence that is it necessary (such as, say, the baby going "AAAAAAHHHH!!!! AAAAAAAHHHHHH!!!!!").

I, on the other hand, don't like the thought of my little girl in pain, and I don't like the thought of her delaying her nap for four hours. I want that nap! She owes me that nap!

So we compromise. Some days, my wife holds back on the Tylenol and keeps Cordelia organic and free range. On other days, I give her a "Pain Vacation." I drug her when she shows signs of unrest, and comfort myself with the knowledge that she can spend an evening free of gum issues.

I don't feel bad about this at all. I mean, it's not like I'm giving her Xanax or Baby Ritalin (yet). It just appeals to my basic sense of fair play. If Mommy gets an epidural, baby gets Tylenol. Daddy can make do with Guinness.

Those Pudgy Little Fingers Can Go Everywhere!

Even if you don't like babies, they make great science experiments. You don't get many opportunities to witness the laborious, step-by-step creation of a human being. It's pretty neat.

This week, I've been holding tempting objects around Cordelia and seeing if she can figure out how to grab them or not. If something is right in front of her, she can always get it. If it's off at even a small angle, however, she can only obtain it by flailing her arms in its general direction and getting lucky.

So this week's lesson is: Figuring out how to grab an item is not enough. You have to relearn the process for every possible position of the item in relation to you. How cool is that?

I feel that, if you don't feel at least a little bit of interest in the steps a blank-brained infant has to take to reach full, complex humanhood, there's something wrong with you.

Her Brain Outweighs Her Body

We're trying to teach Cordelia to crawl. Well, teaching isn't the right word. We're putting her on her stomach, putting a pacifier on the floor in front of her just out of reach, and hoping she figures the shit out. Dude, it's called parenting.

Here are the ways she has attempted to crawl, presented here in soul-deadening detail.

i. Grab the carpet and try to drag herself closer. This is really cute, but futile. First, her fingers are pudgy and weak. Second, she is not actually on the carpet. She is on a blanket, and, when she pulls on it, it just ends up scrunched up around her face. Then she sucks on it and forgets about the pacifier.

Failure.

ii. Attempt to push herself forward with her legs. This is adorable, but futile. Her legs are just too short and there's not enough traction. Also, she invariably ends up lifting both feet and both arms into the air, causing her face to smack into the floor. This sudden reminder of the implacable harshness of gravity causes her to forget about the pacifier.

Failure.

iii. Drag herself forward on her elbows. Basically, in the very best Normandy beach fashion, she stays low to the ground and inches herself forward, a tiny bit at a time, staring at the pacifier with eyes like little lasers. Amazingly, this works. Sometimes, she works herself forward the few inches necessary to reach the pacifier. I hold it in range, she reaches for it, removing the key support her arms are providing, and whap. Her face hits the floor. But she has the pacifier. Success, more or less.

Watching this trial and error process tells me that her brain is developing. Before, if I could read her thoughts, I would hear "Bzzzzzzzzzzzz . . ." Now, I would hear "Bzzzzzzzz . . . Want. Want. Want. Want. Grab. Fall. Whap! Cryyyyyyyyyyyyyy . . ."

Other Trick She Knows

Whenever I blow lightly on her face, she sticks her tongue way out. It's a great trick for amusing friends.

Week 22—Food Cramming!

Being the parent of the world's cutest child is a difficult and sobering experience. (Yes, I'm afraid my child is cuter than your child. If you don't believe me, check out cutechildrankings.org.) Humbly accepting the awed compliments of so many strangers is tiring. As Cordelia sails through her fifth month, it is clear that with great adorability comes great responsibility.

Of course, the random strangers don't get to deal with her when the teething pains are getting her down. Cordelia is always well behaved when outsiders are around. This is because she has already learned the most important goal in this short life of ours: winning the approval of others.

Food Cramming!

In open defiance of the advice of books, the opinions of friends, all that is good and right about the human species, and the Will of God, my wife wants to wean our daughter before she goes out of her goddamn mind.

It's not like it'll be a big loss. Mariann's breasts never produced the amount of milk our little girl desired. Worse, after my wife got a bad cold, her milk production fell by half. So Cordelia has been sustained recently by a healthy diet of formula and parental guilt.

Now Mariann wants Cordelia on solids. Cordelia is ready to go on solids. And that means we have begun that most time-honored of parental traditions: wasting tons of food by smearing it on our child's chin.

It turns out that one of the action items on the infinite list of really basic things a baby has to learn is that "Food must be swallowed." It's not automatic like breathing. When a baby has a mouth full of tasty rice cereal goodness, he or she is probably thinking, "Alert! Alert! I am being invaded by goo!" and out the mouth it comes. With luck, it is not turned into a high velocity mist.

So my wife and I have been spending evenings trying to cram food into the baby's mouth and hoping that she gets the idea. Sometimes, more by accident than design, she swallows. So the goal is to get the food into her mouth in the first place and hope for the best.

The problem here is that damned, vigilant sentinel, Cordelia's tongue. Millennia of evolution have left babies with tongues trained to instantly push unwelcome objects (Spoons. Fingers. Mice.) out of the mouth. How we could survive as a species with infants who eagerly accept into their mouths moldy, skanky stuffed animals but reject spoonfuls of food is, quite frankly, beyond me.

To get the spoon past the tongue and deposit its cereal payload, I sometimes resort to brute force. Well, gentle, kind brute force. Other times, I try trickery, singing to her until she opens her mouth in a broad smile, and then jamming the spoon in there before she realizes what is happening. If you think this is a horrible betrayal of my child's trust, well, um, I . . . ummm . . . She won't remember, and that makes it okay.

The easiest thing to do, in my opinion, would be to try to feed her until she gets upset and starts to cry. Then her mouth will be open all the time, and I can put food into it easily. However, my wife tells me that this is a terrible idea and will give her a "complex" about food. I think "complex" is an unnecessarily negative term. I kind of like the idea of making her have unexplainable, negative feelings about food from early on. If my parents had loved me enough to give me a "complex," I wouldn't be as much of a load as I am now.

Priming the Immune System. Ewwww!

Cordelia jams everything into her mouth. Her level of focus is remarkable. She can take a rattle, meticulously orally moisten every square centimeter of it, and repeat the process indefinitely. Is it possible for a human being to run out of spit?

There are varying theories for why babies do this. Some suggest that this self-inflicted repeated exposure to germs helps strengthen her immune system. I like this theory because it makes my neglect look like good parenting.

"Jeff?"

"Yes?"

"Why is your baby putting that giant dust bunny in her mouth?"

"It's all right. I'm helping to strengthen her immune system."

"Jesus, that thing is huge. And what's that in it? Oh my God! It's a dried-up mouse!"

"It's all right. Mice are very good for strengthening the immune system."

"Don't you ever clean in here?"

"No. I'm trying to strengthen the baby's immune system."

I stand her up against the couch and she sucks on it. I put her on the bed and she turns her head to suck on the pillow. I hold her and she jams my hand in her mouth. I put her on the floor and she sucks the carpet. It's like living with Pac-Man.

So I keep saying "strengthening the immune system." The only other option is to say "Oh God, what's she putting in her mouth now? It's . . . it's . . . blarrrgghhhhhhh."

The Foam Scam

People make a lot of money scamming anxious parents. Even someone as cynical and apathetic as me is not immune.

During one run to Babies "R" Us (also known as "The Mouth of Hell, from Which All Vileness Comes"), I saw these little foam devices you put under your baby when it sleeps. These keep the baby from rolling over and suffocating itself. Nobody wants to enter the nursery one morning and find a blue baby and know it could all have been prevented if only they had given $5.97 plus sales tax to Babies "R" Us (also known as "The Whore of Babylon").

So I bought one. My mother-in-law, who worked as a nanny, took one look at it and said it was useless and I was being scammed. But I didn't listen. I'd bought it, I'd paid for it, and I didn't want a blue baby, so, damn it, I was using it.

Here is what happened. Being an ignorant first-time parent, I did not realize that our one-month-old was as likely to run a four-minute mile as to roll over. She made no rolloverish motions of any sort until she was about five months old. At that point, she rolled over that chintzy six-buck foam piece of shit pretty much as if it wasn't there.

There are whole industries based on prying cash out of parents with the twin tools of fear and guilt. And, if you want to go down that road (as if you have any choice), you can buy everything you'll ever need at Babies "R" Us (also known as "The Favorite Shopping Spot of People Who Have Never Heard of Target").

One More Thought About Babies "R" Us

They are very selective about what they sell. A product must reach a certain high level of price and shoddiness before it has any chance of being considered for their shelves.

Interacting with the Poor, Miserable Childfree

I only recently realized that I am way behind on one of the most important missions of any parent: pressuring the childless into joining me and putting on the same shackles I did. This is necessary because of two key constants of human behavior:

i. If someone has different personal tastes from me, I must convince them to like the things I like.
ii. If someone else makes different choices regarding how they spend their time, those choices (and, indirectly, the person) are inferior.
   And, of course, don't forget that
iii. Having a child is utter ecstasy, but the true joy of it cannot ever be comprehended until a person/victim actually has a child.

Therefore, to be a proper parent, I have to convert others to my bizarre lifestyle. I'm working on it. For example, sometimes, in public places, I sigh loudly and say, "Wow. I can no longer remember how sad and empty my life was before I had a child." When I'm around people without kids, I'll say to Mariann, "You know what I feel when I meet someone who doesn't yet have a child?" (Shake head sadly. Give her a mournful look.) "Pity."

I also look wistfully off into the distance, my eyes unfocusing as I see some hidden future paradise we will all share, and say, "Children are our future."

Then, when some guy rises to the bait and claims he doesn't want a child, I point Cordelia at him. Her cute gaze lances out like some X-Men laser beam, transfixing all it strikes. And, before you can say "Gah gah goo goo," he's running off to have unprotected sex.

It's hard work. But remember. The world can't ever have enough babies.

Babies! Babies! Babies! Babies! Babies!

Week 23—The Angel Slides Smoothly Off into Sleepy Time Ecstasy

The weaning project continues. Mariann and I each have our own parts to play. I keep trying to get unpleasant, pastelike cereal down the baby's throat. Mariann keeps the breasts far away from the baby. She curls up in bed and comforts them, whispering to them quietly and reassuring them that, soon, the monster will never come after them again.

Cordelia is oblivious to the drama. She's been charming this week. She's the cutest little pudge biscuit in the whole wide world, my little cutey wootie pootie bootie happy slappy bugger booger boo.

(Excuse me for that. I'm practicing being a cute parent. Acting like that makes people throw up, and that amuses me.)

Cordelia is growing stronger, smarter, and more advanced in her techniques for demanding constant attention from her parents. She still can't say words, but she can make three different noises: a grunt, a squeal, and a squeak. And all noises mean the same thing: "Pay attention to me or I start screaming."

The Thing I Dread the Most

The thing I dread the most about being a parent is when my daughter can understand what I am saying.

Cordelia often stands around with her mouth hanging open. This makes her look dopey. The other day, when this happened, my wife said:

"Close your mouth, Honey. You look dopey with it open like that."

At which point, I added:

"Yeah, and if you keep your mouth open all the time, a wasp will fly in there. And then it will sting your tongue. And it'll go all numb, and you won't be able to feel it or move it or anything. And then the wasp will lay its eggs in your tongue, and they'll hatch in there, and grow, and then one day you'll open your mouth and hundreds of wasps will fly out."

Since Cordelia is five months old, saying this didn't have much of an effect. But, as I understand it, when she is old enough to understand what I am saying, she will not take the above as a humorous, Shel Silversteinesque flight of fancy. Instead, she will believe it, and not sleep for the following three to five nights, and it will completely f-word her up.

Oh. That reminds me. I will also have to stop saying the f-word five hundred times a day.

Of course, it's not too late to take action. I'm considering not speaking for seventeen years. Maybe she will mistake my utter silence for wisdom and inner peace.

How to Win the Therapy Game

Of course, at this point, it's a given that any child of mine is going to end up needing some serious and expensive therapy. My goal, in this case, is for her to only need the therapy when she is a grown-up, so that it is on her dime. If I can keep her sane until her therapy doesn't have to be paid for by me, I win.

The Giving Tree—A Tale of Terror

Speaking of Shel Silverstein, I only just reread my copy of the children's classic *The Giving Tree*. It's the first time I've read it since I became a parent.

For the unfamiliar, it's about this boy and the tree (read: parent) who loves him. And the boy takes everything from the tree, little by little, and leaves it with NOTHING. He plays in its branches, and he takes its apples, and he carves his initials into its trunk, and eventually he gets an axe and CUTS OFF ALL ITS BRANCHES.

HOLY SHIT!

Does this mean that Cordelia is going to come after my arms someday? Will she come into my room with a hacksaw and say "Give 'em up, Dad. I need to buy a house."

Don't get me wrong. I love my little girl as much as expected. But the day she comes after my limbs, I'm takin' her out.

The Angel Slides Smoothly Off into Sleepy Time Ecstasy

When my daughter goes to sleep, it's like she's been hit with a stun gun.

One night, she fell asleep while pulling her foot up to put it in her mouth. She was frozen in this position. This made more sense than her standard sleeping pose: back arched, neck twisted at an angle that makes me think "broken," and her feet twisted to the side and wedged between the bars of her crib.

When I'm putting her to bed and I put the pacifier in her mouth and turn off the lights, her body instantly stretches out and tenses up and she jams her head to the side as if she was looking over her shoulder. She stretches her head over as far as it can go. Then she grunts as if she's trying to pass a particularly challenging stool.

And then she falls asleep like that.

Sometimes I wish I had more experience with babies. (My actual, practical experience before Cordelia: Zilch.) I want to know whether my baby is weird like other babies or if she is already being a freak in her own little way.

She doesn't like being put to bed. Sometimes I imagine that she regards sleep like her daddy does. Sleep is the life-stealer. Sleeping more makes you live less. Sleeping is something you short yourself of as long as you can get away with it. My daughter acts as if sleep was something to be fought off as long as possible, because each minute spent sleeping is one minute less she can spend drooling, grunting, and staring at random objects.

But I know this is just my imagination. Babies have a strange alien internal logic all their own. Trying to attribute adult motivation to their weirdness just takes up valuable thinking time you could use trying to mentally keep up with the outside world.

Three-Second Naps

I've always gotten Cordelia to nap by feeding her. Sucking on a bottle puts her to sleep in a way nothing else does. When she seems sleepy, I stick a bottle in her mouth. I can only imagine the many ways this completely scrambles up her attitudes toward sleep and her attitudes toward food, and that's without even getting into Freud, so don't tell me. I don't want to hear about it.

Anyway.

Recently, at her regular nap time, she's developed the habit of closing her eyes and nodding off during feeding. Then, three seconds after I pull the bottle out of her mouth, she instantly springs awake. And then stays awake for three hours.

It's the amazing three-second nap. And it pisses me off. It's not fair. She *owes* me that nap, goddammit! After the previous hours of vaguely involved parenting, I have earned those fifteen minutes in which to pursue personal fulfillment.

Week 24—"Could I Have Some Explosives to Set Off Near My Child?"

There's one thing that we haven't had much of since Cordelia was born: holidays. Holidays are great for parents. They give children happy memories they carry into adulthood, providing mental static that will obscure my thoughtlessness and idiocy. And they provide an opportunity to throw all the kids into a bin and let them amuse each other, while I slip off and drink.

Our mighty nation has just celebrated Independence Day, which, for this new parent, means one thing. I got to take my five-month-old daughter Cordelia and let her listen to explosions for the first time. I am pleased to say that she dealt with the firecrackers and bottle rockets with relaxed dignity, up to the point where she completely lost her shit.

I also gave her a chance to spend time around her normal relatives. "Normal," in this case, meaning "Don't write whacked out stuff about their own children and make it into a book."

My parents were also there. Cordelia was sucked into their RV for long periods of time when the explosions got to be too much for her.

"Could I Have Some Explosives to Set Off Near My Child?"

Cordelia is growing up in western Washington state. The Suquamish Indian reservation is conveniently and centrally located here. The local Native American population is allowed to sell all manner of normally illegal fireworks, usually from wooden shacks along the highway that passes through their reservation. This creates a cherished local tradition: families go to the Rez to buy sacks of small explosives to take home and set off near their children.

Of course, it is illegal to buy fireworks on the reservation and carry them off. But everyone does it anyway. This provides a useful and educational example to children, which will help guide their choices for everything from speeding to marijuana.

Anyway, on the way to my grandparents' house, our family was passing through the Suquamish reservation. My wife and I stopped the car at one of the convenient wooden shacks, got out, and bought some small explosives, made in some Asian country with what experience has shown me is minimal concern for quality control. Then we took our baby and our new explosives and joined with my family, each member of which had brought explosives of his or her own. Then we all started eating pork and drinking alcohol.

I still can't get over what was written on the bag the fireworks were placed in when I bought them (again, at the wooden shack along the highway in the Indian reservation). There was a list of safety suggestions given by a character named, I swear to God, Freddy Firework. The first one was:

"Always purchase fireworks from a reliable source."

This brings two questions to my mind:

One. Is a wooden shack by the highway in the Indian reservation a "reliable source"?

Two. What on Earth would it take to *not* be a reliable source? A one-eyed gypsy named Stavros selling M-80s out of the trunk of his Plymouth?

I guess I must consider the shack to be a reliable source, however, since I did buy explosives there. It was necessary. Otherwise, how would Cordelia learn what our nation's freedom is all about?

How Can I Be So Cruel*!?!?*

The holiday meant spending time around relatives, most of which have been reading the installments of this journal. So, of course, I got asked a question I've been asked a lot lately. Namely: "How can you write these things about your daughter? Won't she hate you? Won't she need years of therapy?"

My response to this, of course, is one of utter, shameless lack of remorse. I am very mindful of Cordelia's privacy. I have not revealed anything about her that is not true of pretty much all babies. For example, I have written that:

Cordelia (who is, I remind you, five months old) occasionally cries and has difficulty going to sleep. ("You monster! How can you say such a thing!")

She does not have control over her bodily waste, and sometimes pees and poos unexpectedly. Because of this, she wears a diaper. ("Gasp! How will she ever forgive you for revealing that?")

Her brain has not yet developed very much. She cannot walk or talk. ("You bastard! How can you write such obvious things?")

In fact, even though she is an advanced five months old, she has only the crudest control over her body. ("You have gone beyond the pale by revealing such information.")

Sometimes, especially when teething or tired, she is fussy and moody. ("Aiiiyyyeee! My brain! It is exploding!")

She is cute. ("KAPOW!")

To be honest, I sort of hope that, one day, Cordelia will enjoy reading about what she was like when she was a baby. Like a photo album, but less crushingly dull. And if, somehow, I screw up and mistakenly raise a humorless little prig, well, then her anger at me for writing this will be my punishment.

And, if she's still mad, I'll just throw my arms open wide and say, "Okay. Fair is fair. You get three free punches. Don't hit the nuts."

Doing the Double Breath Check

Mariann was stung on the cheek by a bee. This caused a very mild allergic reaction and, for one night in there, she was feeling a little constriction in her throat.

This fit very well into my schedule. Instead of freaking out and going upstairs every hour or two to see if one girl was still breathing, I went upstairs to see if two girls were still breathing. It made me feel very efficient.

Daddy's Face Is a Torment

Cordelia's favorite activity is still looking around. Look right. Look left. Right. Left. Repeat until time to crap. This makes sense, as learning to see is the most important thing she will ever do. However, I can't help but feel I'm being blown off when I hold her standing up in my lap facing me and she looks absolutely everywhere but at my face.

So I tried an experiment. Whenever she looked anywhere, I rotated her so that she was staring at my face. She would try to twist her neck at an alarming angle so that she could see past me, but I kept turning her so she was always looking at me.

Of course, she completely freaked. Whenever she looked at me, her little face scrunched up in terror, and she burst into bitter tears. And, for a few minutes, she was terrified whenever she caught a glimpse of me.

So I stopped doing that real quick. I don't want her to be filled with anger and resentment whenever she sees me. That shouldn't start for thirteen more years.

Baby Chews the Paper

The daily *New York Times* is the great joy in my life. Even when my wife was in labor, I was still sneaking peeks to see what the editorial page said. I know this is desperately sad and lame. But parents are already lame pretty much by definition.

So it brought joy to my heart to find that Cordelia is in love with the newspaper too. Of course, she is mainly interested in grabbing huge double handfuls of it and cramming it in her mouth, but still. It's a good start. It makes Cordelia ecstatic and buys Daddy a little reading time, so it seems like the perfect activity.

And yet, Cordelia mouthing the newspaper until her chin is black with newsprint does make me feel very slightly ill at ease. First, of course, it's not sanitary. I'm planning to buy an autoclave to sterilize the paper before it gets to her. I just hope that doesn't make it less crinkly.

But then there is the problem of ink. I am trying to convince myself it's acceptable for a baby to eat a certain modest amount of ink every day, but it's not working.

This is why I think Babies "R" Us should supplement the shoddily made, overpriced shit they normally distribute with a line of baby newspapers. It's just like a regular newspaper, but the ink is sweet and full of vitamins and the paper is made of candy. Then I can hold Cordelia in my lap and read one side of a page, while she moistens and shreds the other half. Just like now.

Week 25—The Smile Is Not Happiness

Cordelia is almost six months old now. That's half a year, and she is rounding out this period with a series of small accomplishments. She can now sit up unassisted for several seconds at a time, especially if an amusing object or tasty bit of newspaper is put in front of her. She can now take food off a spoon with her mouth, snapping at it like a little turtle.

But this isn't enough. I won't be able to feel safe until she can defend herself from a small nest of determined ants. This doesn't really have anything to do with anything, but it's still on my mind.

The Smile Is Not Happiness

Some people trust the smile of a child. They are deluded.

Babies are pretty dumb and pretty helpless, but they are not inert. When they emerge from the haze that is their first few months of life, their first ability is to leverage every possible advantage they have to achieve their goal: to be picked up and fussed over.

Cordelia's smile is simply a tool she uses to manipulate us. She doesn't smile when she's happy. She shows happiness by being quiet. She smiles when she wants to be picked up. For example. She had been lying in her crib for a while and was starting to grunt. I walked in and looked at her. The moment she saw me, she busted out her most full, radiant smile, as if to say, "Hooray! It's Daddy! The bestest daddy in the whole world! Just seeing him fills me with bliss!"

Normally, this barrage of cuteness earns several units of attention. So, just out of curiosity, I waited silently to see what she would do.

After a few seconds, she stopped smiling. She looked confused, and gave me a look that I chose to interpret as "What? What's going on? Wasn't that smile enough? That's usually good for a tickle, at least."

So she tried again. She gave another glorious smile for a few seconds. Then she turned it off, stared at me, frowned, and waited.

This process repeated at least five times. I lost count. She smiled and waited for her reward, while I watched her quietly. If the smile means happiness, this makes no sense. I don't think she was becoming deliriously happy for three-second spurts alternating with periods of unexplainable angst. She was trying to buy some parenting.

Anyway, I watched her instead. Eventually, she reverted to the behavior that always earns her instant attention: screaming.

Of course, this experiment was never repeated. I always try to reward her for smiling. Smiling and looking cute to get things out of people is solid, traditional human behavior and should be encouraged.

Sure, my baby knows how to manipulate me; I won't waste my time convincing myself she is doing otherwise. Instead, it is my responsibility as a parent to channel her innate manipulative instincts in profitable directions.

Poo Isn't Gross, You Wimp

Anybody who is grossed out by baby poo or caring for the infant ass is, I have decided, a wimp.

Here's the thing. I, personally, every day or two, at around the same time of evening (though not so precise that you can set your watch by it), have to take a shit. I suspect that you are pretty much the same way. If not, eat more brown bread.

When this happens, I retire to the bathroom, close and securely lock the door, and go about my business. When I am done, I do not avert my eyes from the bowl like a blushing schoolgirl. I take a look in there and see what's going on. And then, and here is the gruesome part, I get some toilet paper and wipe myself clean.

Again, I hope you are the same way.

My point, and I do have one, is that having a baby does not really dramatically change one's exposure to shit and the wiping of asses. Not having a baby would not magically free me from having to wipe an ass, and it's no big deal. Even the most squeamish childless people do not break down into tears of disgust when they go to the bathroom.

In other words, dealing with infant feces is a change of quantity, not quality. You just have to deal with more of what you already deal with on a regular basis. So what?

Of course, I still really wish she wouldn't kick her ankles in the stuff when I'm changing her. But, since I don't kick my ankles in my own waste, this opinion is permissible.

The Littlest Octopus

It does me no good to remember that, for all of the adjusting my wife and I have done, we're still getting through the easy part of parenthood. Cordelia has been slimy and noisy so far, but basically inert. This means that, education-wise, my wife and I haven't had to bring anything to the table. We haven't had to teach her how to add, or not to play with matches, or that you shouldn't stick the ice pick in the power socket.

Of course, I also suspect we shouldn't have let her get her hands on that ice pick, but come on. You can't do everything.

We are now entering the stage where we can't actually teach her anything, but we really want to. Among other things, she has started actively grabbing objects. And I don't mean clumsily latching on to a big rattle we hold still in front of her at chest level. I mean grabbing for everything in reach. My glasses. A full cup of coffee. My computer's wiring. Mommy's eyeball.

Carrying Cordelia right now is like dragging a strip of Velcro through a bag of cotton balls. After a few minutes, all sorts of crap is stuck to her.

The increased level of attention I have had to pay to her because of this alarms me. After six months of being, for all practical purposes, an emotionally needy satchel, Cordelia now has the endlessly inquisitive nature of the human baby. And this leads to behavior that is, to the neutral observer, indistinguishable from a suicide wish.

Jeff's Disturbing Parenting Tip of the Week

"Sometimes, the only thing that separates a hungry, sleepy baby who won't eat or sleep and a hungry, sleepy baby who will eat and then sleep is about two to three minutes of being left to scream."

"Boy, Mom. That One Muppet There Is Really Skinny."

The main punishment for having a child (well, one of dozens of main punishments) is several years of exposure to children's television. This shit is noxious. Having my brains melted by the Teletubbies or Elmo (or the worse things that will invariably succeed them) is the price I will pay. The alternative is constantly playing with and looking after the child every single minute. I can't do that, because it would kill me.

But there are interesting moments. The other day, one of the headlines in the paper was SESAME STREET TO INTRODUCE HIV-POSITIVE MUPPET.

There are times when living in this world fills me with joy. This was definitely one of them. If only every time I read the paper I could see things that filled me with such delight.

Of course, the very, very first thought in my head was, "How would a muppet get HIV?" And the answer is, I think, obvious: needle drugs.

Of course, it's possible that an infected muppet donated felt at the local Felt Bank, and it was mixed in with other felt and infected the supply, and from there infected any muppet it was sewed on to. Or maybe I'm overlooking the obvious. If a puppeteer stuck his hand up my ass every day, I'm sure I'd have health problems too.

(Oh, before you get all heated up and offended that they would dare to have an HIV-positive muppet, they are mainly thinking about this for Sesame Street in South Africa. And if you know anything at all about the situation in Africa, this suddenly makes a hell of a lot of sense.)

Week 26—Horrible, Horrible Disaster Daddy

Six months old! Half a year. It's Celebrate Passage of an Arbitrary Amount of Time Day! Huzzah!

At milestones like this, it is good to look back and take stock of how much progress has been made. Wow. Cordelia is a completely different creature than she was the moment she was first born. For example, she . . . ummm . . . well, all the pink slime has been wiped off. And she doesn't look like a plucked chicken. And she now knows how to be put on my head and worn as a hat.

She is still learning things. This week, she learned how to sit up on her own. And she knows how to tear off a huge chunk of newspaper with her mouth. And, best of all, she has learned how to be taken onto an airplane by her mother for a weeklong vacation leaving Daddy behind at home alone. I'm especially proud of her for learning the third one.

The Thousand-Yard Baby Stare

Nothing makes babies interesting like having one. Parents size up each others' offspring like ranchers eyeing beef on the hoof, gauging, analyzing, guessing ages, looking for signs of development. While a childless person might look at a baby and see a pink, inert lump shaped like a melting scoop of ice cream, a parent would think, "Hmm. Holding head upright. Signs of mouthing. Chapped cheeks . . . must be teething. And my baby is smarter and cuter."

It can be very therapeutic to do this. It is always good to be reassured that your baby's freakish behavior is normal or could even, in fact, be worse. Consider, for example, what I call the Thousand-Yard Baby Stare. Cordelia spends worrying amounts of time just staring at things. Her face goes slack, her mouth hangs open in a particularly dopey way, and she looks at stuff. Very intently. Like a teeny, creepy homeless person.

She especially likes to stare at humans, primarily strangers. When she lets her mouth hang open and stares at people, they think she's adorable. When I do the exact same thing, I found out, it's not so cute. This is one of the many small bits of unfairness that makes being a parent so painful.

I wasn't sure how normal this is. When you're about to become a parent, people tell you about the crying and the peeing and the sleeplack. Nobody says, "Oh, and she will sit and stare at strangers like a shell-shocked trench war veteran." But, now that she has started staring, I have noticed how many other babies of about the same age do it. Same slack jaw, same stare. It's very comforting. My baby isn't broken.

These days, I often look at other babies to reassure myself. For example, right now, Cordelia is on fire. Nothing big. Smoldering. Smoke. Occasional small puffs of flame. Her occasional spontaneous ignition worried me, until I noticed how many other babies were the same way. Most babies just flame a little, but one toddler I saw in a restaurant the other day was totally ablaze. And, if you don't have a child, I bet you never noticed that most infants are constantly on fire.

When you're a parent, you notice these things.

I Know for Sure Nobody Told Me About This

So Mariann and I were having dinner. Baby was sitting in her carrier on the table, playing with a toy and happily minding her own business. The wife and I were valiantly attempting to maintain a human-quality conversation.

Then the baby started to grunt, in an unusually enthusiastic way. She'd go "Unnggghhhh" really loudly, and her face would turn bright red. Then she'd rest. And then she'd do it again. As we watched in horror, we realized that what she was doing was taking a difficult and enthusiastic crap.

The main reason I wrote this journal is that I wanted to record all of the things about parenting that completely took me by surprise, things that nobody bothered to warn me about. And this was definitely one of them.

It doesn't matter how dedicated you are to remaining a civilized, sensible person in the implacable face of parenthood. It is impossible to maintain an adult conversation when someone is taking a noisy, beet-faced crap on the table in front of you.

I was under the impression that my little girl would take her craps in a modest, quiet way, maybe with some cute little, bubbling, farty sounds. Once again, I find I was sadly deluded.

Toys on the Cheap

I've been very apathetic about buying new toys for Cordelia. We got a few from friends. A few at the baby shower. And I just kept handing the same toys to her, and handing them to her, again and again, until even her tiny, undeveloped brain was going, "Yes! Okay! It's a yellow giraffe rattle! *I get it!* Cram it with walnuts, *old man!*"

Sensing her ennui, I started looking around the house for random things to hand her. Things that would engage her infant brain and, simultaneously, not kill her. For example, my wife's big plastic comb worked. I removed her hair from it first.

I tried a bunch of other objects, but the most successful thing, by far, was a highly collectible pack of first edition Pokemon cards. The shininess, bright colors, and exciting shape were enthralling to her. Her teeth made it useless for sale on eBay in mere minutes.

This was very satisfying to me. You see, I own a lot of collectible objects. And I know she's going to annihilate them. So I'm just getting it over with now. At least, this way, I can get a quiet, amused baby out of it.

Of course, this random object destruction process led to letting my baby chew on a newspaper. And that sure didn't work out . . .

Horrible, Horrible Disaster Daddy

Sometimes I think, "I am a horrible, clueless person, a danger to my offspring, and I should not be allowed to have a child. If my child survives me, it will be a miracle."

The other morning, I was eating lunch in the usual way. I was reading the lower half of the paper. Cordelia was tearing and chewing on the upper half. Both of us were very happy. Then Cordelia stopped chewing. She looked at me and starting drooling and making cute little "Keh" noises. She kept staring at me. Being Idiot Disaster Daddy, it took me sixty seconds of adding two and two to get the proper four.

Then I quickly grabbed her, pried her mouth open (turns out, she doesn't like this), and pulled out the square of newspaper that was stuck to her tongue. It was a decently sized chunk, a square over an inch to a side. Not good. Sadly, Cordelia has lost her newspaper privileges.

Of course, I'm sure some people might try to reassure me by saying, "Oh, everyone has times like this. And their kids all get through it just fine." To which I would respond, "Of course they do. Unless, of course, they don't."

Of course, I do have a special safety mechanism that keeps the baby safe from me. It's my wife. When I leave change on the floor. When I put Cordelia in a stroller and don't buckle her down. When I let homeless people hold her. Mariann is there to make sure I know that I am a Bad Daddy.

Okay, I did not actually do one of those three things. See if you can figure out which one. It's like a puzzle.

Fortunately for me, babies never remember the horrible things that happened when they were six months old.

So there is no way Cordelia can ever find out about the newspaper incident. No way at all.

Phew!

Why I Suck

My wife just took Cordelia for a week's vacation with her family on the other side of the country. I am staying behind. Since expressing my true feelings about this week of freedom will only increase the resentment factor in our generally tranquil marriage, I will express my feelings about this event simply by saying "Woo hoo."

Woo hoo.

Intermission—Why Other Parenting Books Are Stupid

Most parenting books are stupid.

Raising children is a difficult and terrifying job. There's a lot of work to do, it's confusing, and parents tend to also be saddled with affection for the helpless little primates. Thus, there are parenting books. Millions of them, filling long sections in every available bookstore. Each with a cover adorned with clip art of a healthy, white baby, staring out at you happily, as if to say "Your child would be as chubby and blissed out as me if you weren't such a tard."

We parents buy a lot of these books, because we need facts. We need to know how often a child should be eating, and why its skin is peeling off like that, and how blue it needs to get before we should call the doctor. So baby books should give information. Some do. Many, however, exist merely to transmit all of the author's unsupported opinions, random ravings, and crackpot theories.

Parents of infants are easy targets. After all, we are hampered by strong affection for our children. Thus, a parenting book can tell us to do just about anything and we'll do it. Say that SIDS is caused by sleeping alone in a crib, or being exposed to grapes, or thinking bad thoughts, and many parents will believe you. After all, these parents haven't been getting much sleep and their brains are soft, and even a slight, implausible chance of making their little sweetums safer will seem irresistible.

Fortunately for you parents out there, you have me. I have systematically gone through most of the most popular parenting books, carefully picking through them for things I can make fun of. Let me catch the stupidity bullet that was meant for you.

Section I: Books with a Large Number of Actual Facts

The "What to Expect" Books (*What to Expect When You're Expecting, What to Expect the First Year,* etc.), by Heidi E. Murkoff, Arlene Eisenberg, and Sandee Hathaway

This is a popular series of very thick books, crammed with actual facts and medical-type information. They're very useful and readable. In addition, each chapter on a specific month of an infant's life comes with lists of things the baby "Should be able to do," "Will probably be able to do," "May possibly be able to do," and so on. Monthly referrals to these lists to grade the quality of your child will provide reliable entertainment and worry.

But it just goes to show, no matter how sensible the authors of a baby book may be, it is very difficult to keep a little crazy from slipping in there somewhere. Early editions of one of the books in the series provided the infamous "Best Odds" diet, a diet so restrictive and unappealing that even vegans and Orthodox Jews will be looking at you and going "Dude, lighten up." To give you an idea, the diet's example of going crazy and cheating would be to eat a bagel with white flour. The horror! The horror!

Fortunately, more recent editions of these books have purged themselves of the hilarity that was the Best Odds diet. So you could do a lot worse than to get them.

Dr. Spock's Baby and Child Care, Revised Seventh Edition, by Benjamin Spock.

Dr. Spock gained great fame by writing parenting books based on the idea that parents are basically smart and will do the right thing on their own most of the time. This theory, in time, led to the raising of a whole generation of stinky hippies. And yet, somehow, his books are still around.

Actually, though the books are around, Dr. Spock isn't. He has lamentably passed on to the next world. Before he went, though, he left stressed-out parents one final gift: In the most recent edition of his book, he said that babies should be raised with a vegan diet. No meat, no eggs, no milk.

Thanks, Doc!

I mean, honestly, what is it about food that makes otherwise sensible writers need a checkup from the neck up?

I have nothing against vegans personally, as long as they shut up and eat their gray paste quietly. But feeding a baby a vegan diet without it turning into a sickly, twitchy twig-child is difficult, at best. Also, a nicely done veal chop is, in my view, the highest pinnacle of human achievement, and no writer has the right to deny that to my child. Anyway, as I understand it, veal cows have it coming. So there.

Of course, Dr. Spock's books also contain a number of factual statements. So if you can still trust him, you might as well use his books. Just feel free to ignore anything he says.

Complete Baby and Child Care, by Dr. Miriam Stoppard.

Another sensible book, mostly filled with basic facts. I'm a big fan of basic facts.

In addition, this book is very heavy on pictures. Speaking as a sensitive and enlightened man of the new millennium, not only do I appreciate the information these photos convey, but I also appreciate the hot, topless, redheaded mom that graces so many of the pages. Those pictures have really taken the edge off of many a long night of parenting.

The Girlfriend's Guide to Surviving the First Year of Motherhood, by Vicki Iovine.

This is actually a humor book that is packed with the author's opinions. It has been promoted to the factual section for two reasons.

First, most of her advice is to ignore what books and your idiot friends tell you and just do what seems right to you. Sounds factual enough to me.

Second, this is the only guide to raising an infant I am aware of that was written by a former Playboy playmate. To me, this lends the book a gravitas that could only be exceeded by having pictures of cute, topless women in the actual book. But since the previous book did have cute, topless women, I'm pretty much set now.

Section 2: Books That Are Mostly Some Dude's Opinions

These books have facts in them. Some more than others. But, more often, they are soapboxes the authors use to tell lucky, lucky you what sort of parent you should be. Sometimes these opinions are sort of sensible. And sometimes they're crazy. Good luck.

The Sears Library (*The Baby Book, The Discipline Book,* and *The Nutrition Book*), edited by William Sears
Thank God for Dr. William Sears.

This country currently suffers from an insidious plague of confident parents. Confidence in a parent is a dangerous thing, resulting as it does in sleepful nights and non-high blood pressure. Fortunately, for parents so afflicted, the Sears library exists to provide the author's strongly held opinions on how everything you believe about parenting is wrong.

Dr. Sears advocates Attachment Parenting. I am not a wise person or a fountain of knowledge. As I understand it, this means that I should wear my child in a sling like a designer handbag, let it sleep in my bed (thus preventing me from getting laid any time before the Earth crashes into the sun), and generally never leaving the baby alone for a minute. It's a systematic method of doubling and redoubling every shred of parental guilt you have until you're capable of doing nothing but clamping your baby tightly to your chest and whimpering.

The main goal of this parenting method is to create and preserve "attachment" to your child, the invisible and nebulously defined bond that is weakened whenever you do something Dr. Sears disagrees with.

To illustrate the horrors of failed attachment, the books deploy the favored weapon in the arsenal of hand-waving parenting books everywhere: "The one-sided anecdote." Thus you can hear the sad tales of parents of difficult children who let others baby-sit for them, breaking the sacred bond of parenting to such an extent that the parents went on vacation for a week. (Gasp!) Or the selfish mother who went back to work, resulting in her occasionally not being there to wear her child in a sling. And this child eventually spent a good portion of his time chopping hitchhikers into bite-sized pieces. That'll teach you to turn your back on Attachment Parenting, you evil, evil working mother!

The truth of the matter is that, Attachment Parenting or not, I am attached to my child. It relies on me to feed it. If I don't, I go to jail. You can't get more attached than that.

But if you feel guilty because the birth of your child hasn't consumed every single micro-moment of your life, you could do worse than to use these books.

Secrets of the Baby Whisperer, by Tracy Hogg

Tracy Hogg is, supposedly, the "Baby Whisperer." She has claimed for herself the magical talent to wordlessly communicate with babies and divine their innermost thoughts, like Spock making contact with some alien rock creature. The purpose of this book is to teach you how to more painlessly raise your infant. Oh, and she is British. Really, really British.

This book never for a moment lets you forget her spooky, Mary Poppinsesque Britishness. It is heavily sprinkled with words like "mum" and "luv" and refers to the reader as (I swear to God) "ducky." If you were wondering if it was possible to write like this without God descending from the Heavens and blasting you with righteous fire, I must report that, sadly, it is.

Tracy Hogg makes her money as a parenting consultant. A consultant is someone who, when you're confused about something, comes and bosses you around in return for a big pile of money. I feel that anyone so flummoxed by dealing with a toddler that they have to shovel cash at a consultant to get through the day is part of a new, highly evolved species of loser. But that may just be me.

At any rate, being a consultant, Tracy Hogg is great at consultant-speak. Her book is full of checklists, action items, and systems referred to by clever acronyms, like S.L.O.W. and E.A.S.Y. And, of course, most of it is W.A.N.K.

Secrets of the Baby Whisperer is pretty much par for the course for parenting books. In other words, it contains a small number of actual, useful facts, interspersed with long sections of the author's opinions. And, no matter how cute your accent is, opinions are still opinions. Listen to everything she says that you agree with, and throw everything else in the dustbin.

The Secret Language of Children, by Dr. Lawrence A. Shapiro

You see books like this a lot. They claim that, behind your child's incoherent babble and glassy-eyed expression, there is an actual brain that is struggling to communicate with you. And they'll teach you how to understand it, for only twenty bucks.

Child psychologists speak of something called "Ego differentiation." This is the process where your child learns that you are an actual human being and not just an extension of it. For the first few years of life, as far as your baby is concerned, you are a tool, like a hammer or a wheelbarrow, except that you are controlled with screaming.

Your kid might be trying to communicate with you. Or you may just have a big, fat case of wishful thinking. Baby communication courses are mainly a way for impatient parents to spin their wheels while waiting for their kid to turn into a human. If that's how you want to spend your time, knock yourself out.

On Becoming Babywise, Revised, by Gary Ezzo and Robert Bucknam

At some point, you may become so secure in your parenting that you feel comfortable dipping your head in a big ol' bucket of crazy. When you get to that point, the Babywise books are there for you. They are, honestly, the very best parenting guides Christian fundamentalism has to offer.

You will notice I made sure, above, to mention I was referring to the "Revised" edition. There's a good reason for that. You see, the Babywise books operate on a principle of strict, rigid parenting, of molding your child into a highly scheduled, non-coddled machine of moral obedience.

Unfortunately, it turned out that when you tell people that, to be good parents, they need to feed their child on a strict schedule (although some babies won't get enough nutrition when fed this way) and that comforting a crying child too often can be damaging (even though the crying might be a way of saying "Why am I not being fed, you *jackass*?"), what you are going to get is doctors noticing an increase of malnourished children being brought to them. Whoops!

And so the earlier editions of the book, with their charming, downhome mix of Christian love and negligent homicide, were revised. Now don't get me wrong. They're still crazy. But the kookiness is buried in enough doubletalk and twisted syntax that it's almost (but not quite) concealed. Parents who want to be told that they can crush their child under their iron will still find everything they need. Wink! Wink!

Don't get me wrong. I love reading books by crazy people. It's always a good laugh. But the Babywise books are too dull to be amusing and too twisted to ever be trusted. Avoid them as if the pages were made of syphilis.

The Third Season: Twenty Percent Human

By the end of Cordelia's sixth month, I was bored with her.

Raising a child, even an inert one, is real work. I'd put in a lot of time on her. I was ready for rewards. I wanted the kid to start doing something. Anything! Say a random syllable. Pick its nose. Set the curtains on fire. Anything to make me feel that a third human was living in our house.

These three months are when the eager parents are rewarded by signs of humanity in their offspring. The first signs of brain activity, as if the child is slowly waking up from a coma. The changes come agonizingly slowly and, when they do, they make you wonder if they are really improvements.

A child that can crawl can also try to escape.

A child that can reach and grab can also hit and claw.

A child that can comprehend what it sees can also demand to be shown lots of television. (Actually, this bit is an improvement.)

I have discovered The Parental Law of Unintended Consequences: every physical or mental advancement your child makes will create a new problem for you.

Week 27—The Thirty-Year Rule

Halfway through Cordelia's first year, I find I have very little to write. Because she is away. Thousands of miles away. Her mother has taken

her for a week of seeing family on the other side of the country, giving me a sweet, succulent week of freedom.

So, for the last few days, I have rediscovered what it is like to be
childfree. I can spend less than six hours watching a two hour movie.
And go out to nice restaurants, alone. And sit staring at the walls
wondering what to do to fill the evening. And just lie around, feeling time grind on, seconds of my life slipping pointlessly away,
because I don't have anything to do and all of the movies out now
are lame.

Eerily, spending a week without a child is also good for remind-
ing you why you had one in the first place.

And Yet

Of course, I've become horribly lonely. I have had to take drastic
steps to recreate the parenting experience in Cordelia's absence. Fortunately, simulating a baby is less difficult than you might think.

i. First, you need to be alerted/awakened at random, irritating
times. Fortunately, our phone is constantly barraged by the
calls from telemarketers, many times a day, morning, noon,
and night. If I run to answer the phone whenever it rings, it's
almost like having a baby. Plus, while screaming furious
obscenities at your child is frowned upon, doing the same to
the jackass who is trying to get you to change your long-
distance service is both expected and satisfying.

ii. Always carrying around a heavy, inert, little person was hard
to simulate convincingly, until I had the good fortune to find
a stuffed monkey at a flea market. It's sort of mangy and one
of the glass eyes is missing, but it's just about the right size
and weight, and it's clear that some taxidermist once loved it
very much.

Of course, the looks I get when carrying the monkey are very
different from the looks I get while carrying a baby. But the horror
of passersby does not deter me. I wuv my widdle monkey baby.

iii. Feeding is easy to simulate. Giving baby food to a stuffed monkey results in as much actual nutrition as giving it to Cordelia. It all ends up in the lap, either way. Cleaning the monkey is easier though, since I can use a hose.

iv. Finally, life just isn't the same without having to wipe someone's messy ass once a day. So I've been eating lots and lots of fresh, ripe fruit.

Of course, I can only keep this up for so long. The stuffed monkey really wasn't made for heavy use or repeated hosing. It's kind of starting to mildew, and the hair is falling off in big clumps. I'm hoping it doesn't decay too much. I'm counting on it eventually saving me the cost of a teddy bear for Cordelia. Or I could put a skirt on it and tell her it's a Barbie.

Wheezy Baby

Then Cordelia came back. While she was gone, she got pudgier. She got a cute little baby tan. She learned a new way to complain (short, loud, chirpy screams, repeated rapidly, from when she wakes up to when she falls asleep). And she learned to make a new noise!

The new noise is, basically, a death rattle. It's a long, slow, ghastly tubercular wheeze. She loves making this noise, even though it freaks out Mommy and Daddy and makes them look in her throat for swallowed dimes.

She loves making this noise in public. Strangers are horrified, as it appears that my daughter is obviously choking to death and I don't seem the least bit concerned. I'm not sure why, but stupid people thinking I'm stupid bugs me.

Baby's First Flying Experience

Trip to: a quiet little angel.

Trip back: four straight hours of practicing her new screams. As I understand it, by the time the flight landed, half of the passengers were ready to join Al-Qaeda.

The Thirty-Year Rule

I have lots of parenting books, and they take great delight in telling me radically different things. No matter what question I have, I can find two books that tell me completely opposite answers. For every single decision I have made, there is a book that says I'm about to shatter Cordelia like spun glass because of it.

I'm supposed to have weaned her off the pacifier by now. Or not. I'm supposed to make her a vegetarian. Or not. Mariann has to breast-feed her until she's ten. Or not. I'm not supposed to let Cordelia sleep in our bed. But one book said sleeping in a crib makes it more likely she'll get the SIDS. (No kidding.)

Being a basically calm, rational, scientifically oriented person, this annoys the hell out of me. I mean, medicine is a science, right? You don't pick up a physics textbook and read, "Oh, and gravity doesn't exist. We are held to the earth by gnomes under the ground," do you? It seems to me like anything in a parenting book has a fifty-fifty chance of having been pulled out of someone's ass. This strikes me as an untidy state of things, to say the least.

It's enough to reduce my already low opinion of reading as a suitable activity for humans.

Of course, when Mariann and I were feeling our way through parenting, the surplus of opinions was confusing. Finally, I snapped. I set up one rule for making all my parenting decisions: "The Thirty-Year Rule." it goes like this:

"If deciding something one way or the other doesn't have a *clear, noticeable* effect on what the kid will be like when she's thirty, I can do whatever I want."

So, for example, basic education. This makes a difference in the long term. So does teaching her to read, and feeding her. So you have no choice there. And you have to think carefully about whether or not to circumcise, as that will certainly be noticed thirty years down the road. (Unless, of course, you have a girl. Not having to think about circumcision is one of the primary advantages of having a girl.)

But pacifiers? I can do what I want. Hey, maybe infant pacifier use will make some difference (who knows what?) when Cordelia turns thirty. But I seriously doubt it. Attachment parenting? Co-sleeping? Organic baby food? Bombarding her with Mozart? These things might make a difference when the kid is thirty. In an infinite universe, everything is possible. But the effect is neither noticeable nor clear. So who gives a shit? The kid will sleep in a crib, eat Gerber's processed apple goo, listen to Led Zeppelin, and *like it*!

And I can guess what you're thinking now. Something along the lines of, "Oh, that's reasonable advice. You can relax and do whatever you want. Though, of course, you are a bad parent unless you make sure to use cloth diapers/carry it around in a sling until it's twelve/only dress it in clothes made of hemp/whatever stupid thing I've decided is the One True Secret of child-rearing that makes the child healthy and a Mensa member and keeps away the SIDS." Everyone has their own Gris-Gris, and that is fine, as long as you don't bother me with it.

New parents, myself included, are twitchy, freaked out souls with the tendency to make dysfunctional mountains out of developmental molehills. I say, to hell with it. Feed the kid. Dress it. Bathe it. Hug it. Beyond that, dowhatchawant. Anything beyond the basics may be as likely to harm as help in the long run, anyway.

Disturbing News Delivered Long Distance

While away, Cordelia stayed in a house with dogs. At first, she was terrified of them. Then she became fascinated with them.

This means I have about eight years to get her to hate dogs again. Because I never went through an "I like dogs" phase, and I don't think I will enter one when my little girl asks me for a puppy every seventeen seconds.

Maybe I'll make her forget she wants a dog by buying her Barbies. Whatever else you can say about Barbie, good or bad, she won't shit in my house.

Thoughts from the Future

By the time she was two, Cordelia could make all sorts of sounds that made strangers think she was choking on a sea urchin. Eventually, whenever someone gave me a look, I'd just shrug and say, "What can you do? You'll lose a few."

As for being bossed around by parenting books, one of the best things about having a second child is that you sort of know what you're doing. Unless it refuses to breathe or has no anus, you never have to crack a parenting book again.

Now That They're Back

Well, anyway, two days after the joy of freedom faded and the loneliness kicked in, my wife and baby returned. We came home from the airport. My wife got in bed and fell asleep. And Cordelia began a crying/fussing/squealing jag that has been continuing for two hours and, as I write this, shows no sign of stopping.

Actually, she did stop squealing for a few seconds, just long enough to say her very first words! They were "So you wanted me back, huh? How do you feel now, JACKASS!?!? Eeeeeeeeeeeeeeeeeeeee!"

Week 28—Stuck with Pacifiers for Good

Cordelia's back from vacation and I've had a good, solid week of parenting. It's gone well. I have done nothing in the past week to put her life in immediate danger. That makes two weeks of safe parenting from Daddy in a row. Of course, one of those weeks, baby was around two thousand miles away. But I'm still counting it. My self-esteem needs all the reinforcement it can get.

Boring progress report. She can sit up unassisted for a long time. She is very well behaved, able to sit and babble happily through an entire dinner. She can pick up a Cheerio, but she cannot then do anything productive with that Cheerio. She thinks that green beans are from Satan.

Outside, the weather is sunny. Cordelia gets taken for lots of walks. Walks are the perfect parenting activity. Just pop a pacifier in her mouth, put her on wheels, and shove. She enjoys the movement. I get to shave a few micrometers off my fat ass. Of course, strangers see that I've given Cordelia a pacifier and look at me like I'm a bad parent. But if I really cared what strangers thought of me, I wouldn't dress like a homeless person, would I?

Stuck with Pacifiers for Good

"To avoid development of a strong habit, begin withdrawal from the pacifier by the time your baby is three months old."—*What to Expect the First Year*

"When the kid is thirty, nobody will give a shit whether she used a pacifier or not."—Me

I had one of those magic parent moments the other day, one of those times when the baby does something new and exciting and smart and reminds you that she won't be an immobile little meat sac forever. Like taking her first steps. Or learning to pick her nose.

Cordelia, with difficulty, reached out, grabbed her pacifier, carefully maneuvered the business end into her mouth, and left it there. She does it often now. It's adorable. It's like her first chemical dependency, just without chemicals.

It's safe to say that, at this point, easily breaking her of the pacifier habit is no longer an option, if it was ever possible at all. Numerous parenting books look with a jaundiced eye on long-term pacifier dependency. However, I'd much rather be a bad parent whose kid goes to sleep at night. My baby can develop a "strong habit" of using a pacifier, just as long as Daddy gets to develop a strong habit of not spending three hours every night begging her to sleep.

The best thing about this development it that Cordelia is learning that, when stressed, she should medicate herself. Happiness, after all, does not come from within, no matter what Hallmark cards and Gandhi tell us. Relief from our internal stresses comes from outside ourselves, be it in the form of pacifiers, Nintendo, food, or grain alcohol.

In the end, your loved one may disappoint you, but you can always achieve happiness by reaching out for something made of plastic. Ask my wife.

A Word About Baby Photos

Recently, we shot a whole roll of photos of our little girl. Sitting up, lying down, doing things, having cute expressions, lying in funny shapes; I relentlessly documented it all. I was really looking forward to getting them developed . . . I was sure that they would be just the most fantastical glorifulous documentation of baby development in the history of anything.

Then, when I got the pictures back and looked at them, all I could think was, "What is this crap?"

It was basically thirty shots of the same baby, in roughly the same pose. They're not interesting! They're dull as hell! How could I have been so deluded? My wife and I spend an hour playing the new, fun game: "What made this seem so interesting that we needed a picture of it?"

"Well, I think I thought this was neat because she was sitting up."
or
"She sort of had a cute smile for this one. Or something."
or
"Well, sure she spends an hour every day playing with this rattle, but when I took this picture, she was doing something really special with it, like holding it upside-down. And it was so cool I absolutely had to document it forever."

Baby pictures are, ninety-four times out of one hundred, crap. I try to be ruthless when editing our baby albums. I try to exclude anything that is not actually interesting, leaving the remnants for gifts to relatives or putting them in a big box labeled, "Only open when the kid leaves home and your heart is breaking and you need something to look at while you drink."

So that leaves me with a huge stack of baby pictures, only four of which I consider interesting enough for posterity. (And that's interesting to me, of course. *You* couldn't give less of a shit.)

On the bright side, none of the new pictures were of excrement. I can look at the whole pile without vomiting.

One More Word About Baby Photos

So you're a parent. You love your Wuggly Snuggly Buggly Uggly Baby Boo. You think she's great. And you might as well. If it dies, you go to jail. I don't.

I don't care about your child. Sure, I think babies are as cute as the next guy. But, when it comes to someone else's child, it takes some serious adorability megawattage to pierce the shell of my intense disinterest.

So, when you are showing baby pictures to anyone who is not actually a relative (a friend, someone at a class reunion, a complete stranger, homeless people), you must limit yourself to three photos. Three. Make it like an audition or a résumé. Show *only* the three most goddamned adorable pictures you can find.

And then, if the victim shows interest and actually asks for more, then and only then can you show more photos. If the person is genuinely interested, you can haul out the albums documenting Poopsie Woopsie (featuring her first smile from eight different angles) and completely destroy your victim's will to live.

And what if you have more than one child? Well, you still get only three pictures. Total. Not three each. Three each starts to add up real quick and, before long, it becomes a war crime.

Don't think that's fair? Don't think that gives you enough coverage of your precious offspring? Tough. Should have kept your dick in your pants, shutterbug.

And Yet Another Word, This Time About Video Tapes of the Baby

These must not be shown to anyone under any circumstances.

Doesn't That Seem Harsh?

Good God, but babies are boring. Staring at the baby while actually caring for it should already be enough for any person. Actually watching films of it wriggle and drool? I shudder to think of it, and I'm the parent!

You ever see one of those anti-drunk driving commercials where they show videos of these cute kids being cute and then it says, "Cute kids, huh? Well they're *dead*! They were *killed* by a drunk driver! Think of that the next time you have a beer, you *sick bastard*!"

This is the only legitimate use of baby videos. Post mortem. If something horrible ever happens to Cordelia, I will watch the baby videos late at night while bawling and drinking Jack Daniels. In any other circumstances, baby videos should *never* be watched.

And why prepare for the worst? Stick with a regular camera. And those three (Three! Preferably less.) perfect snapshots.

"But I hate babies! I really, really hate them! Why should I have to look at even three pictures?"

Oh, come on. Like it would kill you to smile at three lousy pictures. Suck it up. Be a mensch. Who died and made you king of Shit Mountain?

Something I Wish Cordelia Had Done Intentionally

Cordelia hates to be put down for a nap, whether she needs it or not. Sometimes, the only thing she has the energy to do is scream. And yet, we keep making her nap, because that is how mommy and daddy get that precious hour or two a day in which to live our lives.

Lately, Cordelia has started to signify her annoyance at being exiled to a nap by throwing her pacifiers. We leave the nursery and, moments later, hear the unmistakable knocks of furiously flung pacifiers hitting the door. It's as if she's trying to say "You think a pacifier will buy me off? This is *bullshit!*" And then she doesn't have any pacifiers, so she won't sleep.

Fortunately, this wasn't a difficult problem to solve. Now we just put her in her crib with a half dozen pacifiers. We pile them up around her head. Now she runs out of energy before she runs out of ammunition.

Week 29—Progressing from Limpet to Turtle

Cordelia had a good week. Some weeks are bad ones, some are good. This week, she was a smiling, fuzzy, little ball of pudge and, far and away, the cutest baby in our house.

This is despite her weaning. Mariann has mostly liberated herself (or, at least, her breasts). Cordelia is now breast-milk free. I don't think our little girl would be so happy if she realized what a horrible, harmful betrayal this is.

Or maybe she does. Cordelia mainly spent this weekend developing a new scream. It's a real piece of work: long, shrill, and piercing. Going "EEEEEEEEE!" every few seconds is now her primary form of communication. Some books, big on encouraging parents to relate to their offspring, say that I should be trying to figure out exactly what she means when she says this. Well, what I think she means is, "EEEEEEEEEEEE!"

Thanks to the screaming, our options for taking the baby out to dinner with us are becoming very limited. Personally, I think we should be allowed to take Cordelia anyplace, even nice restaurants, as long as that place is also frequented by assholes with cell phones. I think Cordelia is infinitely cuter than a cell phone, even one whose ring is the chorus to "I Want a New Drug." It's not fair.

But, as I will tell Cordelia every time she points out that I'm doing something dumb and indefensible, life is unfair.

Progressing from Limpet to Turtle

The child has become mobile. It turns out, once you know how to roll over, if you repeat that same rolling-over motion enough times, you will get places. Like the stairs.

Cordelia is enjoying her new mobility greatly. Now Daddy is able to watch TV for up to ten uninterrupted minutes while his little girl flops her way across the room. Eventually, of course, she reaches a chair or table leg and gets stuck. The concept of reversing direction is beyond Cordelia's baby brain. To her, I think, changing direction shows a certain fickleness and lack of character. If she hits a wall, she's going through that wall or nowhere at all.

Babies are dopey.

I am pleased to announce, however, that Cordelia has raised her capabilities to the level of the turtle I got in seventh grade. This turtle, whose name was Cannibal (for reasons of little interest), was not a pet that interacted gladly with its owner. To "play" with Cannibal meant to pick it up and put it on the floor in the center of the living room. It would then walk forward until it hit a wall, at which point it would stop and never move again. This is not unlike "playing" with Cordelia now.

Eventually, Cannibal learned a trick. It urinated whenever I picked it up. Again, it has this behavior in common with my daughter. While this pee reflex prevented me from ever playing with Cannibal again (making little diapers out of tissue paper was not successful), duty forces me to keep playing with Cordelia.

The Parade of Ugly Babies

Up until recently, I thought that becoming a parent makes all babies look cute to you. Sadly, this is not true. As it turns out, there are plenty of ugly babies out there, lurking, waiting to spoil your faith in the future. And your meal.

Recently, I went to the local farmer's market. And, I swear, they must have declared Ugly Baby Day. They were everywhere. There were older kids with misshapen skulls, as if the head had been squeezed out of shape during the passage through the vagina (which always happens) and never returned to normal (which usually doesn't). Exhausted babies with big bags under their eyes. Kids with incredibly unappealing facial features, as if they had been rearranged by some sort of evil Infant Head Shaping Mold like they once used on girls in China.

And there was one kid who had this enormous skull. Normal body, normal face, massive skull. He looked like a baby supervillain. Like the kid was going to grow up and get a cape and change his name to Telepatho.

I swear. Every baby I saw, I wanted to hit it with a stick.

So parenthood has not provided me with some sort of brain chemical that makes me see every baby as cute. No reproductive, hormonal equivalent of beer goggles. But it's all right. Heck, you don't even have to think your own kid is cute. You merely have to see your kid as "Deserving of food." Once you got that, you're basically covered.

Awww, What a Pwecious Wittle Bit of Fuzz

Cordelia reached another growth milestone today. She's developing a tiny, soft little bit of brown fuzz on the flat area between her eyes.

That's right. Baby is working on her first little unibrow.

A Rethinking of the Issue of Video Cameras

Last week, I wrote when it was okay to shoot and show video tapes of babies doing cute baby things: never, under any circumstances. Videos of babies are like those tapes you can buy to show to your pet, just two hours of a goldfish swimming in a bowl or something.

However, though I am nearly infallible, every great once in a while I make a mistake. Of course, when this occurs, I almost immediately isolate the flaw in my reasoning and excise it with laserlike precision. This is one of those cases. I have since realized that it is important for any parents, whenever possible, to have a video camera.

Why? Consider the following scenario: I am playing with Cordelia on the floor. I hand her a rattle, or a hat, or whatever. She dutifully plays with it. Then she looks up at me, smiles, and says, for the very first time, "Daddy." And then I suddenly die of a brain aneurysm.

Wouldn't that be horrible!?!? I mean, if *I* didn't have video tapes of a baby, well then I can't look at a baby. Which is good. All babies pretty much look the same, differing only in clothes and skin tone. But I, on the other hand, am really interesting! If I died, how would Cordelia ever get to look and listen and see how neat I am? How cute I am, the neat noises I make, how interesting I am when I play with *my* toys?

So what I am going to do is rent a video camera and make a few films of me playing with her. She'll eventually watch them and get to see how loving and wonderful I was. How I helped her sit up. How I was usually able to catch her when she fell. How skilled I was at simultaneously looking after her and watching TV. How I didn't flinch when I held her up in the air and she drooled on my face. How I wiped up her feces.

It'll be very poignant, of course. But, when I think of the horror that would be her experiencing life without me, well, it seems a small price to pay.

This Week's Final Milestone

Cordelia made her first classic, adult-style poo. Firm. Dry. Rounded. Really a model of craftsmanship.

Well, actually, that's how I imagine it. My wife described it to me after disposing of it, without calling me in so I could see it first, with my own eyes. This was upsetting to me. If I can't get a picture of her first grown-up poo, what on earth am I keeping a baby album for, anyway?

My Current Answering Machine Message:

"Hello. You have reached the home of Jeff Vogel and Mariann Krizsan. We can't answer the phone right now, because we're too busy looking at the *baby*! Babies are *so cute*! We *love* babies! *Babies babies babies!*"

"BAY-BEEEEEEEEESSS!"

"Beep."

It's even starting to disturb me.

Week 30—"But I hate people who bring kids to restaurants. And I hate you!"

Tick. Another month gone by. Cordelia, cherubic bearer of all my hopes and dreams here on this Earth, just turned seven months old. She enjoys standing up (with assistance). She can roll around. Thanks to constantly lifting her legs in the air, she has tight little baby abs.

As I understand it, the fun, low-key period of parenthood is rapidly coming to an end. Soon, I have to start doing actual parenting. Molding her moral sense. Explaining why mommy refuses to allow a Barbie into the house. Plus, one of these days, she'll hit puberty.

I've got parenting books. I've been reading ahead. It appears that one of the most pernicious qualities of parenthood is that every stage makes you miserably realize how easy you had it just months before.

As for other family issues, now that Mariann has stopped breast-feeding, she now has a lot of time on her hands. Time that was previously spent clutching Cordelia to her chest and thinking, "I wish I wasn't doing this." Now she is free to concentrate on her mind, and the way seven months of parenting is making it feel like it is melting.

Mariann works with me making computer games. We are working hard to find small, thought-intensive jobs she can do. The alternative is little bits of her brain crawling out of her ears while she sleeps, trying to escape across the pillow to a place where they can be used.

But it's a pretty decent marriage, overall. With its own milestones . . .

Mommy and Daddy, Happy, with Baby in a Box

This week, Mariann and I celebrated our fourth wedding anniversary. This was a very unusual anniversary for us.

First, we remembered it. We have a long, depressing history of forgetting our anniversaries. Fortunately, when you forget it and then your wife forgets it too, it's a total wash. You don't get in near as much trouble.

Second, we have a baby now. This makes it much more important to celebrate our marriage, since we're totally stuck with it. So we want to go out and do something nice. But, unfortunately, we have a baby. What to do? What to do?

Fortunately, in Seattle, there is a new place called Restaurant Zoë. It's your standard, trendy, fancy, pricey, food-wanker pseudo-French place, the sort that appears in large cities in any empty space that would fit a stove, a pile of scallops, and some scallions. What makes Restaurant Zoë different is that it makes a point to be extremely family friendly. Kids are very welcome there. Which is really, really weird in a place with edible food.

We went. I won't go into detail about how many kids were there (only ours), how friendly the staff was (extremely), how Cordelia behaved (acceptably), or how good the food was (quite). I just want to know why this sort of thing isn't more common.

Look. My wife and I got a kid. We didn't get lobotomies. We are serious, stinky cheese, try the kidneys, restaurants are our lives, hardcore foodies. For us, the most agonizing thing about having a child was losing access to any restaurant that doesn't have a fry vat or some quasi-edible, grease-soaked horror with a name like "Rooty Tooty Fresh and Fruity®."

I shudder in the depths of my being.

There must be a marketing opportunity here. There are a lot of parents in this country, and I am sure my wife and I are not the only ones who want culinary options more challenging than pickles and special sauce. How about places that welcome babies and, at the same time, don't suck?

We had a baby. We didn't have lobotomies. There must be a way.

The Sole Pleasing Solution for Parents Who Like Good Food

Good Chinese restaurants. No place is better for making families feel welcome.

"But I Hate People Who Bring Kids to Restaurants. And I Hate You!"

Bite my ass. Being childfree means you get a life full of freedom and extra cash. You don't have to be a dick about it, too.

There are places you shouldn't take your sprog. Good steak-houses. Most snooty restaurants. Hooters.

But there are places that should be fair game under any circumstances. For example, pizza. If you give me a dirty look when I bring a kid into a pizza place, you're the asshole. I don't care if it's the fanciest, shiniest pizza place in the world. You can bring the kids to a pizza place. Period.

In fact, this applies to just about any restaurant serving food from a non-European ethnicity (with the possible exception of Japanese). If the menu contains any of these words: "fajita," "chai," "curry," or "injera" (Ethiopian flat bread! Look it up!), then you can take the kids.

Damn it, having offspring should not have to mean divorcing oneself from civilization.

A Quick Addition, for the Benefit of Any Idiots Reading This

Of course, manners still apply. If the kid is screaming, take it outside. Don't leave a square mile of rice cake crumbs on the carpet. Don't actually change the baby on the table. And so on. *Of course.*

I'm sorry. I shouldn't have had to say that. But some jackass would otherwise be bound to say, "Well, kids shouldn't be allowed in restaurants because they cry! So there!" Well, of course they cry. And then you pick it up and take it outside. No problem. Jackass.

Look, Commander Childfree. Someday, you'll be old, and those stock options that were going to fuel your trips around the world will be so far underwater that giant squid are screwing them, and pensions are something your great-grandparents and dinosaurs got, and the only thing enabling you to upgrade from generic to name brand cat food ("Look, honey! I got a chunk of meat!") is the money my daughter will put into Social Security.

So, all things considered, I thing you can stand a minute of mild squealing every once in a while. Suck it up.

In other developments . . .

My Little Darling's Newest Skill

She can hold the pacifier in her mouth and scream at the same time.

Our House Is a Complex, Connected Network of Cages

Now that Cordelia can flop herself across the floor, we have to babyproof the house. This means picking a large, suitable room and turning it into a jail. All exits must be blocked with wooden gates. Now Daddy has to be a hurdle jumper to get anywhere in the house.

I honestly don't know how much danger Cordelia is in from falling down stairs. But I am pretty sure that, one of these days, I'm going to be trying to carry her over a baby gate and trip and accidentally break my fall with her squishy little body. So I'm not sure that we have achieved an overall safety benefit here.

Babyproofing Sucks Ass

To get materials for babyproofing the house, we went to the Megaoutlet of All Things Shoddy and Useless. In other words, Babies "R" Us. They sold us a Child Safety Kit, filled with a variety of small, allegedly useful devices. We would have been better off just buying a huge spool of barbed wire and fencing Cordelia in.

The most offensively useless items in the packing were these little rubber bumpers you stick on the corners of the coffee table. In theory, when the baby trips and smacks her head against a sharp corner, her little skull bounces off unharmed. In practice, despite paying scrupulous attention to the instructions, the things fall off whenever someone brushes against them lightly. The glue provided to hold them on is useless.

This would not be a problem if we could just explain to Cordelia that she should be very careful not to knock the rubber bumpers off before she falls against the corner of the table, eyeball first. Alas, since she does not speak English yet, the things are crap. We'd be better off just putting Post-It notes on the table that read, "Cordelia, please do not smack your head against this. Thanks!"

Week 31—Our Child Has Become Emotionally Dependent on Us

Cordelia continues to show more signs of intelligence, on a rudimentary, animal level.

Example. Before, when I tried to feed solid food to her and she didn't want to cooperate, I would make funny noises until she started to laugh. Then I'd dump a payload of oatmeal into her open mouth.

Now, when I do something funny while holding a spoonful of food, she gives me a tight-lipped smile. She's grinning, but the jaw stays firmly clenched.

Seven months old, and already our relationship is a corrupted web of lies and mistrust.

Our Child Has Become Emotionally Dependent on Us

Our little girl has become acutely aware of when we are trying to blow her off.

Our fondest dream, as parents, is a child that is occasionally capable of amusing itself on the floor for a little while. No, wait. That's not right. Our fondest dream as parents is a million dollars and a state-of-the-art Japanese baby-raising robot. And, at this point, we seem as likely to get that as a self-amusing baby.

When we plop her on the living room floor, surrounded by interesting and intriguing toys and the warm, enfolding hug of the baby gates, it usually takes a minute of solitude for her little baby alarm to go off. Then she starts to make little "Eeeeeee" noises, which get louder and louder until Mariann and I can stand it no longer and interrupt what we're doing to go rescue her. We'd let her squeal, but we're afraid that our neighbors would hear and decide that we're bad parents.

Bribes enable the baby to amuse itself. For example, letting her play with her most sacred, fervently desired object, the TV remote, will keep her quiet for several minutes. If I let her chew on our wedding photos, I imagine that'd buy a half an hour.

When the baby starts crying in the middle of the night, I wait for a while in case she goes back to sleep on her own. Now I also wait when she squeals on the living room floor, in case she finds a way to amuse herself. Maybe that yellow plastic ring that totally bored her yesterday and the day before and the day before that will suddenly activate her imagination and explode into a new glorious world of delight for her.

The process of training her to be away from us is a little depressing. Sometimes I feel like I'm trying to wean her off of me and, therefore, love.

On the other hand, if I get it so I can occasionally take two minutes off from parenthood to go take a shit, I feel it will be worth it.

Why I'm Drawing the Line Here

I never want to have to take a crap while my kid is staring at me.

"You're so cuuuute! Cuuuuuuuuuuute!!!!"

The best thing about having a baby is that you can pinch her cute, soft, chubby cheeks freely and without fear of reprisal. When I pinch Cordelia's cheeks and say "Oooooh! OOOOOHHHH!!! Chubbbeeeee cheeeeeeeks! CHUBBBEEEEEEE CHEEEEEEEEEKS!," she just looks sad. When I try to do the same thing to my wife, she sprains my wrist.

But, like I said, Cordelia is starting to grow thoughts. Now, when I pinch her cheek, she reaches up with both hands, grabs my hand, and pushes it away.

She's figured out how to defend herself! Sure, she's a frail, weak little girl. It's not like she's been taking Tae Kwon Do or anything. But she has figured out the basic principles of active resistance.

I am proud. But I had also better get all my cheek pinching in now before she's strong enough to dislocate my thumb.

Now She Can Wound Me

Along those lines, before now when I held or played with Cordelia and she was kicking me, I didn't worry about it. I thought it was cute. Kicky kicky kick. Awwww.

Yesterday, she landed a good solid kick on my chin. It hurt.

Also, when I bent down to razz her belly button, she laughed, as always, but she also clawed the shit out of my face with her cute little baby fingernails.

She's still tiny and unfocused. She couldn't defend herself from a sufficiently determined and hungry mouse. But it's still an improvement.

My Official Opinion on Cloned Babies

Lately, there has been some controversy regarding the issue of human cloning. Some people think that it is wrong to make exact copies of yourself because, apparently, people will inevitably create huge armies of identical copies of themselves and try to take over the Earth, raising all kinds of havoc. As if this would be a bad thing.

People worry too much.

Look. You probably don't know me. But, if you did, you would have to admit that I am pretty much perfect. Sure, my beard is scraggly, my posture is poor, and I'm a little thick around the tummy. But, in general, I am as good an example of fine genetic stock as the human race is likely to produce.

So why shouldn't I clone myself? Why shouldn't I scrape some skin off my arm and run off a few copies? After all, with Cordelia I'm already giving the future someone with half my genetic material. Why shouldn't I let the other shoe drop, biologically speaking, and have a kid with *all* my genetic material? Or eighty of them? And put electric shock bracelets on them and have them serve me on my own private Island of Doctor Moreau. And they will resent and plot against me and eventually rise up and destroy me ironically, and I wouldn't have it any other way! This is how evolution is supposed to *work,* dammit!

Unfortunately for this plan, my wife is essentially perfect as well. Cloning myself takes her genes out of the great game. So right now, I'm having to make do with children with only half of my marvelous genes.

Actually, if my theoretical island had eighty clones of Mariann to go with the eighty clones of me, then we'd really be cooking with gas.

Hmm. Make that one hundred and sixty clones of Mariann for the eighty clones of me. If you know what I'm saying.

The Plague of Ugly Babies

Last week, I noticed how ugly most babies are. Now that I am paying attention, I am seeing ugly babies everywhere. During a walk
today, I just saw one whose head looked like a huge marshmallow
with eyes and a mouth painted on.

His mom smiled adoringly at my own (cute) baby as she walked
by. I smiled at her child. However, while she was smiling because my
child's adorability makes all who witness it feel that there is hope for
humanity, I was smiling because I knew that we weren't going to
trade kids.

"Boo!"

The other night, Cordelia said "Boo." Then, when I said "Boo" back
to her, she thought it was hilarious. I'd say it, and she'd laugh and
laugh, and then she'd stare at me until I said it again. This went on
forever.

Boo.

This makes no sense. What is going on in that brain thing of
hers?

Week 32—How to Bathe a Baby

Age counter: seven months. Tick. This week's result of baby's random emotion generator: happy.

Cordelia is seventeen pounds of burbling, cheery joy. Her happiness provides me with great satisfaction, the sort of sense of
achievement a carpenter must feel after making a really good chair.
Every tiny scrap of happiness she ever experiences, she has because
of us. Everything she ever achieves of value was brought about by my
and my wife's wise parenting and the high innate quality of my
sperm.

Of course, my wife spends more time raising the baby, and she
did have to lug it around for those nine inconvenient months, and

she did have to submit to it milking her. So I think I should only get one-quarter of the credit for Cordelia's happiness. Still, that's enough to make me feel like a god.

Struggling to Move, Part 1

At her current stage of development, it is time for Cordelia to start sitting up on her own. She knows that this is something she wants to do. She just hasn't figured out the exact technique yet.

What she does is lie flat on her back. Then she tries to just sit up, without twisting her body or using her arms. She just tries to sit straight up. Understand, this is quite a trick even with a developed, grown-up body. (Try it.) For babies, it is comically impossible. She tightens her abs, tries to sit up, and grunts pitifully. Then she stops to rest. Then she tries again and again, until she gets frustrated and the screaming starts. Meanwhile, Mommy and Daddy and their friends sit around and laugh at her.

Don't get mad at me because I laugh at her. I'm not a bad man. If there was not an insuperable communication gap between me and my grunty little offspring, I would patiently explain to her what she needs to do to sit up. But I cannot. Sometimes, really, the only reasonable way to react to a baby is to laugh at it.

Struggling to Move, Part 2

Cordelia also knows that she should be crawling. She wants to move, but she can't. It pisses her off. She does a lot of limb swinging and flailing around. I try to encourage her, but the best I can do is place all of her toys just out of reach.

I've been looking forward to her learning to move and crawl because, being an idiot, I thought that this would make her more capable of entertaining herself. And this is true. However, the way mobile babies entertain themselves is by throwing themselves down the stairs. Net time savings for Daddy: none.

How to Bathe a Baby

Mariann recently forced me to watch her give the baby a bath. Being the living embodiment of patience and kindness, she has always done this job herself. However, my wife wanted me to know how to do it in case she is, say, eaten by wolves. So I watched and learned. This is how you bathe a baby.

> Step one. Fill bathtub with a few inches of water. Remember, babies do not feel temperature like we do and are much more sensitive to heat. The water should be cool on your fingertips and icy cold on your inner arm. This will be scalding hot to a baby.
>
> Step two. Take off all of baby's clothes. Do not dislocate baby's shoulder in process, you clumsy dumbass. Remove diaper. Note that the moment the diaper is off, your baby has become a ticking, waste-excreting time bomb.
>
> Step three. Place baby in bathtub. Baby will now be in ecstasy. Hope she doesn't take a shit. You don't just drop the baby into the water, though. You put it in a plastic tray or on a large, flat, spongy mattress specially made for this purpose and sold for money. The best ones are sold under the brand name "Drown Less Soon."
>
> Step four. Wipe down all of baby's extremities with washcloth and a little soap. Try to control your shudders of disgust. Try not to think about how long it takes for baby to turn the bathwater into a weak urine broth. Try to get less shampoo in the baby's eyes next time.

Speaking of the eyes, good visual hygiene is important. I recommend wiping down the baby's eyeballs gently with a soft chamois.

> Step five. Now that baby is clean, let it frolic happily in the water. Remember, babies drown easily, so don't leave it unattended for more than ten minutes.

No, just kidding! A baby can drown in as little as one-thirty-second of an inch of water. You can drown a baby by setting it on a damp table. Babies can drown if you even *think* of water. You ever walk around on a hot day and think, "Man, I could use some iced tea right now"? Well, you just drowned your baby. Good job.

Just to be safe, I recommend that, the moment your baby's body hits the water, you totally freak out.

> Step six. If your baby is an uncircumcised boy, be sure to carefully clean the crusty, foul-smelling smegma out from under his foreskin. Having to do this is how God punishes people who aren't Jews.
>
> Step seven. Remove baby from water. Dry it off quickly, rubbing vigorously to try to restore warmth. Babies lose body heat very quickly. You have ten seconds, or else. Why are you still reading this? The clock is ticking!!! Go, go, GO!!!!!

There. Wasn't that easy? Hope your baby isn't blue.

My Wife's Comment on the Above

First point. According to her, baby shampoo is now formulated to not be painful to baby's eyes. Yeah, right. Just pour the shit in there, then. Knock yourself out. Clean eyeballs are as important as anything else.

Second point. Regarding smegma, she said, "Ewww. Thank God we don't have a boy."

I am only the teller of tales. Don't blame me for how the penis was designed.

"I'll Take the One with the Baby Drowning Box"

Parenthood changes your priorities and perceptions. For example, our house seemed quite pleasant once. No longer. The nice, busy street right by our house, giving quick access to stores and restaurants, now looks like a deathtrap for any four-year-old chasing a ball. The bedrooms are now woefully inadequate to warehouse young life. And the local school districts, which I never gave a moment's thought to before, now appear to be grimy factories designed to churn out burger-flipping mouth breathers.

I try to be hip and cynical and talk a good game, but the tentacles of responsible, boring daddyhood clench me as tightly as everyone else.

So Mariann and I started, in the slowest, most tentative way, shopping for a new house.

I suppose that the reason I bring it up is that we saw a pretty nice house. Big. Plenty of room for our business. A good (read "yuppie") neighborhood with good (read "white people send students there, so they get money") schools. A yard for me to garden badly. An acceptable price.

But it didn't work out. You see, it also had a swimming pool. Or, as I call it, the "baby drowning box."

A swimming pool. Great. Hey, why stop there? Why not just fill the backyard with your antique refrigerator collection?

How can any parent stand to have a swimming pool? I already interrupt Cordelia's sleep to check for signs of life every hour on the hour. The last thing I need is to have to run screaming into the backyard every time the house is quiet for two minutes.

Week 33—"We Wuv Our Widdle Baby Scabby-Face"

Cordelia's spent this week muttering random syllables and trying to move forward. When she's on her stomach, she knows she wants to do this, but she has no idea how. She looks like she's trying to will herself forward with concentration alone. She tries to drag herself forward with her hands. She kicks her legs frantically. She gets incredibly pissed.

We've tried lifting her into a crawling position. We prop her up on all fours and hope she gets the hint, but she just flops over. We push on her butt and hope that some genetic-level crawl programming kicks in. We sneak up behind her and shout, "Snakes!" Nothing gets her moving. Mariann and I are trying to elevate our parenting to a higher level than just food shoveling and waste collection, but so far it's been a big goddamn waste of time.

"We Wuv Our Widdle Baby Scabby-Face"

While little Cordelia seems, in some ways, to be advanced and promising, in other ways she is a terrible underachiever. Teething, for example. She showed the clear signs of teething (excessive drooling, chapped face, chewing on everything, unbelievable bitchiness) months ago. But her teeth have remained cute little bumps, still safely under her pink, moist gumskin.

This worries me greatly, because my wife's genetic line has a predisposition for . . . how do I put this delicately? . . . nightmarish teeth. My wife entertained me on our first date by telling me her orthodontic history. Let's just say that her mouth was to healthy dental formation what Afghanistan is to responsible government. One of her molars came out of her ear. And it runs in her family.

So any sign of tooth trouble in our baby makes me worry.

But lately, Cordelia has shown signs of new, intense teething symptoms. In particular, she is exceeding at drool formation, and the constant moisture has left her face chapped. Insanely chapped. I would go so far as to say "Scabby." No matter how dry we try to keep Cordelia's face and how carefully my wife applies soothing chin salves, our adorable baby's face grows ickier and sorer and crustier with every passing day.

My wife and I have come to rely on the adoration strangers direct toward our offspring to keep our sanity afloat. I shudder to think of how we will cope if people stop saying "Oh, how cute!" and start saying "Oh, dear God! *What have you done?*" And then Cordelia's lower lip will snap off. I feel I should do something to avoid this.

And yet, if I try to encourage the teeth to come out faster, say with a pair of needlenose pliers, then I'm the jerk!

Let's Be Optimistic and Hope It's a Boy

Strangers who coo over our little one almost always assume that she is a boy. I guess, for people to consider the possibility that our child might be a girl, we have to put her in little frilly lace dresses, put her in pigtails, and tether a Barbie to her. But without all these frills,

Cordelia looks as androgynous as, well, any other baby on the planet.

However, when people say things like "Cute boy," I don't bother to correct them. Why, I figure, should I make them feel bad? Though, and I admit this is cynical of me, I suspect they're calling her a boy because they think, deep down, that if you call a girl a boy, it's a compliment, but calling a boy a girl is an insult.

But it's not a bad thing. Having a girl is a great deal! Statistics indicate that you only have to pay a girl 70 percent as much as a boy for being the same child.

There Is No Limit to the Ways We Sell Out

When we started out, we used cloth diapers. It seemed like the right thing to do. Now we have switched entirely to disposables, because cloth diapers are environmentally responsible and virtuous, and therefore a gigantic pain in the ass.

I'm not sure whether this means we're destroying the Earth or not. Since no Ecowarriors from the future have traveled back in time from a ravaged planet to kick my ass, I think we're okay so far. Of course, that may just mean they haven't invented time travel in the future yet. What a bunch of losers.

Actually, when you think about it, I am probably completely safe from the angry revenge of the people of the future, so I can do what I want to them. Ha! They can kiss my ass!

So disposables are okay.

Also, Cordelia is now completely weaned. She shall never again have access to sweet, sweet mother's milk. Mariann wanted to breast-feed for at least six months. She lasted seven. Now Cordelia is on her own. She will no longer be able to eat "the perfect food for babies." Now she has to eat the perfect food for humans: food.

Ceasing to breast-feed is a terrifying process. Backed up milk makes the breasts really huge, really hard, and really uncomfortable. For a few weeks, it was like Mariann had just gotten breast implants. And not in the good way.

But now they're back to normal. Soft and Daddy-friendly. Now I have to provide foreplay again.

Alleged Good Reasons to Have a Baby

I occasionally hear people talk about you should only have a baby for the "right" reasons. This is crazy. I strongly maintain that There Are No Bad Reasons to Have a Baby.

Okay. I have to take that back, a little. There are exactly three bad reasons to have a baby:

  i. For a source of valuable minerals and oils. And protein.
 ii. To wrap in duct tape and use as a doorstop.
iii. Ballast.

But as long as you aren't doing one of these things, there are no bad reasons to have a baby.

How can this be? Does this make sense? Sure. You see, for there to be "Bad" reasons to have a baby, that implies that there are "Good" reasons to have a baby. Bad is a relative term, after all. For something to be bad means there must be something better.

So, an exercise. Think, in your head, of a "Good" reason to have a baby. Something someone could say without fear of public disapproval or, in rare cases, a Geneva Convention violation.

Got a reason? Good. I can pretty much guarantee that your "Good" reason falls into at least one of two categories: Selfish or Delusional. For example:

Selfish

  i. I wanted someone to love.
 ii. My life was too boring, and I needed something to take up time.
iii. I didn't want to be alone when I was old.
 iv. I wanted a source of organs for emergency transplant.

These are all perfectly reasonable, understandable reasons to have a baby. But they're all pretty darn self-involved, and therefore not good. On the other hand, there are reasons that are just nuts . . .

Delusional

i. I love kids, and I love babies.
ii. I wanted to create someone who could feel a lifetime of happiness and joy.
iii. I wanted to make the world a better place by adding another human to suck its resources. My child would make the world better since it will be imprinted with my incredibly sensitive and valuable moral system.

These are all worthwhile sentiments, all lovely and nebulous, and all will evaporate into nothingness the first time the kid is screaming at three in the morning and you want to hit it with a rock. But it could be worse. Some reasons are both . . .

Selfish and Delusional

i. Having a child will strengthen our marriage.
ii. Having a child will keep my loved one from leaving me.
iii. Having a child will make me happier.

Nothing makes the normal, unending hassles of parenthood a bitter experience like having the kid because you thought it would make things better.

"So What You're Saying Is Nobody Should Ever Have Kids? Nice Try, Extinction Boy."

Do not misunderstand. I believe that kids can add fulfillment and richness in one's life, somewhere in my weird, distant, science-fiction future. But that eventual long-term gain has nothing to do with the reasons why we have them in the first place. Let's take a real world example. It's like if I throw a rock at some hippie, and I miss and kill

Thoughts from the Future

I started feeling guilty about using disposable diapers. To deal with it, I've started putting a photocopied note in every bag of Cordelia-waste I haul to the curb. It says, "Dear Future—Sorry for the trash. I hope you have come up with a convenient way to either convert it into pure energy, compress it into a teeny, tiny cube, or launch it into the sun. If not, well, what have you been up to in the years since my death? Losers. Good luck keeping the ants from taking over."

"Best regards, Jeff Vogel (Deceased)"

Hitler instead. Good result, having nothing to do with my original intentions.

I'm sure, in the long run, parenthood is worth it. But when you're deciding to have a kid, the good things are pretty nebulous. As I am fond of saying, I have no real idea what a lifetime of knowing and loving one's child is like. But I have a damn good guess what it's like to have someone piss on me.

Week 34—Trust, Once Lost, Can Never Be Regained

I'd write what Cordelia did this week, but I'd just have to copy and paste what Cordelia did last week. Random noises. Failure to crawl. I've been writing this so that, someday, Cordelia could read it and find out what she and her parents were like. Well dear, I'm not sure about us, but you were pretty dull.

Of course, most of my knowledge about what she's been doing was received secondhand. My mom and dad are in town, their RV a reassuring, monolithic presence in the driveway. As usual, they are enchanted by my daughter to the exclusion of all else, including food and air. Sometimes, I'll walk in on them caring for Cordelia and notice that they're turning blue. I have to remind them to breathe. It's so cute.

Of course, I don't walk in on them much. My parents being around enables Mariann and me to hand off the baby and vanish for lengths of time that would horrify actual good parents. Other people get a big kick out of babies, with their mood swings and their inertness. Me, not so much. I'm just hanging on until I can teach her how to kick her friends' asses at Nintendo.

I Am the Bad Cop

To best analyze my and Mariann's parenting technique, one best looks at police procedures. Namely Good Cop/Bad Cop. I'm the second one.

Mariann looks after Cordelia during the day while I work. She puts in the long hours on the parenting thing. Feeding, bathing, rescuing the baby from her crib. The things that make Cordelia happy.

I, on the other hand, look after Cordelia in the evening, when she is most likely to be in a shitty mood. And, more importantly, I am the person who puts her to bed. In other words, I am The Hammer. Eventually, someone has to go, "That's it. You've been conscious long enough. Be in your box. Have a nice scream." That person is me.

When Cordelia is exhausted and wailing in her crib and someone walks into the room, she immediately flips on her belly, lifts herself up with her arms, and flashes her most radiant "You are my God, now please pick me up" smile. If Mariann walks in, this smile is usually at least good for quick pick up and hug. But if Cordelia looks up and sees me, she knows all hope is lost.

Sure, it would be nice to pick her up and comfort her every time she cries. But it would also be nice to not have a baby who cries for Attention on Demand every hour every night until she's thirty-two. I cry to my wife for comfort every few hours every night. (Well, "comfort" is the term I have for it.) Believe me, it's not always appreciated. So I want to spare whoever ends up with my baby the same horrifying fate.

But it's sad. Babies are fast learners. They have to be. Otherwise, we'd have a lot of immobile, corpulent teenagers in diapers. And Cordelia has learned where to turn for comfort and solace. She knows from where the good things come. When she's crying and I'm holding her, if Mariann isn't in the room, I can comfort her just fine. If my wife is in the room, however, Cordelia will completely freak out until I hand her over. Cordelia latches onto the most reliable source of comfort like a fly looks for a fresh corpse, and my wife is generally the most alluring body in the room.

I suppose this should bother me and I should be jealous or something. I'm not. Cordelia is young, and the race is long. I have all the time in the world to buy her affection. After all, Mariann is determined to never buy our daughter a Barbie. As far as I'm concerned, all it will take is one carefully timed Dream House to fully restore myself to my daughter's good graces.

If that doesn't work, I'll escalate to a Playstation. A pony. Earrings at age seven. Whatever it takes. What price is too high to pay for the love of one's child?

Actually, I think a few grand might be a bit on the expensive side. But I'll bribe that bridge when I come to it.

And the Baby Gets a New Food

My wife tried out a new food on Cordelia. Prunes and Oatmeal flavored baby food. Cordelia loves it. This is such a bad idea.

When I found that Cordelia was being fed prunes, all I could think was: What? Why are we feeding her food that encourages her to crap? She doesn't shit enough? She's already voiding out her entire body weight through her ass every day. To get more stuff to crap out, she'll have to start absorbing nitrogen through her skin.

Soon, Cordelia will poop out her entire body. There'll be nothing left. I'll look into the diaper, and the whole baby will be in there.

My wife, on the other hand, is content to have found something the baby will deign to eat, and I can shut up about it any time now, thank you. Meanwhile, I'm feeling obligated to find a baby food with a name like "Colon-Spray Fiber Chunkz."

Why Prunes and Oatmeal in the First Place?

I hate it when I shop for baby food and the store hasn't gotten a new shipment for a while. That's when the only flavors left are things so bizarre and unappealing you wouldn't even feed them to a helpless baby. "Chicken and Oats." "Veal Liver and Bread Pudding." "Sand."

I went shopping for baby food late Sunday night. The only flavors they had left were "Shredded Monkey" and "Ass." I bought two of each. Cordelia will eat anything if you mix a little applesauce with it.

Trust, Once Lost, Can Never Be Regained

Cordelia has definite food preferences. Apples and pears are great. Pureed corn and squash mix is very much not. Sounds like a sensible girl to me.

But a jar of corn and squash mix was already open, and I didn't want to waste food. So I tried feeding her pear until she was eagerly opening her mouth for more, and then I surprised her with a big spoonful of corn and squash.

After that, it almost took a crowbar to pry her mouth open. I had to put some pear on the spoon and shove it in past her pursed lips to communicate to her, "Hey, don't worry. The pear is back. No need to starve yourself."

Then, a few mouthfuls of pear later, I gave her another scoop of ambush corn and squash. It took even more work to get her to open her mouth after that.

I suppose I should be glad Cordelia is developing her brain enough to have preferences and react rationally to unpleasant stimuli (unpleasant stimuli, in this case, means "Daddy"). But how could I have possibly known that my child would ever use her newfound mental powers to defy me?

Actual Baby Foods Advertised on Gerber.com, Which Invited Comment

Lamb & Lamb Gravy (The word "Gravy" makes everything more disturbing.)

Veal & Veal Gravy (There is a pleasing symmetry to feeding milk-fed babies to milk-fed babies.)

Lasagna with Meat Sauce Dinner (Lasagna? It's been pureed! I do not believe that someone carefully assembled and baked a dish of lasagna, let it cool, and then threw the whole thing into some giant industrial blender. It should be called what it is: "Liquefied tomato and dough." Gerber, I call bullshit on you!)

Prunes with Apples (Something else to make your baby shit more, this week guest-starring Apples.)

Hearty Chicken & Rice Dinner (Hearty? This was the only food they had with the word "Hearty" in the name. What are they adding to that chicken to make it so exceptional? Actual meat? Protein powder? Lard?)

Banana Plum Granola, Apple Mango Kiwi (From Gerber's "organic" line. I think they are just showing off with these. My daughter is currently trying to see how much floor lint she can jam into her mouth. She would not appreciate "Apple Mango Kiwi" any more than dogs appreciate flavored dog food.)

Thoughts from the Future

Being the Firm Hand is not without cost. A full year later, I was still the parent of last resort. Cordelia will turn to just about anyone else for nurturing before me.

However, if I am the only person around, Cordelia shows instant affection toward me. She's a practical little girl. I sometimes send everyone else away so that I can experience what it's like to have a child who likes me.

One Other Baby Food Flavor I Found

Peach Apricot Muesli.

This was from Earth's Best Baby Food. I don't see why they don't just let the other shoe drop and put "Perfect for Raising Your Young Homosexual" right there on the label.

Week 35—Horrifying Introduction to Children's TV

My parents left again. Cordelia was dramatically improved by their stay here.

My parents are bundles of energy and optimism. Whereas it takes most of Mariann's and my energy to just keep the kid alive and the house free of festering refuse, the grandparents are already trying to teach our seven-month old numbers and the alphabet. Sure, this is crazy. But it's the sort of craziness I should probably partake of more often.

Now that the grandparents have driven their house away, I have taken stock of where the baby is at now.

She is a spine-stressing twenty pounds and two feet tall. She is nowhere near as chubby as she used to be, as her body has been busily converting her baby fat into baby. She says "Da da" and "Ma ma" all the time, although she shows no signs of knowing what they mean. She can't crawl, but she can roll over well enough to maneuver herself into the fireplace, if she wants to.

She has her mother's funky eyes, which are blue in places and brown in others and change colors according to the light. She has her father's dull, pedestrian brown hair. She produces firm, well formed, forest-green stools. I'm not sure whether she got her stool formation from her mother or her father.

There. That's pretty much everything about our baby. We're caught up now. Enjoy.

The Ugly Baby Solution

Saw another ugly baby today. This one had Bloated Head Syndrome. That's the one where the kid has this enormous, puffy melon, and you're constantly worrying that it'll try to turn its head too quickly and its neck will snap like the stem of a fine crystal wine glass.

Seeing this baby, however, put me in a philosophical mood. As I opined to Mariann, are we not at risk of our baby losing its perfect adorability? Babies change so quickly. Any morning, might we wake up to find that our baby has become a little monster? What then?

My wife instantly responded, "Well, we could put a bag over her head."

This would be a good solution, I felt. However, the bag would annoy the baby. And the baby would cry. And strangers would walk over and say, "What are you doing? Take off that bag!" And then we would, the stranger would see our baby and go "Oh, God, put it back! Put it back!" And we would put the bag back and the stranger would be satisfied, but, by that time, my wife and I would have been inconvenienced, and that would be terrible.

Fortunately, in the case of the child we saw while walking, it's a moot issue. No bag would have fit over that kid's head.

One Problem with Baby Appearances in General

My daughter's arms have no muscle tone at all. They're totally round and soft and chubby. Sloppy, sloppy, sloppy.

Horrifying Introduction to Children's TV

I can't remember where I read this, but I'm pretty sure one of my parenting books says that it's okay to distract your child by showing it lots of TV. Considering how excruciating it is to watch a tiny sprog every goddamn minute of every day, this makes sense. So probably all the parenting books say it.

Of course, Cordelia is hypnotized by TV. Anything, I suppose, to distract her from Daddy's awkward and pathetic attempts to entertain her. And, surprisingly, her attention is held most strongly by children's TV. *Teletubbies. Sesame Street.* That sort of thing. I would have guessed that, for an eight-month-old, any TV show would do, but it turns out that, while there may be an outer limit to what I don't know about children, we aren't there yet.

So, to learn and be enlightened, I watched some kiddie TV. *Teletubbies*, mainly, and some nightmare show where biplanes with computer animated faces say supportive things to each other. And some videotape someone gave me with this carrot that tells me about Jesus. And I can't get over how disturbing these shows are. They're perfect for the wee ones, but fifteen seconds of *Teletubbies* makes me feel like my skin is crawling off my body.

With some thought, I figured out why.

In these shows, everyone is nice to each other. Perfectly nice. Perfectly supportive. Everyone forgives each other. Everyone laughs at each other's jokes. Males can be hugged by females and not try to parlay that hug into a lay later that evening.

If I met someone in real life this supernaturally nice, calm, and supportive, I would worry. Two such people, and I'd fear that I'd fallen into the sinister clutch of the Mormons. A half dozen, and I'd grab my wallet and start screaming. While this behavior is great and comforting for kids, to adults, it's just Wrong. *Wrong, wrong, wrong!*

On one hand, you might say, this means I've lost my childish spirit. You might say that I've been consumed by cynicism, and that I should try to recapture some of the naive joy of youth. But, on the other hand, blow me.

The All-Pajamas-All-the-Time Paradigm

Baby clothes should be designed for convenience.

Cordelia's genitalia expel noxious substances on a regular and rapid schedule. Therefore, all baby clothes must be designed to provide easy access to said genitalia.

The best pants are the ones with buttons running up the inside of the thigh and down the inside of the other thigh. These sorts of pants can be ripped open to provide access to the baby's undercarriage in mere moments.

In fact, I think they should make pants like these for grownups too. When the kid is asleep and you're trying to squeeze out a quick lay before the screaming resumes, you need to save all the time you can.

Baby pants without easy access, however, are evil. It is already a horrible imposition to have to clean up human waste. But to have to completely take off the pants and then put them back on again? No. Babies are dopey, and, as far as they are concerned, the only thing clothes need to do is keep them from freezing solid. Therefore, parental convenience is the third most important quality good baby clothes have. The only things more important are warmth and being clean enough that Cordelia's grandparents aren't getting up my ass about it.

Alas, Mariann has started dressing Cordelia in real clothes, smaller versions of the clothes grown-ups wear, with quiet dignity and a modicum of style. If I had my way, the baby would only wear pajamas, and she would keep wearing pajamas until she's old enough to actually ask me for something else. And if that means that she goes to the Prom in pink, fuzzy jam-jams with Wonder Woman on the chest, well, that is the sort of iconoclastic individualism that is prized in this fast-moving, technological, Internet-time world of ours.

Week 36—More Thoughts on the Merciful Glories of Television

Raising an eight-month-old is grueling, thankless work. Mariann and I have pretty much exhausted the entertainment possibilities of a child that can't actually do anything, and Cordelia stubbornly refuses to learn to do tricks for our benefit.

How sharper than a serpent's tooth, etc.

Of course, my wife is still enthralled by the baby. She has no choice. She still has residual birthing mommy hormones ping-ponging around in her system. I, on the other hand, am still waiting for when I can teach Cordelia to play Nintendo.

Of course, this doesn't mean that I don't help with parenting now. I do stuff! For example, I just bought a Nintendo.

More Thoughts on the Merciful Glories of Television

I decided to get out my parenting books. I wanted fresh information about how much TV I should be showing my child. One book contained an excellent summary of this tricky and controversial topic:

"Television—When your tiny baby is being difficult and overly demanding of your attention, it is a good idea to take a break by placing it in front of the television for a while. I mean, have you seen how much attention those little vampires want to suck up? Plop that kid in front of the boob tube, before you go nuts. What are you waiting for? What are you, some kind of loser Nader voter!?!?

"Oh. Make sure that the TV is on."

I'm sure we can all agree with this advice. I can't remember exactly what book I found it in, but it was a thick one, and it had an index, so I'm sure it was right.

And why not? Whether we're putting her in front of the tube or strolling her around the lake, our parental contribution pretty much boils down to giving Cordelia an amusing variety of things to stare at. So why is TV watching inherently a bad choice? In fact, TV watching is better than a walk for three reasons. First, she watches TV sitting up, which I guess is exercise of a sort. Second, instead of breaking a sweat pushing Cordelia around, Daddy gets to lie on the couch and stare at the ceiling. Oh, sweet immobility. You are the peace-bringing goddess that sustains me.

Third, television really is educational! Why, just today, I put in DVDs that showed Cordelia a child learning a Valuable Lesson About Life and an old man learning the True Meaning of Christmas. Then Mariann showed her a movie that taught her that, if you are a bad person, you can easily be brought down by the power of Shaolin Kung Fu. Between the two of us, Cordelia will learn that there is no problem that can't be solved with honesty, openness, and extreme, mind-bending violence.

Also, if Cordelia takes a shorter nap than usual, why not let her spend the time she'd normally spend napping in front of the TV? I mean, the Teletubbies must be better for her development than lying alone in the dark, right?

(And let's be honest. If she naps a half hour less than usual, she *owes* me that half hour.)

In conclusion, the proper parental attitude toward TV can best be summed up thusly: The only time it is ever appropriate to show TV to a baby is when it would make things more convenient for Mommy and Daddy.

The Teletubbies Take Control

The show disturbs the shit out of me, but Cordelia can't get enough of it. When I pause it, she stares fixedly at the immobile figures, trusting them to start moving again at any moment. And if I turn off the TV, she keeps watching the dark screen, just in case they come back on.

I'm so proud of my little girl. Only eight months old, and she already has a hobby.

My Baby's Toys Make Me Want to Twitch

There is a certain sort of baby toy that isn't happy merely being fun. It has aspirations of being (ugh) educational. It attempts this by covering its surface with as many colors, patterns, numbers, letters, and symbols per square inch as it can. These toys are the most ghastly looking objects I've ever seen. They're so garish that they actually make space warp around them. I can't look into Cordelia's toybox without having a seizure.

Baby toys are ugly objects that make my head hurt. And that's me. A grown-up. I have over thirty years of experience looking at things. For a baby, who is still learning how to use her eyes and process information received through them, an object with such a riotous array of patterns and colors must be pure static.

Why is this? Why does every baby toy I own look like a migraine hallucination? Do people really feel that this makes them prettier to babies? Well, we have no idea what looks pretty or not pretty to babies. Babies have different eyes and different brains. If I could remember what my aesthetic tastes were like when I was five months old, I would tell you.

However, I do know what is pretty to humans in general. When I bought my car, I selected it in a lovely monochrome shade of blue green. I did not ask them to paint the front third red with white stars, the middle in alternating yellow and purple stripes, and the back third in a chartreuse and black checkerboard pattern, with the alphabet on the hood and numbers on the tires. That would look like shit. Do babies want to spend time around things that look like shit any more than adults do?

So I say, give the babies something lovely and monochrome every once in a while. Do them a favor. I can't say for sure, but it really seems that Cordelia most prefers to stare at and play with objects that are *simple*. A white tube of hand cream. A wooden spoon. A metal fork.

She rapidly discards those freakish Dali-plus color samplers. I am so proud to have a baby with taste.

"Let's Go See the Rival Baby!"

When I'm left to play with Cordelia, I don't have a whole lot of material. I don't have a knack for babies. "Playing" for me, generally involves handing the little girl a toy, watching as she disinterestedly throws it away, and then picking up that same toy and handing it back to her. Plus peek-a-boo. That's it.

The one I can do that always delights her is taking her to see the Rival Baby. To play the Rival Baby game, I take her into the bathroom, turn on the light, and hold her in front of the mirror.

Then I saw "Look, honey! There's the rival baby! Look how cute she is. Wave at the rival baby! Look at it smile! And look . . . there's the Other Daddy. Look how much the Other Daddy enjoys the Rival Baby. You better watch out, or that Rival Baby will come after your job!" Cordelia laughs and giggles through all of this because, of course, she can't speak English.

When she can speak English, the Rival Baby game will become even more useful, because I can use it to prepare her for real life. "Oh, look honey! There's the Rival Baby! You'd better smile at that Rival Baby, wave at her, giggle, make her think she's your friend. Because someday, you'll be competing against that Rival Baby for getting into college. And jobs. And boys. And, if things get really bad, food. And if the Rival Baby likes you enough, maybe you'll have an edge up on her! You'll need it, because look how cute she is! She's adorable! That's tough to compete against."

After all, if I don't try to prepare her for grown-up life, what sort of a parent am I?

When the Rival Baby Game Goes Wrong

Of course, I'm a loving parent and not a bad person. That's why I wouldn't ever say, "And look how chubby the Rival Baby is. You should always try to be a tiny bit thinner than the Rival Baby."

"Honey, Please Stop Injuring the Baby."

Finally, on the subject of new tricks. When I put Cordelia in her car seat, there is a plastic buckle I have to snap shut in the middle of her chest. She has gotten very good at lurching forward and trying to put her lips and tongue into the buckle just as I am fastening it. Then she looks up at me, blaming me for her self-inflicted injury.

The worst thing about raising an infant is not the harm they do to themselves. It's that, in their dopey little brains, they're blaming you.

Week 37—Chicken Soup for the Lost Soul

Our baby daughter Cordelia is over eight months now and . . . blah, blah, blah. Who cares? We have a Nintendo now!

Surprisingly, it is my wife that is addicted to the Nintendo, not me. This is a huge relief, because I am no longer the only source of distracted, diffident parenting in our family. My wife will play a game and Cordelia will watch the TV happily. Or she will flip through a baby book. Or she'll try to fit a stapler into her mouth. Whatever keeps her occupied. Nintendo helps us not worry about these things so much.

Cordelia takes this all with good grace. She's as quiet, focused, and calm a baby as anyone could ever want. Sometimes, even at eight months, she'll sit up and happily watch TV for a while. She'll occasionally look around to make sure a parent is nearby, then she'll take some sips of her drink and watch more TV.

Eight months old, and she already takes after Daddy.

Now She Can Make It to the Stairs

Cordelia can crawl now.

It's a crude, undeveloped form of crawling, with a variety of different approaches. Sometimes she curls up both legs under her torso and push off with them simultaneously. She will go forward a good six inches and land on her face. When she does try to push off with one leg at a time (proper, correct, according-to-Hoyle crawling), she is much better with one leg than the other, so a more accurate description of the activity might be "directed flailing."

But she does lie on her stomach, hoist her chubby little torso on all four limbs, and propel herself forward. Looks like crawling to me.

I was heavily involved in getting her to this point. She started to crawl only because I kept occasionally putting all her favorite toys just out of reach. Only when I was satisfied with her progress did the rude little objects allow themselves to be caught and chewed.

Cordelia must picture the world as full of desirable but malevolent objects, mocking her and endlessly fleeing. A nightmare world, in which nothing is fixed and nothing can be relied upon. Only the greatest of effort will enable her to grasp an object, imprisoning it and, just for a moment, prying it free from the chaos that swirls around her. Dear God, I hope she doesn't realize that it's my fault.

Of course, when left on her own, she doesn't crawl at all. She rolls around sometimes, but she's usually content to lie quietly, flip through picture books, and fill diapers. The good life.

FGS (Fecal Grout Syndrome)

Now that Cordelia is not eating any baby milk, she is crapping a lot more. I'm sure you want to hear more about this.

Normally, these days, her solid waste comes out in solid, well-formed chunks, the sort of easily gathered pieces that look up and say, "You see? She didn't want to cause you a lot of trouble."

But sometimes, we still get a bad one. She unleashes these sticky, nasty nightmare poos that ooze around and then solidify like concrete. I open up the diaper and see a line of solidified shit between the lips of her labia like grout between floor tiles.

When that happens, there's only one thing you can do: Grab a moist towelette and start mining.

The worst part is checking afterward to make sure I got everything out.

I don't know how much therapy she'll need because of all of this, but I do know that she's not going to get any. I'm taking all of her share of the therapy. I need it more.

Chicken Soup for the Lost Soul

Why do I spend all this time writing all this stuff about my baby? It's not as if there is any shortage of writing about babies. Go to any decently sized bookstore, and you'll find a whole forest's worth of books with names like *Secrets of the Baby Whisperer* and *Forging a Trusting Love Bond with Your Fetus* and *Recharging Your Toddler's Soul Batteries*. I'm not saying I'm in favor of book burning. But I am saying that, with some books, the only useful things they could ever provide are light and heat.

The reason I am writing this journal is that all parenting books are stupid. . . . Well, to be fair, almost all. . . No. Let's be unfair. All. To enter the baby book aisle is to descend into a dank, pastel-colored underworld of the judgmental, the saccharin, and the outright delusional. Whether you're looking at the *Babywise* books at one end of the spectrum (books that suggest that spanking an eight-month-old could possibly be a good idea) and the Sears books at the other end (books that, if they had their way, would have your sixteen-year-old sleeping in your bed), one could easily be forgiven for feeling that the only way to deal with the baby book aisle is with fire.

As Exhibit One, I would like to present *Chicken Soup for the Parent's Soul.*

For those unfamiliar with the Chicken Soup books, each one focuses on a specific demographic (Parents. Pet Owners. Teenagers. Fishermen. Freemasons. Osteopaths. Anti-Semites.) and presents a purely irony-free series of stories explaining how life is a rich cavalcade and people are basically good and, I don't know, Jesus saves, I guess. Being as there are 800,000,000 books in this series, I'm amazed that there aren't twelve for parents alone.

(There is one for grandparents. Not one for great grandparents or great-great-grandparents, though. All of the stories would end with "And then they died.")

For research purposes, I picked up *Chicken Soup for the Parent's Soul* (using rubber gloves, as I don't like to touch that stuff with my hands), opened it, and recorded a selection of the chapters:

The Joys of Parenting
A Mother's Love
A Father's Love
Special Connections
Special Moments
(Here's where it starts getting darker.)
Insights and Lessons
Surviving Loss
Letting Go

Based on this, I would guess that parenthood is a cavalcade of joy, wisdom, and love, which continues up until the point where your kids die or flee.

I was hoping that having a child would free me, even temporarily, from my mental prison of cynicism and ironic detachment. It is becoming clear that this will not be the case, at least until I get hooked up in some sort of *Clockwork Orange*–style mental reconditioning chair where my eyes are held open with hooks and I watch bunnies and *Veggie Tales* for days.

A Brief Unnecessary Digression on the Subject of the Chicken Soup Books

When flipping through a bunch of the Chicken Soup books, I noticed an interesting pattern. They all have about ten chapters, and, in each book, Chapter 7 or 8 was a downer chapter. All the other sections were full of uplifting stories about stuff, and Chapter 8 would always be called something like "Surviving Loss" or "The Tough Times" or "Struggling Through Sadness" or "Sadness of Struggling" or "When the Bunny Passes On" or "Turning That Frown-Shaped Tumor Upside-Down."

If I had my way (and I won't) I would come up with an omnibus collection of all of the obligatory sad chapters from Chicken Soup books. It'd be great. A thousand straight pages of untimely death, failed relationships, and exploding puppies.

Week 38—Cordelia and Daddy Versus the Hippies

Soon, Cordelia will be nine months old. This is a great milestone. She'll have spent more time out of the uterus than in it.

Cordelia learned another new trick this week. If we leave her in her crib with a full bottle, she can find it, lift it, and drain it all on her own. No more getting up in the middle of the night to feed her!

This is a development of awe-inspiring convenience. I feel like someone who has just been handed a knife for the first time, having spent years carving roast turkeys with a brick.

As I understand it, leaving a bottle in a crib with a baby is a bad thing, because the milk rots their teeth or something. Well, she doesn't have any teeth worth noticing. And, even if sleeping with the bottle is bad for her, exhausted, zombie-like parents aren't so good either.

Jamming Fingers into Our Baby's Mouth

Several months after she actually started teething (or, at least, screaming as if she was teething), Cordelia finally has her first tooth. That sharp little fellow has finally cut its way through her gum and started scouting around, seeing if the coast is clear. Then the others nineteen will erupt and Cordelia can really start doing damage to Daddy's fingers.

Mariann and I were really excited about this. So much so that we took turns jamming our fingers into Cordelia's mouth, feeling that little calcium nub. Our baby, having a finely honed sense of infant dignity, was enraged by this process. However, since that tooth caused us months of arbitrary bouts of screaming, wakefulness, and unpleasant facial scabs, we felt we deserved it.

It is the ability to occasionally engage in such degrading and consequence-free exercises of raw power that is one of the best things about raising a very small child. The infant's total lack of long-term memory is the greatest gift nature gives to parents. This won't last for long. Soon, Cordelia will be able to remember things, and, with my luck, she will inherit my ability to hold a grudge for decades.

Sometimes I remember something stupid or unfair my parents said or did when I was, like, eight, and I remind them of it. In great detail. And I'm sure Cordelia will do the same thing to me. She is sure to also inherit my capacity for evil.

So I'm going to enjoy my parental power now. Because soon, all of this crap will be recorded in my daughter's little mental ledger, and, before you know it, I'll be eighty and Cordelia will be "forgetting" to make my lime Jell-O because of some minor disagreement regarding her stuffed bunny when she was six.

My Opinion of Dental Care for Babies

"Shit. She's gonna lose all them teeth anyway. Taking care of baby teeth is like washing a rental car."

I Would Rather Die than Eat Her Food

The fruit is fine. The vegetables are okay.

But that rice oatmeal they sell. Jesus! That stuff smells like liquid paper on a pig's ass.

Cordelia eats it. But I'm sure she sure don't like it.

Cordelia and Daddy Versus the Hippies

Today, at the Farmer's Market, I pushed Cordelia in her stroller past a street musician. He was a crusty, bearded, old hippie, singing old folk standards and playing some weird-ass mandolin thing. The aura of a life misspent hung heavily in the air.

As I walked by, the fellow decided to introduce my daughter to his Happy World of Whimsy and Merriment. He turned, bent down, and strummed his instrument at her.

Cordelia looked up at him with a dismissive look of pure contempt.

I was so proud. Never before have I been so sure that she is her father's daughter.

Street musicians are my arch-nemesis. Street musicians, and white people with dreadlocks.

Avoiding SIDS

My favorite thing about Cordelia reaching the age of nine months is that she is getting out of the SIDS Danger Zone. Now I say fewer things like, "Hang on. I have to make sure the baby is still breathing," and more things like, "Oh, just put the blanket in there with her. If she's going to commit suicide with a baby blanket, it's time for her to get on with it."

But the danger has not yet ended. Babies can get SIDS up to one year of age, or so I'm told. And our baby is now determined to do the worst thing a baby can do (besides taking up smoking): sleep on her belly.

Our kid is a tummy sleeper. And there is nothing we can do about it. Those foam things they sell to keep the kid from rolling over? What a sick, overpriced joke. She flops out of it, chews on it for a little while, and throws it out of the crib. Then she lies on her stomach. Because she hates me.

We're out of the "Baby can die and it'll be *my fault*" stage. We're now in the less dangerous but more unnerving "Baby might die and Daddy can go piss up a rope for all he can do" stage. The belly sleeping is good preparation for the next few years. Or, at least, the large portion of the next few years I'll totally hate.

Less Holding, More Restraining

Sometimes, I miss the early days when holding Cordelia was basically cradling a ten-pound bag of butter and sticks. While I am looking forward to when she can walk (and my spine can recover), holding my daughter is now less a happy moment of parental love than an effort to restrain a small, writhing, squealing primate.

She does not like being in laps. She does not like being held. The moment she sees something interesting, she tries to launch herself in its general direction, pushing off against my torso with her legs. When she is in my lap, she wriggles in all directions like a spiny little worm. She also tries to scratch my eyes out. Unintentionally. I think.

This is another thing the books never warned me about. When Cordelia is not being held, she's a smiling little angel, putting on all the adorable expressions she has developed to get me to lift her. Being a sucker and hoping for some sort of loving Daddy-daughter moment, I do so. Once she's been picked up, however, I basically become secondhand furniture, the sort you don't worry about scratching because you'll get something better at IKEA later. The moment I hold her, she places her hand firmly on my cheek, digs her nails into my skin for better leverage, and pushes herself around so she can grab and devour pieces of lint.

I hope I never accidentally drop her. Then she would learn another of life's precious lessons: Gravity is a lot less forgiving than Daddy is.

Week 39—Get Her Happy. But Not Too Happy.

Cordelia is now a full nine months old. She scares me.

When I first thought about having a baby (well, having my wife have a baby), I didn't realize how single-mindedly inquisitive infants are.

Thoughts from the Future

Cordelia never got SIDS. However, in the years since I wrote this, she had several close calls with TADS: Toddler Automotive Death Syndrome. This is where the toddler attempts to evade Daddy's grasp and jump into traffic and, for once, succeeds. I think the reason so few of us can remember our toddler years is that, if we could, the shock of how suicidally stupid we were would kill us.

For example, when I amuse her by making animal noises, she responds by reaching out and touching my mouth. She pokes at my lips. Then she jams her entire hand inside my mouth. Why? How does that seem like a good idea? How does evolution condition a small primate to react to a creature much larger and with many more teeth by actually putting tender morsels of succulent hand-flesh into its mouth?

That really strikes me as a suboptimal life strategy.

Along these lines, last night was a chilly fall evening, so we lit a fire in the fireplace. We then got to spend the rest of the evening keeping Cordelia from crawling into it.

Humanity is programmed for self-destruction.

Baby's First Signs of Good Taste

The most evil object I own is a snow globe that can play "It's a Small World." Again and again. Truly, it is a tchotchke spawned in the deepest pit of Hell.

But Cordelia is amused by new objects and kids love Disney, so I thought I'd try it out on her. I put the globe on the floor in front of the baby and started it playing its nightmarish little tune. Cordelia was fascinated. For about five seconds. And then she totally freaked out. She wouldn't stop screaming until the orb was far away.

Daddy comforted her, saying things like, "There, there," and "It's okay." and "You're right, dear. Disney is shit." And inside, I silently rejoiced at her good taste. It's more reassuring evidence that she is, in fact, my daughter.

Learning This Particular Baby's Language

I have discovered an actual advantage to being a parent.

Have you ever had a three-year-old walk up and start talking to you? The kid says something like, "I am wamma foop." And you have no idea what that means, so you say, like a reasonable person, "What did you say?" And the kid says, "I am wamma foop!" So you say, "I'm sorry. I don't understand you." And the kid looks at you like YOU'RE the jerk and gets angry and says "I AM WAMMA FOOP!"

And then the parent walks over and says, "Oh, my little angel is just saying he wants food. Why didn't you give it to him? Jackass." And takes the child away. And the child thinks you're an IDIOT.

I hate that.

But now I get my revenge. Now, I will have a kid whose language I understand. Now my daughter will walk up to my friends and go "Barble Baggle Bobble Boo!" and they won't understand and will get all upset and I get to walk over and say, "Cordelia was asking you to take her to the bathroom. Why didn't you, you bastard?"

Ahhhh. That's going to be sweet.

Get Her Happy. But Not Too Happy.

We occasionally take Cordelia to restaurants, generally right after naps when her scream frequency is the lowest. She will scream if she gets too unhappy, but also if she gets too happy. We have to perform a delicate high-wire act of emotion modulation to keep our daughter feeling as bland as possible.

We only give her toys that she is tired of and read books that have lost their appeal. We play tedious games with her that only barely hold her interest. And we sit her facing the least interesting corner of the room.

Parenting books don't give much advice for making your child less happy. This strikes me as an oversight.

Learn from My Mistakes

Mayonnaise has the same consistency as baby food. It smells like it could be baby food. It comes in jars, just like baby food.

It is NOT baby food.

Brief Words on the Alleged Meat in Baby Food

You ever see gyro meat? You know. That rotating meat log in Greek restaurants and state fairs? Granules of flesh from mysterious animals, compressed like particle board? Meat that has been ground and rendered and processed and rerendered and reprocessed until it's basically a collection of individual meat molecules? Meat that's been so heavily altered it should be considered vegetarian?

I strongly suspect that the meat in baby food is the stuff they won't even put in gyros.

And that's all I have to say about that.

No. It Isn't.

And consider cow anus. I imagine, when they put cow anus in gyro meat, they only use the succulent, moist, fresh cow anus. On the other hand, the cow anus that they dropped on the floor, and picked up, and wiped the lint off it, and dropped it again, and picked it up, and decided not to bother wiping it off? That's the cow anus they grind up and put into baby food.

Baby food meat is boiled, then pureed. To find something worse to do to a piece of meat, you have to go to Ireland.

Along those lines, baby formula is a source of great worry to me. I really don't want to know where they get that white powder. My guess it that it's a concentrated chemical slurry, bound together with powdered horse bone.

The First Law of Probabilistic Likelihood of Painkiller Application

The odds of bringing out the Baby Tylenol before a nap are directly proportional to the desire of Mommy and Daddy to squeeze in some quick intimacy.

"Quick Intimacy"? What Is This? A Jane Austen Novel?

Believe me, I wrote a different term before. Then Mariann made it clear that I had to change it, or face horrible consequences.

Intermission—The Whole, Problematic God Thing

The moral instruction of one's child is a tricky business. Trying to shape Cordelia's ethical structure is a no-win proposition. I can't make her turn out how I want, but I can totally screw her up for life. However, since the only other alternative is letting other people teach her their moral codes, and other people are stupid, I have no choice.

Which brings us to God.

I have pretty much worked out in advance my goals for her moral instruction. (Don't hurt other people needlessly, except for my enemies, who must be crushed. Pay taxes, within reason. Clean up your own messes. You kill it, you eat it. And so on.)

But the question of religion is a tricky one. You see, I am an agnostic. I have no beliefs about God's existence, pro or con, and will continue to be that way until someone proves to me there's a God out there. Photos will do. Or he could drop by the house. But I suspect that won't happen anytime soon.

But I come from a somewhat religious family, and I live in a somewhat religious world. Which brings us back to my daughter. Do I raise her in a religion? Which one? What do I tell her is true? What would enable me to continue sleeping in Sunday morning?

The questions are many. And they break down as follows . . .

Question 1: Should I teach her about the idea of God, without saying whether there is one?

Advantages—While honesty to children is not high on my priority list, I suppose, all things being equal, it's probably the better route. In the interest of full disclosure, my kid needs to know that there are religions out there and that some people believe in "God."

Also, she needs to be properly warned. When she hears her Catholic friends talk about Communion, she needs to know that they are not actually, literally describing a horrible, cannibalistic blood ritual. And when she meets Mormons, she needs to know to RUN.

Disadvantages—First, teaching her about religion will take up Daddy's valuable time, which could be spent in more enjoyable pursuits. Video games don't play themselves. And heck, she'll hear about God along the way anyway. I'm sure she can learn everything she needs to know about the nature of the Divine from Pokemon.

Decision—She should at least learn about the idea of God. I'll teach her what other people believe. Sure, it'll be a pain. But she really needs to be warned about the Mormons.

Question 2: Should I tell her that God exists?

Advantages—It'll keep me from getting crap from my family. And it'll keep her from getting crap in school.

Plus, to be honest, the belief in a supreme being is an incredible comfort to a huge number of people. Who am I to decide to deny that to her? For a lot of folks, belief in a Heaven where things are less messed up and Grandma and Grandpa are there is the only thing that keeps them from living their entire lives curled up in a fetal ball.

And I have no moral problem with lying to my daughter. I'll tell her about Santa, for example. And, when you think about it, there is very little difference between teaching your child about Santa and teaching your child about God.

Disadvantages—I won't actually believe what I'm saying. Maybe I'm being idealistic and naive, but I should at least kind of think that things I'm telling her aren't bullshit.

Decision—Probably not. If she needs to believe in God, she'll believe in God.

Question 3: Should I take her to church?

Advantages—Church gives you something to do on those lazy Sundays when you just can't get moving. And you get doughnuts and coffee afterward. And there are songs.

Also, visiting church is entertainment, like going to the zoo or something. You get to see the believers in their natural environment. The only problem is that the fun tends to fade around the hundredth visit or so.

Disadvantages—Church is ass. You have to get up early on Sunday. The sermons tend to be painfully simpleminded. And I can buy my own doughnuts, thank you. I don't want to have to fight for the apple fritters.

Plus, if you never go to church, you never get involved in church politics. You think the situation in the West Bank is bad? Get involved in the process to pick a new pastor. You'll see a normally placid granny try to stab a Shriner in the face with a broken bottle of Communion wine.

Decision—Hell, no! Religion or no religion, it'll take blasting powder to get me out of bed before noon on Sunday.

Question 4: Should I pick a religion and follow it without actually believing any of it (i.e., the Catholic path)?

Advantages—You get to be on a team! You get structure in your life! You get to spend time with your fellow believers! If there is a Heaven, and you've picked the right belief set, you get in!

Disadvantages—You get to be on a team. You get structure in your life. You get to spend time with your fellow believers. If there is a Hell, and you've picked the wrong belief set, you get in. My kid is going to lay enough guilt trips on me. Getting her damned to Hell is a pretty heavy rap.

Decision—If I can't even decide whether to teach her that there's a God, I certainly am not going to pick what flavor God is. Plus, if we belong to some religion, we'll eventually have to go take part in it. And here we are again, up before noon on Sunday.

Question 5: Should I raise her as an agnostic?

Advantages—Honest. I can get behind it. Quick to explain. Minimal time commitment. Agnostics don't need to tithe.

Disadvantages—Major schoolyard beatings. Aunts and uncles freaking out all over the place.

Plus, to be honest, the phrase "I am an agnostic" has a high Wanker Factor. This means that, when a person says "I am an agnostic," he or she has a much higher chance of turning out to be a wanker. Other phrases with high Wanker Factors are "brand identity," "worship the Goddess," and "bisexual visibility." I have no right to saddle my daughter with that.

Decision—No. If I'm not going to give my kid a set of religious beliefs, I'm not going to give her nonreligious beliefs either. I'm going to mess her up in plenty of ways. In this one, she can screw herself up.

Question 6: Should we celebrate Christmas?

Advantages—Everyone loves Christmas! People give you dry goods! And there are TV specials and you get a tree and everything.

Disadvantages—None.

Decision—Of course we will celebrate Christmas. But, damn it, we're going to call it Christmas. Not the Solstice, or Yulemass, or the Festival of Miranda, or the Dance of the Frozen Stars, or whatever PC nutjobs are calling it. It's Christmas. We'll have candy canes. And a tree. Screw you.

In Conclusion:

There. I feel much better now. I have settled what we are going to do, except for all the most important parts.

Now all I need to do is check this over, correct the punctuation, and show it to Mariann. And, when all the screaming stops, she'll tell me exactly what we're going to do, and the problem will be solved.

Ending the Year—The Baby Actually Does Something

And then we approached the end of our first year. The first birthday isn't entirely an arbitrary event. Babies grow and change very quickly. Their bodies are like calendars, clearly marking the passage of each month. The first tooth was July, and saying "Da da" was September, and standing up was December.

The first birthday, therefore, is a real transition, in the way that the thirtieth or the forty-seventh birthday isn't. The first birthday marks the child's imminent change from "baby" to "nightmare."

We saw the signs during these three months, and we knew what they meant. We watched her stand up, knowing that this would lead to walking, running, and attempting to fly. We saw her develop preferences (chocolate over gruel, being bathed over being left in her crib, television over anything), and we knew that preferences would soon change into demands.

It's still exciting. Watching a baby's humanity develop during this period is like unwrapping a package. You can't wait to see what sort of personality and abilities you will find inside. Of course, invariably, this metaphorical box contains a metaphorical alien bug monster, which metaphorically leaps out, clings to your face, and starts chewing.

But at this point, the baby is still a baby. It's gaining power, but it is still easy to control. And, in the end, that is what marks the change from a baby into a toddler: the realization that one is being controlled, and that one doesn't like it. And that is what these last three months are about: the dwindling of our delightful, total control.

Week 40—"Just Because She's Helpless, Doesn't Mean She's Harmless."

This week, that investment in baby gates really paid off in infant survival dividends.

Cordelia's crawling speed has doubled in the last week. She can really scuttle now. And she has thus learned that those big, looming, white objects (which are technically referred to as "walls") are not, in fact, theoretical abstractions but actual objects that require actual maneuvering to avoid.

When Cordelia bonks her head and cries, I do the expected and pick her up and comfort her and all that crap. But I feel a strange lack of concern and sympathy. I have this sad, merciless, Darwinian element in my brain that says, "Next time don't smack your head like that, goofball!"

But it's all right. It's like dating. As long as you create the plausible illusion of interest and concern, you can get through just about anything.

Nonconsensual Ham

Cordelia is a hearty eater, cheerfully wolfing down limitless quantities of oatmeal and pureed fruit. However, like all growing bodies, she needs protein. And, like all sensible creatures, she is horrified by the boiled, chemically treated meat slime they sell in those little jars.

I suppose we could solve this problem by preparing meat and processing it on our own. But we have found it to be much easier and more amusing to find ways to trick Cordelia into opening her mouth so we could scoop the stuff in. The best way was getting her to laugh by lightly pinching her belly with salad tongs. (Don't call Child Protective Services. She really seems to like this. Babies are dopey.)

Recently, my wife, in a moment of peculiar empathy, discovered that the baby likes yogurt and yogurt contains protein. She doesn't have any problem feeding Cordelia big, creamy spoonfuls of live bacteria (which I picture as multitudes of pale, microscopic cockroaches).

So we're giving the meat a rest for now. It's a pity. The sooner we get Cordelia to believe that meat is a necessary part of life, the less chance that she'll get a bee in her bonnet and turn into some sort of freakish vegetarian in her teen years. If I can get her to share my view that a perfectly done veal chop is the highest pinnacle of human achievement, I have done my job as a parent.

My Playing with the Baby Warning

People love holding our adorable baby. They grab her and hug her and immediately forget what harm sharp little baby fingernails can do to the human cornea. They don't realize that those chubby little legs pack surprising force and can do things to your jaw. Or your poor, hapless testicles.

Therefore, when a new person grabs our baby, I've started giving a standard warning:

"Remember, just because she's helpless doesn't mean she's harmless."

Sometimes, the Brain Can Store Two Things at Once

Today, when I was feeding her, she absentmindedly tried to grab the spoon I was holding while she was staring out the window.

It was nice to see her trying to do two things at the same time. You can't do something absentmindedly without having a little bit of mind to begin with.

The Beautiful Future That Will Be Brought to Us by Cloning

Cloning is still in the news. People are bothered by it. Whenever someone clones a monkey or a cultist or something, all the sob sisters and worrywarts come out of the woodwork and piss and moan about the horrible nightmare future that awaits us if we tamper in God's domain.

Well, they can get bent. The sooner we tamper in God's domain, the better. God's domain could, frankly, use the work. My greatest fear is that I will die before I see a world populated by bizarre, mutated products of the warped human mind. And that is why I want to get a cloned Teletubby.

Why, you may ask, do I want a cloned Teletubby?

People who know me personally may suspect that I want a cloned Teletubby so I can have sex with it. That's a good guess but, believe me, if I could choose anything to clone for sex, it would *not* be a Teletubby. (The first thing I would clone for sex would, of course, be me.)

No, I want a cloned Teletubby for my daughter, because she loves *Teletubbies*. My favorite trick of hers to show off to friends is the concentration trick. At nine months, she can already be fascinated by the TV for up to fifteen minutes at a time, thanks to those adorable Teletubbies.

She deserves to live in a world where she can see something charming and loving on TV and then have one in her bedroom, sleeping at her feet, hugging her, making those aggravating little noises they make. Mommy occasionally having to comb bits of Teletubby waste out of the creature's matted fur seems a small price to pay for my little girl's happiness. Plus I suspect that, once we could mass-produce them, they would be cheaper than ponies.

And, when she tires of it, I'd put it in the trunk, drive up the Interstate an hour or two, and leave it on the side of the road. It could run into the woods and frolic and find its own people and eat squirrels or whatever. And then I'd go out and buy my daughter a cloned living Barbie.

My honest opinion? People who oppose cloning just don't love their children as much as I love mine.

Week 41—"Awww! She Gave You a Love! I'll Call 911."

This has been another of those weeks when visiting grandparents made sure I never had contact with my daughter. Before she was taken away, she made the standard incremental improvements in movement, thought, and recreation.

She is crawling better: She is now using her arms and legs to hoist her pudgy torso off of the floor. She is clapping better: She will now clap in response to us clapping. And she is watching TV better: When she sits and watches *Teletubbies,* if we put a pillow behind her, she will lean back to watch more comfortably.

She has also, with great difficulty, sat up on her own for the first time. I wasn't in the room when it happened, but my mother obligingly shoved Cordelia down onto her back so I could see it happen again.

The Festivale Parentale

As I write this chapter, my family and I are in the middle of what I have dubbed the Festivale Parentale. My parents are living in an RV in our driveway. My mother-in-law is staying in the guest room. Between the three of them, if I try very hard and run into just the right room at just the right time, I can catch a glimpse of my daughter.

My parents are staying with us for a week because my father is recovering from having his gall bladder removed. At least, that is what I have been told. The alleged surgery may just be a very clever ruse to enable them to stay near their only grandchild longer. All I can say is that I'm glad my dad only has two kidneys.

My mother-in-law Ilona, on the other hand, just wants to keep her old nanny skills sharp. Her experiences raising children on a professional basis have given her a wide variety of opinions about how things are best done, and she has no problem sharing them with me, at great length and volume and at every opportunity. Fine with me. You could tell me that babies are disguised lizard creatures from Venus, and if you say it while changing my child's shitty diaper, I'll not only nod agreeably but also admit that up is down and freedom is slavery.

The best thing about grandparents is that their experience and enthusiasm enable them to play with the baby. They know how to do this. I still have not developed the ability to play with very, very small children. I can hand her toys. I can recite the alphabet. I can sing "Dust in the Wind." And that's pretty much the extent of my material. I'm not very interesting to her, and I sort of bore myself too. Playing with babies is like making small talk, another thing that I never developed a knack for.

Her grandparents, on the other hand, are amazing. They can pick up a toy she tired of months before and, through pure force of enthusiasm, make it a fresh source of amazement. They make up games. They swing Cordelia around. They sing. They dance. They form human pyramids. They taught her to count to six. Thank goodness someone around here knows what to do, because I feel like a jackass.

"Awww! She Gave You a Love! I'll Call 911."

My parents see things differently than I do. Really, really differently.

Cordelia really hates having things near or against her face. Being kissed bugs her. She can defend herself, though. Sometimes, when I kiss her cheek, she turns her head, presses her forehead against my face and shoves. Surprisingly hard.

When she started doing this, my mother said "Awwww. She gave you a love." This completely broke my brain.

And then my wife Mariann picked up Cordelia. Cordelia turned her head and smacked my wife a really good one in the nose with her forehead. As Mariann checked to make sure no cartilage had been damaged, my mother again said, "She gave you a love!"

What is that about?

My parents have the ability to read the most benign or beneficial motivations into any of our child's actions. I expect conversations like this in the near future:

"What a cute baby! I'd love to hold . . ."

"You may not want to get that close."

"Ahhh! My eye! My eye!"

"Awwwww. She gave you a love with her fingernails."

"I've never been in this much pain!"

Or . . .

"Let me give Cordelia a big kiss."

"Whack!"

"How cute! She gave you a forehead love."

"Arrrhhhhggghhhgggggrrrr."

"Oh. When we find your teeth, a dentist can put them back in. I suspect they'll turn up in your stool in a day or two."

"Ghhhhhuuuhhhhh."

"Children are our future."

Taking This Process to Its Natural Conclusion

Based on my parents' example, I have decided to read the best possible outcome into anything Cordelia does.

Action: Cordelia waves her arms around randomly.

Interpretation: "Oh, look! She's playing pat-a-cake!"

Action: Cordelia picks up a block.

Interpretation: "She wants to give you a gift."

Action: Cordelia tries to touch a hot oven.

Interpretation: "Come here, honey! Our little girl wants to cook us a fantastic seven-course meal!"

Action: Cordelia tries to roll into the fireplace.

Interpretation: "Awwww! She wants to determine if her clothes are really fireproof! I bet she'll grow up to be a certified safety engineer."

It feels so nice to give her the benefit of the doubt.

Developing My New Career Writing Children's Books

Sometimes, well-meaning relatives who know that I am writing a baby journal suggest that I write some children's books.

Tellingly, nobody who has actually read some of my writing has ever suggested this.

But I am nothing if not accommodating, so I have developed a proposal for a series of books about "The Three Fluffy Bunnies." These will be short and lovingly illustrated tomes which will both entertain children and teach them a number of lessons. They will detail the adventures of:

Peter Fluffytail: A happy-go-lucky scamp whose curiosity and energy get him in a variety of wild scrapes.

Susie Longear: The studious bunny, who wants ever so muchly to know everything about all the creatures and plants of Happyforest Glen.

Roger Grumpygus: A cranky rabbit who likes to sleep in his den all day, but whose rough exterior conceals a heart of goodness.

And these three lovable little bunny rabbits will have a number of adventures, carefully described and sold in book form, such as:

The Three Fluffy Bunnies and the Haunted Farm: The three bunnies discover a farmhouse that they are sure is haunted. The explore it and find that, actually, it's just abandoned.

The Three Fluffy Bunnies and the Candy Factory: The three bunnies wander into a chocolate factory and find some candy. They eat it and become very ill. But then they get better. They resolve not to go back to the candy factory.

The Three Fluffy Bunnies and the Difficult Decision: The three bunnies have a hard time deciding whether to bake a cake. In the end, they decide to.

The Three Fluffy Bunnies Get It, But Good: The three fluffy bunnies are getting older now, and they feel compelled to do what bunnies naturally do. A lot.

The Three Fluffy Bunnies Shiv Buggsy the Squirrel: In which we learn that all the good little animals of Happyforest Glen should know when to keep their mouths shut. If they know what's good for them.

The Three Fluffy Bunnies Get It, But Good: Very similar to the fourth book in the series, but with a number of additional new characters.

The Three Fluffy Bunnies and the Lunchtime Surprise: Rabbits, in extremis, eat their young. Let's all read and learn together!

Oh, but I do love those three fluffy bunnies so. Hope and dream with me, and perhaps I might someday be giving my Bunnies books five-star ratings on amazon.com.

Week 42—The Horrific Torment That Is Daddy

The house is still packed with grandparents. I am currently a father only in a sort of cosmic, theoretical sense. I parent by observation. Every once in a while, Cordelia is carried into the room and some grandparent shows me her new trick. I nod approvingly, and the baby is taken away again.

It's a Roman Emperor–style parenting system. "Yes. This plucky child has pleased me. Take it away and feed it."

Among the demonstrations I have pretended to be thrilled at, Cordelia can pull herself up from an almost standing position to a standing position. She can also perform both the "Bake me a cake as fast as you can" and "Toss 'em up" portions of pat-a-cake. She can't do "Roll 'em up" yet, but I am assured that this major, vital baby skill is soon to be acquired.

Away for the Weekend. Not Missed.

Since our house was crammed with family, my wife and I took the opportunity to get away for a weekend together. While the grandparents fought a grim, unending deathmatch to prove who loved our daughter the most, my wife and I went up to Canada. Vancouver, British Columbia, to be exact.

A brief word about Vancouver. It's western North America's answer to Amsterdam. Prostitution is legal. Pot might as well be. In the space of four blocks late Friday night, my wife and I walked by three clouds of pot smoke, one guy who tried to sell us weed, three bustling nightclubs, one porno theater, and a brothel. And all of this was by the *supreme court.*

It's a great town for getting away from the family.

Of course, we worried. Of course, we called home repeatedly. And, when we did, we always got the same response: "Don't worry. Your daughter is doing just fine without you. In fact, as far as we can tell, she hasn't even noticed that you are gone."

If possible, a brief vacation is an experience I recommend highly for all parents of newborns. It really makes clear how little space you actually take up in that tiny, undeveloped brain.

Completely Unrelated Vacation Tangent

I saw Michael Stipe in a restaurant. He blew his nose on a paper towel in the bathroom, right next to me. I could have, had I wanted, fished the paper towel out of the trash and sold it on eBay.

This is the sort of rich life experience having a child usually denies you.

The Horrific Torment That Is Daddy

Cordelia loves her mother much more than she loves me. This only makes sense, as Mommy is the bringer of all good things and Daddy is mainly the bringer of awkward play and *Teletubbies.* But having grandparents around has totally bumped me down on my daughter's Love List.

Sometimes, when I picked her up and there were several other relatives around, Cordelia would immediately start to cry.

This *totally* will not do. I may not be the Best Daddy in the World, but I'm not some damn Klingon either. So whenever my presence makes Cordelia cry, I pull her away from everyone, run into my bedroom, and shut the door. Then I play with her in all the ways she loves most (tossing around, bouncing on the bed, and other things that make my back crumble).

Then, when she is laughing and happy, I return her to the other relatives. Sure, I may be a gruesome ogre. But I'm not going to give up on her liking me just yet. That is why I have begun a campaign of Daughter Love Development . . .

The Art of Love Transference

What I am currently trying to do is transfer at least a certain amount of my daughter's love from her mother to me. My wife can afford it. She has adoration to spare. The question is: How do I best win some daughter love for myself?

The solution, as I see it, is to give her the things she likes.

The way I figure it, if whenever she wants a pacifier or toy or Cheerio or something, I am the one who hands it to her, she will be happier when she sees me. So that is the basic plan, which I have refined in several phases:

Phase 1—Watch daughter when she crawls around. When she drops her toy or pacifier, pick it up, say her name to get her attention, and hand the object to her. I make sure, of course, that she sees that it is me that is handing it to her. Thus the association is made in her tiny, tiny baby brain between me and good things.

Phase 2—However, watching the baby move around and hoping she drops something became too time-consuming, and I did not feel I was getting enough chances to prove my worth for the message to sink in. So, when she was playing and not looking at me, I would quickly reach in and pull the toy out of her hands. Then I would get her attention and hand it back to her, making sure that she saw it was me who was giving it.

As long as the tiny baby brain does not realize that I was the one who took the object in the first place, we're safe.

Phase 3—Of course, the best way to make myself look better is to make everyone around me look worse. I have found that, when my wife is playing with Cordelia, I can sometimes duck in, grab my wife's hand, and use it to knock the toy out of Cordelia's hands. Then I grab the toy and make a big show of returning it to Cordelia. Mean mommy, nice daddy.

My wife has made it clear that this behavior will result in my getting my wrist broken. But what sort of a man would not gladly pay any price to win his daughter's love?

Phase 4—I also feed Cordelia little bits of chocolate.

It's hard work, but I am keeping the faith. There's no problem that can't be solved with a carefully planned program of emotional engineering.

Week 43—Jam Fleshy Tab A into Canvas Slot B

Cordelia turned ten months old today. She has been having a growth spurt in the brain region. Every day, she becomes visibly better at basic person things. She can stand on her knees. She can achieve even higher crawling speeds. She will eat crackers when we hand them to her. Just a few more of the basic human tasks that seem desperately uninteresting until you see how much work it takes to learn them for the first time.

On the downside, all of the grandparents have left our house. Cordelia's days of constant loving attention have come to an end, and the painful period of unspoiling her has begun. Hotel heiresses and movie stars get their every wish fulfilled instantly. Cordelia, not so much.

Unspoiling is a difficult process. It involves Mommy and Daddy leaving the child alone for a few seconds, at which point she starts screaming for the attention that she feels she is entitled to. Remember, babies have no long-term memory. (Think about it. How much do you remember from when you were ten months old?) They only have short-term memory, which means that all Cordelia can ever remember is a world in which she was the center of attention. Now, for the first time in her life (that she knows of), she is being left to entertain herself. And thus, she wails her angst to the world.

The amazing thing is how little time it takes for her screaming to settle into the background and join the ambient noise of the room. It's sort of like Anguish Muzak.

On the bright side, Cordelia seems to have realized that she is stuck with us, and she has adjusted properly. After two weeks of my being beneath her notice, she now bothers to smile at me when I enter the room. Even at ten months, she knows that a smart prisoner sucks up to the jailers.

Jam Fleshy Tab A into Canvas Slot B

Since my wife tends to take care of most of the day-to-day baby maintenance, Cordelia has largely been spared being dressed by me. Considering how indifferent I am to the appearance and quality of the clothes I put on my own sorry self, this is a lucky break for her.

So I have only a few things to say about the whole, ugly process.

One

I am not really a person who approves of Velcro on kids' shoes. As far as I am concerned, the need to learn to tie your shoes is the only thing that keeps us from returning to the trees and throwing crap at each other.

That having been said, putting laces and not Velcro straps on baby shoes is completely idiotic.

Two

Baby clothes are always made with the soft, fuzzy, nice side on the outside, where Mommy and Daddy can feel it, instead of on the inside, against baby's tender skin. Some sob sisters have complained that this is not how it should be.

Bullshit. That is *exactly* how it should be. If I'm going to lug this twenty-pound lump of wriggle-meat around, I am glad that someone is making the effort to make the experience as pleasant as possible for me.

Three

No. Really. Putting laces on baby shoes is just *dumb*.

Four

Unless the baby is being taken out into cold weather, I have to be forced to put her into anything but pajamas. Pajamas are great. She's in them when she wakes up, they're warm, she can be put down to naps in them, she can be left in them when she wakes up from her naps, and she can be put to bed in them.

The question here is not, "So when do I ever change her clothes?" The question here is, "Why have I spent all this time changing my own clothes like a sucker?" I'd go to the mall right now and try to buy man-sized pajamas with the feet on, if it wouldn't make people think I'm some sort of sex pervert.

Five

I have not and will never look into any of my parenting books for advice on how to dress my child. They'll just try to scare me. I know how those things work. They'll say things like, "Infants should only be allowed to wear pants under strict supervision. Pants can suffocate children below the age of four. Do not let an unsupervised child wear pants, even for a moment!"

I don't need to read any of that. I have enough problems trying to get shoes on her without twisting her ankle.

Babies Are Not Happy

When my grandmother was staying with us, poking and examining her great-grandchild for the first time, she looked at Cordelia and said, "She's so happy! What a happy baby."

Now, I hate to disagree with my grandmother. My grandmother was wonderful to me when I was young. She took me repeatedly to the mall, without fail. She bought me a number of Atari cartridges. She made brownies. She was first rate.

But I do not understand how it is possible to think that babies are happy. While I'm not sure we can truly understand the crude emotions in their undeveloped brains, I am quite confident that "happy" is not one of the words we should be using.

Look at it this way. Suppose you couldn't walk. Couldn't speak. Couldn't understand anything going on around you. You were subject to the arbitrary whims of these giant, babbling creatures to obtain even your most basic needs. And whenever you took a pee, that fluid that started out so nice and warm and soothing always got cold and irritating within minutes.

Sure doesn't sound happy to me. Being a quadriplegic doesn't necessarily prevent one from being a productive member of society, but it's no bed of roses either.

Well, you might say, babies' brains are different, simpler instruments, and their helplessness doesn't bother them like it does us. Well, *good*! Thank goodness for that. It is only the simplicity of their minds that protects them from being driven mad by their helplessness!

And Hell yes, their helplessness bothers them. Watch a baby. Babies are not content creatures. Watch a baby struggle to learn to crawl, trying desperately to dig its fingers into the rug to drag itself a tiny bit forward. Look at how intently babies stare at things, struggling to tease some meaning out of the flood of colors and shapes their eyes deliver. Watch how fanatically infants grab and mouth everything in sight, using their hands and mouth to the point of fetishism because they're the only body parts they can actually control.

Nothing works and struggles to learn like a baby. And nobody who is truly content, I don't care how old it is (or what species it is), works that hard.

Babies can be happy during those brief, fleeting moments of intense, parental affection. But most of the time, they just want to be able to survive on their own, thank you.

Oh, Wait. I'm Breaking the Rules.

Sorry. Forgot myself for a second there. Parents aren't supposed to talk like that. Let me try again.

Babies are so happy! Especially our cutesy wootsy pudding pie! Goo.

Developing Other Life Skills

Cordelia has started to occasionally jam her finger down her throat. The gagging noises she then makes are good for attracting instant and thorough dual-parent attention.

I'll set aside the bulimia issue for the moment. I don't really think Cordelia will start being bulimic in a serious way until she gets into Barbie.

No, this worries me because I am afraid we will condition Cordelia to jam her finger down her throat whenever she wants attention. We have enough shit to explain to the grandparents without having to sort through that one.

But I think that it is important for babies to jam their fingers down their throats occasionally. It teaches a valuable lesson. Namely: Don't do that.

Daddy's Getting into Barbie

Thinking about Barbie filled me with an instant and overwhelming compulsion to go to the Barbie Web site. (http://www.barbie.com. Make sure your monitor can display the color pink.) Once there, I learned two things.

The first thing I learned was that, to enjoy the Barbie Web site, I had to seek out and install new software. Barbie's head and upper torso actually popped up to tell me this. Barbie also suggested that I get my parents' help, which is idiotic. Based on what I know about my parents, asking them to track down, download, install, and configure Shockwave would make their heads implode.

So now I know that Mattel is right. Barbie really is a good learning influence on young girls. For example, Barbie forced me to learn how to reconfigure my Web browser.

Once I bypassed all of the error messages and related abuse (written, of course, in hot pink letters), I managed to reach the online store, where I found for sale "MERMAID FANTASY™ BARBIE® Doll." That was when I learned the second thing: Years of subjecting myself to the Internet have forever warped the way my brain reacts when exposed to the words "Mermaid Fantasy."

This Week's Greatest Parental Trauma
My Web browser was dissed by Barbie.

Week 44—Adventures in Feeding Cordelia Badly

I'm sort of ashamed of how much more I like Cordelia these days. I feel like it shouldn't have taken evidence of an actual brain existing inside her skull to make me feel so warm toward her, but here we are.

I've never liked babies. Having an actual, helpless, oozing infant in my house destroying my carpets did not give me evidence that my initial opinion was unjustified. Fortunately, since only a small fraction of the parental experience is spent with a baby, I figured I could just gut it out.

But now Cordelia can understand (in a painfully limited way) some things I say. She can also say "Da Da." I'm sure she doesn't understand what it means. But instead of going, "DaDaDaDaDa-DaDaDaeeeeeaaaahhhhhhhhhhh," she says, "Da. Da (full stop)." This is endearing.

Also, she stood up on her own. She only did it once, pulling herself up using her toy box. My wife didn't actually see it happen. She just caught Cordelia standing. This creates the uneasy suspicion in my mind that Cordelia is capable of doing lots of interesting things, and she just stops whenever we're around. She might not be dopey. She might just be really, really devious.

Anyway, she seems to be trying hard to meet me halfway on the whole father-daughter thing, so I feel I should be giving her positive reinforcement. I'm considering spoon-feeding her sugar. Though, just to be healthier, I'd use brown sugar.

Our New Parental Low Point

The other night, just after a late dinner, I had a sudden, overwhelming craving to go out to my favorite ice cream parlor. The problem was that the trip would have to be during Cordelia's feeding time. Even in a dessert place, I don't want to subject others to my baby's noisy, squealing woe.

So Mariann, who is normally the fount of parental wisdom and sanity in our relationship, suggested that we simply feed Cordelia ice cream for dinner.

It turns out that this works well. Very, very well. Dangerously well.

How Did Cordelia Like Ice Cream?

How do you think?

The Awe-Inspiring Justification My Normally Responsible Wife Gave for Feeding Cordelia Ice Cream for Dinner

"Well it's just like yogurt, only without the bacteria."

Other Adventures in Feeding Cordelia Badly

The next night, we discovered that tiny bits of fortune cookie, rationed and carefully parceled out, will keep our daughter quietly happy during dinner at a Chinese restaurant.

Boy, and I thought the television was a dangerous temptation to the labor-saving parent. Sugar is like portable television.

Today's Deduction About the Baby's Thought Process

"She must not want to have any brothers and sisters. That's why she tries to kick me in the testicles so often."

"Hello, baby. Blah Blah Blah Blah Blah."

In those blissful days when Mariann and I didn't have kids, we made fun of our friends with offspring behind their backs all the time. One couple we knew had their toddler over and they insisted on speaking to it. A lot. In complex sentences. In a quiet, reasonable tone. As in, "Now, honey, you know that you aren't supposed to jab forks into other peoples' bodies unless they say that you can. Also, while I'm on the topic, you know Mommy appreciates it when you don't light matches you find. Please stop. Please stop. Stop. Stop. Please stop. Please stop. Please stop."

And the toddler reacted exactly as if it was being spoken to in one of those parent voices from an old Peanuts special. "Mwah mwah, mwah mwah mwah, mwah mwah." It continued to try to light matches with all body parts that weren't holding forks.

Mariann and I thought this was HILARIOUS. We'd endlessly act the scene out ourselves, always ending by saying, "WHO DID THEY THINK THEY WERE TALKING TO!?!?"

We were being dumb. Things nonparents say about children should always be ignored.

The other day, when looking after my ten-month-old, I said, in all seriousness, "Now honey, you'll have to be patient. I'll take you out for a walk in a second, but I have to get stuff together first." And then I said, "WHO AM I TALKING TO!?!?"

Sometimes, other people say to me "Why are you saying those things to her? She can't understand a word you're saying."

And I say, "Yes, you're right. She can't understand. And she'll go on not understanding, up until the day she does."

Week 45—"Mom! Daddy Is Entrapping Me!"

Every day, Cordelia's desperate quest for mobility moves visibly closer to completion.

A mere week ago, she was able to stand up only through a combination of anger, desperation, and dumb luck. Now she is standing up all the time, using anything within reach to support herself. It is now very hazardous to lie on the floor in our house, as one's delicate body parts will be used by Cordelia to pull herself up. My wife's breasts, which are only now getting over the horrible trauma of breast-feeding, have repeatedly found themselves used by our daughter in a much more painful and less dignified fashion.

Since babies have teeny, teeny brains, the whole standing-up thing has driven everything else out of Cordelia's mind. Clapping her hands? Gone. Saying "Da da"? Gone. Now she is completely focused on movement and hoping against hope that somehow, when Mommy and Daddy are distracted for just a moment, she can climb into the refrigerator.

"Mom! Daddy Is Entrapping Me!"

Like many parents, I own a copy of the omnipresent tome *What to Expect the First Year*. And thus, like many parents, I religiously check the milestone lists at the beginning of the chapter for each month. I read what my baby "Should be able to," "Will probably be able to," and "May even be able to" do, trying to gauge whether my little angel is dumb or not.

And I have watched with horror as my daughter went from a baby who could do just about everything on all the lists to someone who could barely hang on to the "probably be able to." I started to suspect that the ever more difficult lists near the end of the book were just a conspiracy to make parents feel like jackasses.

At least Cordelia has always managed everything in the "Should be able to" section. This is the section where, if the baby can't do it, you are advised to "check with the doctor." This is the list with things like "Breathe" and "Blink." And, after eight months or so, "Move."

But now my most paranoid suspicions have turned out to be true. I looked at what Cordelia should be learning this month and found this in the "Should be able to" section: "Understand word 'no' (but not always obey it)."

Wow. This is bullshit in so many ways.

First, how the hell am I supposed to check whether Cordelia understands "no" or not? I mean, it's not like I'll say "No." and she'll look up at me and say "Oh, I am sorry, Father. I had no idea that I was not supposed to stick my tongue in the power socket. I shalt remove it forthwith."

Plus, she's a baby. We aren't talking laserlike focus here. She will stop doing anything she's doing in a few seconds, whether I say "No" or not.

Second, unlike pretty much any baby milestone (like sitting up), the word "no" is something we have to specifically teach to her. And how are we supposed to do that? Even if Cordelia is the Bad Seed and a malevolent creature of pure evil, she doesn't have the physical capability to do anything wrong. We haven't had any reasons to say "No" to her! What? Am I supposed to set up situations where she can be bad, just so I can tell her not to?

Anyway, this is exactly what I've started doing. All my bottles of liquor are still on a shelf at floor level, so I occasionally let Cordelia see the booze. Interested, she crawls toward it. Then, at the last moment, I swoop down, say "No!," pick her up, carry her away, and drop her in the corner.

It's the baby equivalent of playing fetch with your dog and faking the throw.

It's entrapment, plain and simple. Normally, I wouldn't resort to this, but the book makes it very clear that Cordelia has two weeks to understand the word "no" (but not always obey it). And if I fail, the book says I have to take her to the doctor, and Cordelia will get whatever pills or injections make her more obedient.

Time for Her Dose of Vitamin T

Instead of the generally orderly teething progression described by the books (four teeth every four months or so, progressing in an orderly fashion from front of mouth to back), Cordelia's teeth are coming in in a bizarre, semi-random order, accompanied by unpredictable periods of pained, screaming fury. We had thought that her teeth weren't coming in. It turns out they were just farther back in. We couldn't check for them because, when we tried, Cordelia went for our eyes.

(To me, one of the most disappointing things about babies is the way they refuse to meekly accept anything their parent decides is good for them. I assume this changes later on.)

Her teeth are coming in weirdly. If the current pattern holds, she's going to have one tooth sprout out of her chin soon and another out her nose. And that will suck, because if anyone has invented a teething ring you can jam up a baby's nostril, I haven't seen it for sale yet.

Since she was in so much discomfort, we started giving her more chemical vacations. I started to give her a shot of Baby Tylenol (or, as I call it, Vitamin T) before she went to sleep. The alternative is an all-natural, purely undrugged, organic baby who stayed asleep for a whole thirty minutes before waking up and completely freaking out.

But my wife and I are now concerned. Cordelia used to dread Baby Tylenol, and the "Scrape the sticky goo off the face into her mouth with the dropper" game was one I was getting very good at.

But Cordelia has since developed a taste for Tylenol. It's sort of creepy. She sees it coming, and her mouth springs wide open. When she can, she grabs the bottle and gnaws on it, no doubt trying to get that sweet red elixir to pour forth.

I know I come across as a very casual, unconcerned father, but there are limits. TV is one thing, but I don't want to be raising a cute little year-old druggie. If she wants to get herself all crazy with mind-altering chemicals later, fine. That's what college is for.

Week 46—Scientifically Measuring Exactly How Irritating Your Child Is

Cordelia is cute. So cute. I could write about all the cute things she does. Or I would, but it would be so mind-numbingly boring that your eyes would spontaneously explode to protect your brain.

I will say, though, that when she wants attention, she crawls up to us and rams our shins with her head like a little rhino. And whenever Daddy holds a latte, she tries to grab it out of his hands and sip it. And when we put her on the changing table, she tries as hard as she can to flip herself off of it. And . . .

(Kapow!) (Kapow!)

Sorry about your eyes.

Children are boring. Especially other peoples' children. Fortunately, disease is interesting . . .

The Coming of Disease

Cordelia had her first cold over the weekend. Much to my relief, she seems to have inherited my constitution (colds fade almost as soon as they have begun) instead of my wife's. (Colds set up shop and run amuck in her system for weeks. If you listen carefully, you can hear the cheery, raspy sound of billions of hostile bacteria in her system, laughing and mocking her as they make snot.)

Cordelia got over her cold in only two to three days. It didn't have a big effect. There were only two observable changes in her behavior:

First, she took more and longer naps. She slept a lot. This, I have to say, wasn't so bad.

Second, her nose ran a bit. Booger formation was high, and she would occasionally sneeze out a big snot icicle. Several times, daddy had to do a leap and barehanded catch to grab the goo before it landed on our upholstery.

Looking back, when I weigh the advantages and the disadvantages, I have to say that Cordelia's illness really worked out for us. If only it was possible to genetically engineer light, sleep-inducing colds and release them into the population at large. This would give all lucky enough to catch it a much-needed, completely mandatory rest.

Why Do People Have Pets?

Having a baby makes me wonder why anyone ever keeps pets.

Pets, like babies, are dirty, noisy creatures who don't really care about you and have empty minds and minimal bladder control. And yet, while my baby will most likely grow up and become interesting and eventually be around after I die to make sure my body gets properly buried instead of eaten by rats, a pet stays stupid for its entire, very short life, and then it dies and you have to mourn and dispose of it.

Babies and pets are both annoying responsibilities. Both wake you up in the middle of the night. Both require training. But babies have so many more advantages. First, babies help your genetic material stay in the great evolutionary game, and that's pretty important. Let's not forget the whole Goal of All Life thing here. I wouldn't have had children if I didn't realize that I, on many levels, am just better than other people. The world needs more people like me, so I bred.

If I have a cat though, and the cat has kittens, then the world just has more cats. Who needs that?

In addition, babies, eventually, are capable of expressing some love toward their parents. On the other hand, it is now well established that the endearing behavior of dogs is simply an illusion generated by evolution to play on the emotions of gullible humans. And cats, of course, couldn't care less whether you live or die as long as the food bowl stays full.

(I know these hard facts will irritate some people. These are probably the same people who are convinced that babies recognize, imitate, and care for their parents the moment the head clears the vulva. I picture such people as occasionally needing to be convinced that the toaster doesn't love them.)

Admittedly, babies are more work than pets. And, if you have a really bad day, you can be really mean to your pet without it eventually blabbing to a therapist. But I firmly believe that if you're going to spend a lot of time cleaning up something's shit, it might as well be something that can someday clean up your shit in return.

One Admitted Advantage of Pets Over Children

You don't have to kick pets out of the room before you have sex.

Scientifically Measuring Exactly How Irritating Your Child Is

So it turns out babies have personalities. Who knew?

A few decades ago, psychiatrists Stella Chess and Alexander Thomas developed a list of nine "Temperament Traits," which can be used to analyze and quantify baby personalities.

Now, it's okay to be scared here. I understand. Whenever the words "psychiatrists" and "analyze personalities" come up, the sentences "Take this pill once a day and you will lose your negative emotional peaks, along with your ability to maintain a boner" and "You think your mother is a monster who wants to steal your penis" can't be far behind. But this particular theory makes a little sense.

It states that babies have nine basic temperament traits. They are:

Approaching/Withdrawing: How much your child wants to engage in the dubiously rewarding activity of meeting new people.

Fast Adapting/Slow Adapting: How likely your kid is to be freaked out when you light a fire in the fireplace.

Low Intensity/High Intensity: How loud your kid screams when you light the fire.

High Persistence/Low Persistence: How hard the kid tries to crawl into the fireplace.

Low Distractibility/High Distractibility: The degree to which you will have to struggle to keep your kid out of the fireplace.

Low Activity/High Activity: A measure of general wriggliness.

Positive Mood/Negative Mood: A measure of general bitchiness.

Predictable/Unpredictable: How likely your sex is to be interrupted by a child's screaming.

High Sensory Threshold/Low Sensory Threshold: The extent to which your child is upset by anything and everything around it.

This is my favorite part: Based on these nine measurements, a child can then be evaluated as an "Easy Child," "Slow to Warm Up Child," or a "Difficult Child." (Or, as one Web site memorably put it, a "mother-killer.")

The book *The New Father—A Dad's Guide to the First Year* goes a step farther, even providing a chart where you can rate your kid from 1 to 5 on each of the nine scales, tally the results, and see if you win. If you have a score of 1 to 9, it says, "Congratulations! You can just coast for eighteen years!" and if the score is 36 to 45, the book says, "You have spawned the Bad Seed. All of your worst fears have come true. You are lost."

Or something like that.

The best thing about this scale is that each of the nine temperament traits has a "Good" direction and a "Bad" direction. This is the wonderful thing that science offers us. For Chess and Thomas, it's not enough that babies are a big pain in the ass. They had to explicitly and rigorously break down all the specific ways in which your child can be a pain in the ass. Thank you, Science!

Week 47—The Proper Way to Drop the Baby

Cordelia is a normal baby, and she has been hitting all of the expected normal baby milestones. For example, she has developed "stranger anxiety." This is the awareness that the world contains, in addition to Mommy and Daddy, multitudes of alien people who could squish her like a bug. Therefore, the only proper way to deal with a stranger is to totally freak out. Especially when Mommy and Daddy go to a friend's house for actual human contact.

Stranger anxiety starts when you are one year old and ends, if you are sensible, when you die. Some people bemoan the alienation of our society, the way we all live in our private homes and avoid our families and don't know our neighbors. I, on the other hand, think that this is a great way to live. The less time you spend interacting with other people, the less chance you have to realize how stupid they are.

This is, I suspect, the core cause of "stranger anxiety." It's merely the child's perfectly sensible hostile reaction to other humans. In a perfect world, one where every human being who didn't actually give the child food or gifts was kept a minimum distance of a hundred feet away at all times, the child would never be forced to lose the blessed stranger anxiety, and the world would be a happier place.

The Proper Way to Drop the Baby

There are several rites of passage every parent must go through. The first time the kid keeps you awake all night. The first time it gets a disgusting bodily fluid on you. The first time you have to catch something foul with your bare hands to keep it off the rug.

Add to that list the first time you trip while carrying the baby.

Holding a baby makes you top heavy and blocks your vision. Combine this with toys on the floor and baby gates to climb over, and you're pretty much guaranteed to go ass over teakettle sooner or later.

(Speaking of baby gates, those things are a menace. A friend of ours has her toes taped up because she tripped climbing over a baby gate. Granted, they're useful. But they're mainly a highly efficient vector for transferring injuries from babies to parents.)

My turn came last night. I was going over the gate, taking Cordelia to bed, when one of my grotesquely huge feet caught the top of the damn thing and over I went.

When you're falling, you don't have a lot of time to plan. You only have enough time between "Oops" and "Wham!" to protect one person from falling. And, due to the gruesome and unsympathetic urges of evolution, that person is going to be your baby, not you.

It's sad and painful, but true. Babies are fragile and valuable. Think about it this way. Carrying a baby is like carrying a rare, original, mint condition, toy Millennium Falcon, except that the baby is much harder to replace on eBay.

So I'm falling, and I'm doing my best to slow my fall by ramming my body against solid objects on the way down. The result was that Cordelia was only in free fall for about a foot before she impacted the carpet. She was both unharmed and extremely pissed. I, on the other hand, managed to sprain components of three out of four of my limbs. Which is a pretty good trick, when you think about it.

And I was lucky. I've heard nightmarish horror stories of broken bones and exploded kneecaps. Because when you trip while carrying the baby (and you WILL), you're likely to end up more damaged than if you tripped while walking alone. While you're airborne, you will make sure that you are the cushion the baby lands on. Your lizard brain won't give you any choice in the matter.

So if you're reading this to find good reasons not to have kids, that's a good one right there. They sprain you.

More on Dropping

I have a friend who is a family therapist. His new patients have to fill out a form with background on the children involved, and the form asks whether the baby has ever been dropped.

I am assured that I would be surprised how many babies get dropped at some point in their infant career. A lot of the time, they leap off their changing tables. Other times, they just wriggle loose.

Lots of parents slip up. Almost nobody admits it, except in strictest confidentiality. And, I suspect, often not even then.

I will let my openness serve as an example for other dumbass parents around the globe. Sorry, Cordelia. I dropped you.

The Final Lasting Effect of the Dropping Incident, Beside Me Having a Six-Inch Wide Bruise on My Leg

I now approach baby gates with the terrified preparation of a climber approaching the Everest summit.

The Proper Way to Interact with an Eleven-Month-Old

Lately, my primary mode of interaction with Cordelia is to make stacks of blocks and let her knock them over.

I feel like I'm training her to be a mad scientist.

The Perils of "Thinking About Things"

So I am watching, as I now often do, an episode of *Teletubbies*. It started inside the furry creatures' hobbit hole, where the Noo-noo, the intelligent vacuum cleaner that loyally serves them, hears them coming. It then flees and hides behind the stove.

Tinky Winky, the first and largest Teletubby, enters. Its knees are very muddy.

About a minute later, Dipsy, the next largest Teletubby enters. Its knees are also very muddy.

About a minute later, Laa-Laa, the next largest Teletubby enters. Once again, its knees are very muddy. Cut to the Noo-noo, still hiding and rolling its eyes.

Finally, Po, the smallest Teletubby, enters. The entire front of its body is muddy.

The creatures proceed to cleanse each other with Tubby sponges, but I am no longer able to absorb any of what I am seeing. The first three come in with dirty knees, and the fourth with her front completely covered?

It doesn't take a brainstorming session between Albert Einstein and John Holmes to figure out what was going on there.

No wonder the Noo-noo was hiding and rolling its eyes. I was, too.

"Yeah, Children's TV Can Seem Creepy. You're Thinking About It Too Much."

Exactly! I have been told I shouldn't think about these things so much. Thinking during shows for kids is a dangerous thing.

Because then you notice that Bert and Ernie have a very suggestive living arrangement. And you start to wonder how a frog can mate with a pig. And you realize that, if you knew a middle-aged man who still lives alone and wants to introduce children to his "Land of Make-Believe," you might be more than a little concerned. And if you put a dinosaur, purple or not, around soft, delicious children for long enough, someone's gonna wind up short a head. And why does every Disney movie start the kids on the journey to success and personal fulfillment by offing their parents, anyway?

If you think about these things, they are creepy. But the alternative is worse. Not think about things? To Hell with that!

The day I stop recognizing the seething cesspool of barely concealed perversity and interspecies flirtation that is children's TV is the day parenthood has totally eaten my brain. I don't want to see those shows the way a kid sees them. I don't want to see anything like a kid anymore. I've done that already. It made me believe in Santa and stupid shit like that. I'm cynical and cranky, and I'll stay that way.

Week 48—Learning to Shut My Big, Fat Mouth

It won't be long now before Cordelia downshifts her brain. The frenetic level of brain construction that babies go through doesn't last forever. It seems like every day she picks up some tiny, indispensable skill she'll need to get through life. As time passes, the rate of learning will slow down. Eventually, she will be like me and be able to go years without learning anything more taxing than changes in the TV schedule.

But for now, she develops before our eyes. She just figured out how to lick her lips. I bet you hadn't thought lip licking was something that needed to actually be figured out? Well, it is. She can roll a ball now. She can tell when I'm unwrapping a piece of chocolate and scuttle over to beg for some.

I know the books say I'm not supposed to give her chocolate, but it is so hard to resist. No matter how much of a rush she gets from the sugar and caffeine, it is nothing compared to the pure hit of baby affection I get when I give her the candy. I am not made of stone. My daughter's joy is very addictive. Now maybe I should find a way to get my fix of baby happiness in a way that isn't, like, really bad for her.

Also, one more bit of news. Cordelia managed to use her tiny baby claws to give both me and her mommy bloody face gashes on the same day. Another developmental milestone reached.

Learning to Shut My Big, Fat Mouth

We are getting ever closer to the dreaded day when Cordelia can understand the things I say.

This is a real problem. I don't know if she is going to be able to properly process all the slurs on people of different religions, sexes, races, cultures, belief systems, and sexual orientations I need just to get through the day.

For example, the other day I opined that the rest of humanity was, on average, a bunch of "slack-jawed, mouth-breathing, tardtastic shit-for-brains" Now, I'm not saying that's an inappropriate viewpoint for my daughter to be exposed to. I just feel she should be allowed to come to that opinion on her own.

A poorly placed comment can break a child's brain. You can never tell what random statement will lodge in the kid's mental gears and jam things up forever.

For example, when I was around ten, my grandmother was talking to some other relatives about people who didn't have children. As I listened, she said that people who never had kids were more selfish than other people. All the mothers and grandmothers in attendance nodded solemnly at this wisdom.

At this point in my life, it had never occurred to me that not having children was something you were allowed to do. This was my very first introduction to that possibility. It came attached irrevocably to the word "selfish" and the stern disapproval of my elders.

I want to say now that all the late nights, the dirty diapers, the stress of having to fill time playing with the baby, the worry, these are all my grandmother's fault. She planted the seeds of shame, which grew into a tree of obligation, which then shed the bitter fruit of not being able to go out to dinner. All the fear and torment parenthood brings, all my grandmother's fault.

This makes me feel much better. And it is yet another in the rapidly growing list of things I have to be sure never to say around the child.

Spreading My Sweet, Sweet DNA

I think I figured out the main reason I wanted to have a baby: to spread my DNA to future generations. Considering how terrific a person I am, this is all to the good.

What I have discovered, however, is that this won't work. You see, each child I have contains only half of my DNA. And it turns out that having children is extremely inconvenient for me. I am given to understand that it is even more inconvenient for women.

So if I gut it out and have two kids, I have only replicated my DNA once. I can try to improve my odds by raising my children to have lots of children of their own, by indoctrinating them into some crackpot faith that encourages them to have lots of kids (Mormonism, etc.). But this is unreliable and forces me to have more contact with religion than I would normally choose.

I could try to get my DNA out there by donating sperm, but I don't think I would be accepted as a donor. Turns out, there's no shortage of sperm. I could try to create more children through a series of sleazy one-night stands, but I think there may be some ethical problems there. I could clone myself, but it's a sin against God and Nature.

Evolution is a tough game to play. I just hope that, as Cordelia lives her life, she realizes that she isn't just an independent human being, with hopes and dreams and beliefs. She is also a mobile, self-directing packet of my DNA, and she needs to take good care of it.

Taking Credit for All Things Good

And yet, there are reasons to have children that aren't horribly selfish, driven by guilt, or involve knocking up as many random strangers as possible.

One of the nonevil reasons to have children is that you get to introduce them to new things. I don't mean new things like vaccinations or toilet training. I mean the good things, the things that make life worth living.

For example, we have given Cordelia her first chocolate. Just a few tiny bits, every once in a while. Of course, she loves it. Loves it to a frightening extent. When I put down a candy wrapper she'll grab it and suck on it desperately. When I pry it out of her mouth, she has the cutest possible screaming fit.

Of course, it's a big relief that she likes chocolate. If she didn't, I would have to disown her. (Hmmm. I should add that to the list of things I shouldn't say around her.)

It's going to be great introducing her to all the things she's sure to love. Pizza. Bugs Bunny. *Taxi Driver*. Chicken liver pâté. Foul-smelling French cheeses.

All these things she will love, and that happiness (and all happiness she ever has) will be because of me. It's like I'm a *god*.

Week 49—Cordelia's First Christmas. Aww.

Christmas happened. Christmas is this huge, huge thing for kids, a long celebration of food, family, and greed. I understand it has some religious significance too.

I was wondering if presents and holiday festivities would be enough to crack through my daughter's Infant Shell of Utter Obliviousness. The answer is: No. The tree and the presents were just a slightly different background for some strange, inner baby drama I can't begin to comprehend.

This week Cordelia learned to "cruise" (i.e., walk while holding onto the couch). Also, by experimenting very, very carefully, I found that Cordelia has realized that it is possible to "fall," and thus crawling off the edge of the bed is a bad idea.

(You could repeat my experiment with your own child putting it on the edge of a bed, getting a *very* firm grip on its shirt, and waiting. You could test it this way. You really, really shouldn't. But you could.)

Cordelia's First Christmas. Aww.

Some guy in a store saw me pushing Cordelia around and said, "It's her first Christmas! How nice!"

Thanks, jerk. More pressure on me.

Since we have a child and children actually give a shit about the holidays, Mariann and I have to start putting some real flash and spin on this whole Christmas thing. This is easy for Mariann. She loves Christmas. She puts up lights and a tree and everything. Me, I just buy people some dry goods, open my own gifts, and spend the birthday of our Lord and Savior sitting around in shorts, scratching my parts, and watching DVDs.

But with a child around, I'll only be able to do two of those things.

One great thing about kids is that they make you freshly appreciate holidays that had long since become dull and stupid. Consider Easter. For grown-ups, what could be more horrible than Easter? (Or, as I call it, "Big Christian Snuff Day.") All the stores are closed, and the best celebration you can hope for is a double-length church grind in the morning.

But with kids around, you get to fill the house with chocolate and hard-boiled eggs! I love hard-boiled eggs! Now that we have Cordelia, I may actually start paying attention to Easter again! Now refresh my memory. That's the day the rabbit got nailed to a cross, right? Those Romans were messed up.

But I digress. Christmas. We tried to celebrate it. We got a small tree and put it up on a table, in a futile effort to keep Cordelia from swallowing parts of it. My daughter got eight hundred presents, all nicely wrapped.

Considering how much she likes tearing paper, we thought we could get her to unwrap them. Of course, she just tore off a tiny corner of wrapping paper, ate it, and ignored everything else. And that was the sum total of Cordelia's Christmas experience.

Don't worry, though. I got to sit, scratch, eat beef, and play Nintendo. So the day worked out pretty well.

What Cordelia "Wants" for Christmas

Here is a pre-Christmas conversation I had with my long-suffering mother.

Mom: What do you think Cordelia wants for Christmas?
(This is a reasonable question, I suppose. It should be interpreted to mean, "We have bought Cordelia fifteen things. What do you think the sixteenth should be?")

Me: What does Cordelia *want?* Hmmm. What she wants is Metroid Prime for the Nintendo GameCube.

(Since Cordelia is an oblivious little thing with a surplus of toys, I think she has enough of a kind spirit to not mind Daddy getting a little something too.)

Mom: (Sounding dubious.) Really?

Me: Oh, yes. Nintendo has started to make computer games for one-year-olds. It's like *TeleTubbies,* but video games.

Mom: I don't know about that.

Me: Sure! Cordelia loves the GameCube. She loves wiggling around the controller and watching the funny shapes move around the screen. And Metroid Prime has . . . uhhh . . . exceptionally pretty shapes.

Mom: I don't think so.

Me: Okay, fine. What Cordelia really wants is a sheet of newspaper. So she can eat it.

I don't know what Cordelia wants. All I know is what she should be getting. Socks. This is just about the last Christmas that I can give her socks without sowing seeds of bitter resentment in fertile mental soil.

The Gift of Terror

My aunt and uncle sent us a Barney doll. Holding a banjo. If you press a button, Barney plays the banjo. This is a diabolical combination of the two most annoying things on Earth.

When we played it for Cordelia, it completely freaked her out. She crawled to Mommy, started screaming, and didn't stop until the evil banjo doll was far away.

Good girl. Good, good girl.

A Side Note About Santa

Some parents don't teach their children about Santa because they don't want to lie to them. They are afraid that this teaches kids that authority figures, get this, might not always tell the whole truth.

Interestingly, I feel this is exactly why you *should* teach kids about Santa.

If she hasn't been inoculated by figuring out that there's no "Santa," "Easter Bunny," "Tooth Fairy," or "Yoda," what will my poor darling do when she has to figure out if there is a "God"?

Another Bit of Intelligence Progress

When Cordelia wakes up from a nap, she sits up in her crib and stares sadly at the door, hoping each moment might be the moment a parent comes through it.

Thus, having passed through the intelligence stages of limpet and turtle, she has reached puppy.

"Awww. A Little Brown Bath Toy."

Cordelia has just reached one of the more important infant milestones described in *What to Expect the First Year*. She shit in the bathtub.

Fortunately, I was not present when my wife noticed that there were a few tiny bath toys too many floating in the water. It really broke her brain, though. I realized something had happened when I poked my head into the bathroom and saw the thick layer of borax coating the bathtub. My wife kept those noxious, searing chemicals there all day to make sure the fecal cooties were utterly destroyed. Through some exercise of self-restraint, she kept from going over the tub one more time with a wave of cleansing fire.

Plus, she soaked the bath toys all day in the sink with water and more chemicals. I think she should have put bleach and ammonia in there. That'd give those naughty toys a lesson they won't soon forget.

On one hand, Mariann and I want to be fair. We don't want to punish our daughter for innocent actions completely out of her control. On the other hand, I think Cordelia has completely shit herself out of getting a pony.

Thoughts From the Future

Mariann read what I wrote. The next time Cordelia shit in the tub, my wife's reaction was much different. She drained the tub, dumped all the soiled toys in the sink, sprinkled a half inch of borax on every surface, and said to me, "You're so smart. You deal with it."

Week 50—Each Baby Is Irritating in Its Own Special Way

Cordelia is almost a year old. She learned nothing that I feel is of sufficient interest to write down.

Also, she lived through her first New Year's Eve. Normally, this is a night for celebration, wild partying, and savoring life. Thus, it is the first holiday that having a baby really screws up.

How I Spent New Year's Eve, Pre-Baby

Drinking.
Playing poker.
Chatting with friends.
Living life the way it was meant to be lived.

How I Spent My First Post-Parental New Year's Eve

10:00 P.M.: Leave party, taking pissed-off baby with me. Leaving wife behind to experience refreshing human contact.
10:15 P.M.: Put baby to bed.
10:16 P.M.: Play computer games alone in basement.
11:50 P.M.: Go upstairs. Do dishes.
11:59 P.M.: Drink tequila alone. Watch countdown on TV.
Midnight: Woo hoo.

12:01 A.M.: Walk outdoors. Drink more tequila.

12:02 A.M.: Get cold. Go inside and stare at sleeping baby. She rests soundly, oblivious to her creepy daddy.

12:05 A.M.: Go back downstairs. Play computer games until 5 A.M.

Every once in a while, I get one of my parenting books, read about the richness of life becoming a parent was supposed to give me, and laugh and laugh and laugh.

Another Advance in Our Baby's Life

Cordelia can now stand alone, without holding on to anything. This was, of course, big news in the household.

When she manages to stand up, her little infant brain always goes through the same several steps:

i. Hey! I am standing!
ii. This is really great!
iii. I will now scream and wave my arms around frantically, to signal my joy to all nearby.

The act of waving her arms upsets her balance, however, causing her to fall over. So she tries to stand back up, and the process begins again.

If Cordelia could speak English, I would explain to her that standing up is a very Zen thing. The only way she can do it is to not care too much that she is doing it. Only then can she succeed.

Yet Another Great Advance in Our Baby's Life

She tried to pick her nose and eat it for the very first time.

She didn't have much luck. She rubbed her nose and a booger came off on her fingers. She looked at it, intrigued, and then tried to get it into her mouth. Her aim was poor, so she only managed to smear it all over her face.

At this time, Daddy, struggling to control the surge of bile rising in his throat, stepped in and took control of the situation. Babies are generally gross in this low-level, bearable sort of way. But no matter how much you like any particular child, seeing her pick her nose and eat it makes you want to put her in a sack for a little while.

Caring for the Anus

I have been informed by my wife that, when changing the baby, I should occasionally apply soothing cream to her anus, which was getting red and annoyed. When I tried to find out what tool or implement was provided for this task, I was told that my finger would do nicely.

I do not like this. I do not want to deal with my own anus, let alone the anus of another. I figure, in this free market, service-driven society, where there are tools and equipment and Sharper Image gear to deal with just about any conceivable need, someone could at least come up with something I could use to apply cream to this unspeakable area. Say, a little sponge stuck to the end of a chopstick.

In fact, I do not think people should have anuses at all. I think I should just have a little drawer down there. And every once in a while, I'd hear a ringing noise and I'd open the drawer and there would be several small, rocklike nodules in there, and I'd take them out and give them away and they'd be used to pave roads or something.

But, as it is, the human body is gross and stupid. And because of this, my fingers are being forced to go places no finger should ever have to go. For the sake of my own sanity, I can no longer regard them as parts of my own body. Sometimes I look down at them, all pink and sausage-shaped and bereft, and weep for times that are lost forever.

Week 51—Teaching Children Wisdom Is Stupid

Only one week shy of Cordelia's first birthday, and it's like someone gave her smart pills or something. She's showing real signs of brain activity. She can stand up unsupported for much longer. She can put her toy blocks back into their box and put the lid on the box. (Though not always in that order.)

She still has a very short attention span. However, I feel that saying babies have short attention spans is unfair. Maybe they stop doing things quickly because the things they can do are so boring. If you had to spend time doing the things babies do, you'd lose interest quickly, too.

For example, I could not bring myself to play with blocks for more than, say, a minute. I am not very interested in sucking on a spoon. And, compared to me, Cordelia's endurance when watching *Sesame Street* is positively heroic. So I guess, based on all that, my baby has a longer attention span than I do.

Descending Farther into Being Parents

We got a video camera.

Though Cordelia is young and her brain is tiny, she already has the uncanny ability to sense when she is filmed and immediately stop doing anything interesting. We have already developed a formidable library of videos of our daughter staring blankly into the camera. Off-camera, you can hear us pleading for Cordelia to do whatever she was just doing. It's gripping film-making.

If I died right this very moment and Cordelia watched the tapes to try to divine what I was like, she would come to the conclusion that I was an ineffectual idiot who spent all my time begging for her to knock over a stack of blocks. The poor impression I am making on hypothetical future Cordelia is starting to haunt me.

Because the World Can Never Have Enough Baby

But it gets worse. Mariann has used the power of Macintosh to make DVDs out of our baby tapes. This will make Cordelia's grandparents happy beyond words. They can put a disc in a machine and be rewarded with fifteen grinding minutes of pure, uncut baby.

To me, it's a great money-making opportunity. I'm thinking of a full press run of the DVDs for ten bucks each. They're perfect for anyone who wants to be stripped of the will to live. You built your suicide machine, hooked yourself in, and can't bring yourself to push the red button? I promise that a few hours of home movies of babies will be all it takes to push you to victory.

This is an ugly sentiment, but it's true. I mean, I'm her father. She's my flesh and blood. I adore her. And yet I can only watch about five minutes of her staring back into the camera before I'm fast-forwarding looking for car chases.

The Accumulated Wisdom of My Life

I feel that I should record some poignant final video message to Cordelia, in which I pass my life's wisdom on to her. I mean, I could be hit by a car, or get anthrax, or be found impaled on a baby gate. And I feel I should tape something so that, when Cordelia is lonely and bereft, she can watch it and it will *totally improve her life*.

So I've been writing down all of the wisdom I have learned. Here's what I got so far:

"Life is like a crap sandwich. The more bread you got, the less crap you gotta eat."

"Go to bed with itchy butt, wake up with stinky finger."

And that's basically it. If Cordelia was a boy, I would also add, "Don't boff freaky chicks." I would hope that my son would be the first male in the history of humanity to obey this advice.

But as it is, I'm stuck. I don't know enough. I'm thinking of using Google to find some good, hard-earned life wisdom. In the meantime, to create a inspirational legacy for Cordelia, I took a Forrest Gump DVD, tucked it into a copy of *Chicken Soup for the Soul*, and called it a day.

My Hungarian Immigrant Wife's Final Advice for the Baby

In the interest of fairness and equal time, I asked my wife what wisdom she would pass on to Cordelia:

"Don't ever marry a Hungarian. (long pause) Or a European."

"Don't ever shave your pubic hair."

Teaching Children Wisdom Is Stupid

Often, when people are really reaching for a good reason to have children and they want to make themselves sound good, they say they're doing it to make the world a better place by passing on their values and wisdom. They're going to give to the world a child raised *right,* to go out and fix the Bad Things.

Sure.

This is really the most selfish reason to have kids I can think of. It is basically saying, "I will have children so they can go out and crush the children of those who dare to disagree with me." Or, more accurately, "Children will finally provide me with a captive audience who will have no mental defenses when I inflict my crackpot ideas upon them."

My father was better than most in this area. His life philosophy is one of extreme, intense, utterly maddening even-handedness. And he infected me with it. The tenets we will pass from generation to generation can be easily summed up:

  i. Other people may be stupid, but they're stupid in a way that lets them get through life, so it's probably okay as long as they don't burn crosses or something. So don't act like you're better than them. You're not so hot.

 ii. There's no point in getting in arguments with people. Nobody ever ended an argument by saying, "Oh my God! You are so right and I am so wrong! I will change my opinions right away! Thank you for taking the time to show me the error of my ways."

I imagine that this is what I will teach Cordelia. I could do worse. Come to think of it, I'm sure I will.

A Final Thought on Passing Down the Wisdom of the Ages

Even a quick inspection of history reveals that things in the world get better when young people ignore the wisdom of their elders, not follow it. The constant removal of older people and creation of younger people is the mechanism through which Nature encourages progress.

Week 52—Having Struggled Desperately to Reach One End, Are We Stupid Enough to Want Another Beginning?

Our little girl Cordelia is now one year old. Fifty-two long weeks of not turning blue.

We did the occasion right. We took a vacation. We flew south to spend the holiday in a mobile home. In the middle of a desert. Within walking distance of the San Andreas Fault.

Of course, I'm using a very loose definition of the word "vacation."

First, the Terrors of Flight

First, to visit the family, we had to give Cordelia her first flight on a plane.

Well, okay, technically Cordelia flew somewhere else with my wife a few months ago. However, since I was not there, I feel that that trip a) was not a problem at all, and b) doesn't count.

So, as I was saying, Cordelia's first flight. You ever been on one of those flights where there was this one kid who cried and cried and drove everyone nuts? And you loathed that kid's stupid parents for not being able to control their squalling brat?

Well, screw you. Screw you for not being in my place. Screw you, screw you, screw you. In your ear.

Flying with infants is miserable and stupid. But when you consider the alternative, namely being trapped in a house with them without respite for month after gruesome month, we really have no choice. I hope the nice businesswoman who was sitting next to us understood that. Probably not, though, since she spent the whole flight looking like she couldn't decide whether to kill herself or the baby.

Then again, we were flying on Southwest. Anyone who flies on a bargain airline deserves what they get. A crying baby? Come on. They should have felt lucky the stewardesses weren't spitting on them.

But anyway. Hours. Baby. Screaming.

So was it a good flight? Well, like I always say, there are two sorts of airplane flights. Flights where you fly into the ground at five hundred miles an hour, and good flights. We had the second sort. Though there were moments in there where I was really hoping for the first.

First Birthday

We had a first birthday party for Cordelia. There was cake. She got an obscenely huge pile of toys to be brought home and set next to her other obscenely huge pile of toys. I had no idea so much molded plastic existed on this planet.

A first birthday party is, of course, for the parents' benefit only. The baby is still only emerging from the pure, crystalline dopeyness of infancy into the more refined, irritating dopeyness of childhood, and she has no idea what a birthday is. All our daughter knew was that there were lots more people cluttering the room than usual, and someone was shoveling cake into her mouth.

Thanks to the miracle of refined sugar, the day worked out well for her, overall.

I know that I'm supposed to get some feeling of accomplishment from having reached this great milestone, but I don't. I wish I did. But the thought of the toddler years ahead weighs me down. I'm given to understand that they totally suck. At least, that's what my relatives spent the weekend telling me. Again and again and again.

But hey, at least I got cake.

The Best Thing About Spending a Baby's First Birthday Around All Your Older Relatives:

When they sit around and tell all of their "the time my baby almost died" stories. If you're the parent of a baby, hearing this shit is more fun than anyone should be allowed to have.

"Once, I didn't pay attention and handed little Enid a Lifesaver. She almost choked to death right there."

"I gave little Billy a piece of ham the size of a flea's asshole, and he almost choked to death on it. I'll always remember the first thing he said when I got the ham out: 'WHAT THE HELL WAS THAT!?!?' They were the most beautiful words I'd ever heard."

"My baby was almost exactly the same as little Cordelia. When I fed her some carrot baby food, just like what you're feeding to her now, she almost choked to death. It was a miracle she survived."

"My baby almost choked to death on nitrogen."

Speaking as someone who would really prefer that his child survives, believe me, this gets old real fast.

One Reason This Birthday Thrills Me

I call it "SIDS Liberation Day." I no longer have to worry about this at all.

Now, when I stand over the sleeping baby and listen to make sure she's still breathing, I'll know for sure I'm being an idiot, instead of just suspecting it.

Baby's First Dunking

We spent Cordelia's first birthday in the town of Desert Hot Springs. This is a small, cozy desert village in southern California where old people go to live in modular homes and soak in hot tubs. Since some of the hot tubs were not too warm, we took this opportunity to let Cordelia swim for the first time.

Of course, she did not actually "swim." Instead, my wife or I submerged her to neck level in a weak, salty, warm broth with a gentle old person flavor, while the other one of us watched mistrustfully for any signs of the baby being about to drown.

Cordelia loved it, of course. And she learned a valuable lesson: Don't dip your head down and drink mineral water old people have been soaking in. The flavor is non-optimal.

Actually, we were breaking the rules bringing her into the hot tub. The posted rules clearly forbade any infant still in diapers from being in the pools. I feel pretty bad about this. After a year of scrupulously trying to be good, responsible, polite parents, we totally slid into obnoxiousness when we were so close to a full year of virtue.

But come on! We put Cordelia in the family pool. The one that four-year-olds were in all day. Who do they think they're kidding? Everyone knows that pool is half urine already.

Plus, it's really prejudiced. Old people in diapers can use the pool, no problem.

So anyway, just to make a statement, I pissed in the pool a few times myself. It's not something I would normally do, mind you. But it was a matter of principle.

The Demonic Birthday Present

Some relative, in a moment of madness or malice, gave Cordelia a Playskool brand toy cell phone. A cell phone.

At first, I wasn't sure why on earth anyone would buy a child a toy cell phone. Then I figured it out. It's so she has something to do while driving her toy car.

When you push one of the buttons on the phone, it rings and a little robot voice asks how you're doing. Then, and this is the best part, a few seconds later the phone calls you back. It then says one of two things:

"Hi, it's me again! You're my best friend. Bye!" [Click.]
(That's nice! They think she'll have a best friend.)

Or

"Hi, it's me again! I love you. Bye!" [Click.]
(Cordelia is now being stalked by one of her toys. I swear I've been in relationships like this.)

Unfortunately, Cordelia really likes her toy cell phone. Now we have to get her a toy calling plan.

Having Struggled Desperately to Reach One End, Are We Stupid Enough to Want Another Beginning?

At Cordelia's birthday party, after dinner, during tequila, and before cake, my parents and grandparents stunned me by asking when we were planning to have another baby.

As I reeled in shock and horror, the elders debated how long it was best to wait before the next child. One year? (Also known as "[Insert ethnic group here] twins.") Two years? (So we never get a chance to torment ourselves by briefly enjoying life again.) Four years? (Giving the older sibling absolute physical power over the younger.) Forty years? (Which, speaking as the current parent of a one-year-old, seems optimal.)

But what gets me is that, after such a short period of time, we're already being hounded for more offspring! I would have thought squeezing out one sprog would have bought us at least two years of grace! Now I see that I was a fool. My relatives will not be satisfied until my wife's uterus falls out of her body and she drags it behind her like a poodle on a leash.

My grandparents did give us an excellent reason to want another child: because the first one might die. Being an only child myself, I can appreciate the harsh but sensible rationale behind this argument. There is a very real and constant pressure that comes from knowing you are your parents' only shot at posterity.

On the other hand, you really, really can't tell the second kid that you had it so it could be your redundancy system. But, I figure, why hide it? I'll name the next two kids "Backup" and "Backup 2" and be done with it.

I can't even bear to think about it. We have a real, live girl. She's adorable. So far, we've managed to keep her alive. And the thought of having another makes me very, very, very tired.

And that's all I have to say about the first year.

Epilogue—The Three Main Reasons Being a Parent Sucks

That's it. We've had our baby girl Cordelia one full year. I've written a book's worth of text about the creature. And since that's more than I would ever actually want to read about babies in general, let alone one particular baby, that's enough.

I have observed that it is customary, when writing a record of one's offspring, no matter how fuzzy or how dark, to end with a bit of sentimental twaddle. I'm supposed to write about how, even though I occasionally sounded pessimistic or bleak, I still really, really wuv my Snuggly Wuggly Widdle Babykins. And how she has changed my life for the better and I am a new person, and blah, blah, blah.

Hell with that. Frankly, if you need to be reassured that a parent loves his child, you should stop reading this, because this book probably has one too many moving parts for you.

And if you need to be told that having to spend all your time, 24-7, chasing down a highly mobile ball of dopeyness and keeping it from eating carpet tacks changes your outlook on life, well, you're an idiot.

But refraining from dunking our heads in a vat of treacle doesn't mean that I am entirely done. I still have something I want to close with:

The Three Main Reasons Being a Parent Sucks.

1. Your Life Is Over.

If you are the sort of blissful shut-in who can't imagine anything nicer than shutting yourself up in your home with a pack of off-spring, looking at their vacant faces for day after day while the world continues on its merry way outside your door, skip to Reason 2. You are already lost.

The rest of us, sometimes, obtain joy from interacting with the world around us. Movies. Plays. Going out with friends at midnight for coffee and dessert. (Or beer.) (Or drugs. Whatever.) Following current events. Dancing. Swinger clubs. Paintball. Barhopping. Blowjobs. Long distance running. Creating and hoarding weapons of mass destruction. Just relaxing. Living life the way it was meant to be lived.

And that is OVER. O. V. E. R. Over! Even if you are ever able to take an active part in civilization again, you will be doing it alone. Your partner will be at home parenting, stewing in resentment, and plotting revenge.

And let's not even get into what happens to the sex. You're going to have to slip out of the house at 3 A.M. and hide in the garden shed just to jack off.

It's a gruesome situation. And that's even without the occasional childfree wanker who'll gloat at you.

2. You Are Doomed to Disappointment.

I believe that practically every parent has this moment: You go into your child's room, late at night, and stare down at his or her slumbering form. And you imagine what that child might be. Every parent (well, I *hope* every parent) looks at the kid and thinks: "This one might be president. Or an author, or a scientist. This might be the child that *changes everything*."

No. It won't.

Think, for a moment, about how stupid and irritating other people are. And realize that your child is, despite its dependency on you and the genetic material you provided, one of those *other people*.

Forget about raising the child that changes everything. Instead, I suggest you aim for raising a child who doesn't end up married to someone in the sex or lard rendering industries. Forget about grandchildren, forget about raising a doctor or lawyer. Just aim for a kid who knows the difference between bricks and dinner rolls. Heck, forget about your child even liking you when it gets old. Just aim for it not hating you.

My guess is, if most guys saw how their relationships with their children would turn out, they'd give themselves vasectomies with ballpoint pens the moment they got their first boner.

I may sound a tiny bit pessimistic now. It's okay, though. Reality is far, far worse.

3. You Will Never Feel Safe Again.

I know now that I did not truly understand terror until I got myself in a position where I loved someone who thought staples were food.

Children are perverse, self-destructive creatures. They run out into traffic. They climb onto the roof and jump off. Sometimes they just stop breathing. And, just when you think you are finally safe, they end up like me, with an unexpected brain tumor at the age of nineteen. I lived. Many don't.

There are a lot of important relationships in my life. With my wife. Friends. Parents. Licensed massage practitioners. These people all have one thing in common. They were all capable of looking after themselves. My wife is exceptionally good at looking after herself. She can go unsupervised for whole days at a time without killing herself. That was why I was so kind as to let her have sex with me.

But Cordelia is different. She is completely at the mercy of, well, pretty much everything. One minute of my inattention, at the wrong time, could be the end. That's so stupid! How did I let myself get into this position? What could I possibly have been thinking?

Even if you don't care about becoming a prisoner for eighteen years, even if you don't care that your child might grow up to despise you and everything you stand for, there is always this. Children are fragile and dopey, and you will not always be there to look after them. You only have to look away for one minute . . .

Try not to think about it. You'll fail. But try.

In Sum. You don't have kids?

Then count your blessings. They are not a magic spell that brings happiness or fulfillment. Though, I must admit, they do have their points.

And That's It.

Thanks for listening.